THE AMERICAN
TRAVELER'S
GUIDE TO
ISRAEL

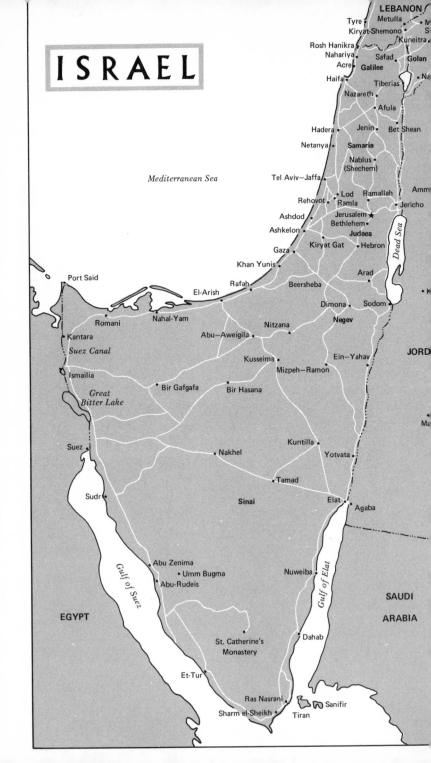

Abby Rand

The
American
Traveler's
Guide to
ISRAEL

Charles Scribner's Sons
New York

CONTENTS

PART I. What to Expect

PART II. Before You Leave Home

PART III. Enjoying Israel

APPENDICES

INDEX

Part I

WHAT TO

EXPECT

1
How to Use This Book

This book has the official endorsement of absolutely no one. Written by an American for other Americans, it is simply a reporter's appraisal of what awaits the increasing numbers of Christians and Jews who spend their vacations traveling in Israel. There are several current directories and guides to Israel's tourist facilities, but I do not know of one that is written from the point of view of the mature American traveler who hopes to have a comfortable, pleasant trip, with a due amount of enlightenment and inspiration and—if possible—a little relaxation and fun.

Fun possible? It is inevitable. There are those Americans who have postponed going to Israel because they dreaded the thought of nonstop edification. But, to visit Israel is to learn, experience, feel, reflect—and laugh a lot. It is one of the few spots left on earth where short-term visitors actually can make friends with the residents.

Here are presented the facts about Israel as I saw them, traveling 4,000 miles throughout the country, to be read by you before you leave home, so that you know what to expect and can plan accordingly, and to be consulted as you travel day by day. However, I suggest you postpone reading the portion on pretrip preparations until after you have clarified your ideas of what to see and do.

Every statement about Israel should be read as though it were preceded by the words: "It is estimated that . . ." Prices, facilities, managements, political situations—everything changes continuously. What is presented here are my estimates, based on experience, of what you are likely to find within the next few years. Designed merely to guide your planning, these are not exact quotations and most assuredly not offers by the various enterprises. By the time you arrive in Israel, the actuality might be different. Nor can I—or any writer—be certain what proposed new facilities will be realized. I have mentioned several key projects. I may have missed some that will be completed before you land, but I have not described anything as being in existence unless I myself saw it.

Since Hebrew is written in its own alphabet and there is no single universally observed system for transliterating it into Latin letters, I have adopted the system used by a national institution committed to clarity and brevity, the English edition of Israel's telephone directory, a nationwide volume published by the Ministry of Posts. However, some proper names have been established with English spellings that the telephone book does not employ. Ashkelon, for instance, will never be Ashqelon to readers of English-language Bibles. In general I have used the letter *k* instead of the Ministry's u-less *q,* which Israelis consider very mod. Other names are often spelled differently on maps. For those names not found in the telephone book, I chose transliterations that would seem right to American ears. Purists will object, but I have tried to help readers "hear" the names.

This book is not meant for historians or for Israeli patriots. They would find important sites missing or treated with insufficient solemnity. That is all right. Instead of ticking off everything that could be seen, I have focused on those sights that vacationing foreigners, with varied backgrounds and diverse interests, might realistically settle for in a limited time.

By the time you read this, the dimensions of Israel may have changed once more. East Jerusalem, the Golan Heights, Sinai, and the West Bank (Bethlehem, Hebron, Jericho, Qumran) are included in this book as though there were no question about their future. That is not the case. Nobody knows when, if, or where history will tear on the dotted line. However, as I write, these are places you can visit as part of a trip to Israel.

Among the many individuals and organizations who were generous with their time and knowledge, I owe special thanks to the Israeli Ministry of Tourism, notably Nate Freidman in New York, Ilana de Perelstein and Ilana Ron in Jerusalem, and Yohanan Erez and Herta Lakshin in Haifa; Haim Avissar of Arkia Israel Inland Airlines, Ltd.; Dan Erlich and A. M. Arbib of Bank Leumi Le-Israel; Gershon de Haas of the

Israel Camping Union; and Ethel Broida of Tel Aviv and New York for her excellent guidance in the field of art. The entire Egged organization was enormously helpful, led by Zvi Marom of Egged Tours. Shimon Palistrant of Kibbutz Hagoshrim, Naomi Wall of the Mount Hermon Ski School, and Elliot Lapinsky of the Caesarea Golf Club deserve special thanks, as do Neil Greenberg of En Bokek, Marian Solomon of Bet Zayit, and the entire Bernea family of Bet Yannai.

For their guidance and direction, I am also grateful to Shirley and Haskell Tydor, General Tours; Mel Carr, Histadrut Foundation for Educational Travel; Kay Schattman, Janet Cushner, and David O'Connor of Trans World Airlines; Susan Nissim, Tower Travel; Haim A. Goren, Tourstars, Inc.; and Dr. Leon A. Feldman, Rutgers University.

*"Our tourists work hard. They
use their feet and they use their
heads all day."*
                    —JERUSALEM HOTELMAN

2
Something Different

The most important thing to grasp about Israel is that it is not merely a Jewish country, but a *country,* with all the trappings of modern democratic nationhood, from traffic congestion to football scandals. It is not a road show of *Fiddler on the Roof;* neither is it illustrated Bible stories nor a nonstop experiment in human nobility. It is one of the world's oldest countries, or one of the youngest, depending on how you figure it (Israelis figure it either way, considering the argument at hand). The past is always visible. About half of the country's visitors are Christians, many of them pilgrims who come to relive the days of the Bible. Driving through the Galilee, it is easy to picture the shores as they were twenty centuries ago. But even the pilgrims find themselves attracted to the new scenes.

In Israel everybody asks everybody else his religion. If you are asked directions in Old Jerusalem, you tick off one set of landmarks if your questioner is Catholic, another if he is a Jew. This is a highly cosmopolitan crossroads country where the Semitic faces most easy to identify are usually those of the half million inhabitants who happen to be Arabs. Over two and one half million Israelis are Jews, but above all they are Israelis, a new blend of idealism, courage, pragmatism, and warmth, carefully disguised as brusqueness. Many Americans are shocked to find that Israelis are not particularly religious. Seldom inclined to Orthodoxy, Israeli Jews represent as wide a range of thought as do American Jews.

If this were a guidebook to France, there would be no need to satisfy your curiosity about my background. Our subject, however, is Israel, and so you should know that I am an American Jew born of Lithuanian and Polish parents. I was born in Baltimore and attended a Conservative synagogue and Sunday School. At the age of five, I stood on street corners selling felt cornflowers to raise money for the Jewish National Fund, but by age fifteen, I was an ex-Zionist, with no ties to organized Judaism. My first trip to Israel, in 1964, was made in fear and trembling. I was afraid I would hate the place. I didn't. Instead, I did what most visitors do—I came away with a happy glow, a wealth of new information, and more color photographs than friends care to look at.

Getting around in Israel is safe and easy. You can rent a car and drive almost anyplace completely on your own or with a licensed driver guide, or you can easily get around by the efficient and inexpensive public transportation. Many tourists, however, arrive in organized groups and spend their entire time on tour buses, being shepherded through rigid itineraries. There are practical reasons why they travel this way: it saves time and money, provides constant companionship and continual information, and eliminates the need to cope with baggage, schedules, menus, and tips.

So many Americans choose organized tours that prospective tourists believe it is the only system that is permitted or possible. Of course, you are free to travel competely alone or to join organized tours for selected segments of your trip, ranging from a half-day to a week. Facilities are proliferating and so are the number of Americans making their second, third, or fourth trips to Israel. Many are venturing beyond the guided tour circuit to pursue their own special interests and whims. The pros, cons, and intricacies of group touring are explored in Chapter 12.

Israel is the birthplace of three great religions, but it is not necessary to spend all your time on bent knees. The Israelis certainly do not. True, they spend more time visiting their own nation's tourist attractions and they know more about them than do people elsewhere, but they also use their free time picnicking, swimming, skin-diving, golfing, playing tennis, and going to movies, concerts, and plays. Join them. The facilities are excellent. It is more enlightening to pursue your own interests in a foreign land than to follow the "cookie cutter" itinerary. Besides, beaches and tennis courts are great places to become acquainted with the locals.

There is an organized "Meet the Israelis" program, but all you really have to do is extricate yourself from the tourist bus treadmill and stand in a likely spot. Israelis are not much nosier than anybody else in the world, but they are very much freer about speaking up and making friends with visitors, often in the guise of offering help. Stand on Ben Yehuda Street (any Ben Yehuda; every town has a major thoroughfare named for the father of modern Hebrew). Display a puzzled look and a street map. Within 20 seconds, you will "Get Met."

Some sights are interesting to everyone. These are covered by the standard preplanned tours. (Alas, so are some sights that no one seems anxious to see.) Tourists with strong special interests should count on arranging additional expeditions. The true archaeology buff will not be satisfied with the standard quick visits. Music lovers might rather hear one concert in Caesarea's Roman amphitheater than see all the other wonders left by Rome. There is no need to accept the usual sightseeing menu. Build your own.

As an English speaker, you will find the language barrier virtually nonexistent. If you know a little Hebrew, or at least the letters of the alphabet, the sailing will be even smoother. Yiddish is not as useful as it used to be, but you will still find some older residents who speak it fluently. Thanks to the large number of new immigrants from Africa, French is widely understood. Young Israelis tend to be fluent only in Hebrew, although they might have a schoolbook knowledge of English or other tongues.

Signs are often—not always—printed in English, or at least in Latin letters, as well as in Hebrew.

American dollars are not used in normal, everyday transactions, although stores and restaurants often accept them as a courtesy to the customer. The money used within the country is the Israeli pound, or the *lira,* as it is known in Hebrew.

The international calendar is used for secular purposes, but Saturday is the Sabbath, the New Year is in the fall, and Christmas is not a national holiday. The one day on which everything is closed is *Yom Kippur,* the Day of Atonement. The metric system is used here, with distances measured in meters and kilometers, weights in kilograms, and temperatures in Centigrade.

Now let's have a look at where you are going.

*"I have two sons in the Army.
How Jewish could I be?"*

—JERUSALEM HOTELKEEPER

3

The People—What They're Like and Why

Israelis are the pushingest, shovingest, shoutingest, snappingest, kindest, warmest, friendliest people on earth. They move down Tel Aviv's Dizengoff Street at a pace other nationalities reserve for chasing buses. Unable to grasp the concept of the waiting line, they don't join a "queue" by getting behind the last person; they get behind the first, blocking out competitors with their elbows and crying *Rega achod* *—"One minute, wait!" Nobody waits, not for one second. Everybody rushes, as though another 2,000-year intermission could be called before they bought their movie ticket or chose their groceries.

The whole country lives at the top of its voice, but angry feelings are unloaded quickly, effectively, and frequently, leaving a lot of time for smiles and pleasant exchanges. Even kindnesses are dealt out efficiently. A few seconds' conversation produces a series of blunt questions, brusque comments, and an invitation for a drink.

The country's greatest national resource is *chutzpa,* meaning nerve, guts, unmitigated gall. No other word could characterize an unarmed handful of city dwellers who democratically decided to make the desert bloom, made it bloom, and then proceeded to defend it—after proper democratic discussion, of course—against increasingly larger armies with increasingly sophisticated weapons. In reference to such gallant devotion, *chutzpa* is a lovable thing. When applied to the bus driver who deliberately shuts the door on your foot, *chutzpa* loses its charm.

Arrogance is pretty thoroughly distributed among the older populace, but it is most visible (or rather, audible) in their children, the *sabras.* Sabras are native-born Israelis, named for

* The Hebrew "ch" is not that of the "ch" in in *church;* it is a guttural sound, as in the German *machen* or *nacht.*

9

the prickly fruit of the cactus, which is tough on the outside, but sweet inside. The occasional hostility does not bother visitors so much as the way it alternates with genuine consideration. Conventional manners are ignored; true concern for others is what counts. A Safad hotelkeeper told of how she had stopped a guest from wearing an ugly dress by telling her she looked "like a second-rate prostitute, not even a first-rate one." The Safad lady attributed this skill in human relations to her sabra-hood.

Daily life is hard. Many offices open at 7:30 A.M., some earlier. The traffic jams have thinned by 5 P.M., although many stores observe a three-hour siesta and stay open until 7 or 8 P.M. Housing is still scarce. Apartments are small, and their distribution is regulated by several systems of priority, which reflect size and age of family, date of immigration (newcomers are favored), occupation, affiliation with a sponsoring group and, of course, *protectia,* "pull" (also referred to as Vitamin P). Most, but not all, now have electric refrigeration in their homes. Washing machines and automobiles are still thought of as luxuries. In many homes the first appliances to be squeezed into the budget are the television set, radio-phonograph, and tape recorder. Since people cannot afford to go out much, visiting friends, reading, and watching TV are the chief entertainments. The average Israeli earns under $4,000 a year and pays about 50 percent in taxes. How do they manage? Credit. It is hard to compare their standard of living with ours. One is struck by the abundance of fresh foods, but meat and fish are high in price and convenience foods are beyond the reach of most. Rents seem cheap, but most people have to buy their small apartments, with the prices ranging from $18,000 to $30,000 and up. Their insurance, pension plans, and the national health organization help Israelis in the very areas that can spell catastrophe in America. Israelis have learned to be great copers. Since Independence, they have had three wars and almost constant crisis, such as threats of more war or of economic disaster, the school problem, the immigrant absorption problem or, at the very least, a postal strike.

Military service is a permanent part of everyone's life. On weekends the roads are crowded with soldiers, girls as well as boys, trying to hitchhike home. Everyone stops to give them lifts, even though the boys always carry their Uzzi, the Israeli-made automatic rifle, and at least one plastic shopping bag filled with food. At eighteen, men enter the army for 30 months, and women for 20 months. Married women and mothers are exempt. Women whose religious convictions prevent them from serving in the defense forces work as teachers or nurses instead. Women soldiers learn how to use weapons but, like our WAC's, they specialize in support duties rather than combat. After they are released, both men and women remain in the Reserves (men until fifty-five, childless women until they are thirty-four). Each year the men spend several weeks (14 days to more than 40) training, away from their homes and jobs.

For many Israelis, Hebrew is a second, third, fourth, or even tenth language, painfully learned in adulthood. Fewer than half the present citizenry were born there. Some 56 percent are immigrants, from 100 different countries, roughly half from Africa and Asia, with the balance from Europe, the Americas, and Australia. Immigrants from English-speaking countries are generally referred to as Anglo-Saxons, a gorgeous irony. One American arrival commented: "After 30 years of being labeled a Jew, I finally made it. Today I am an Anglo-Saxon."

The large number of Oriental Jews—those from Morocco, Iraq, Yemen, India, Ethiopia—explains the declining percentage of Yiddish speakers (the spurt of Russians arriving in the 1970's gives a minimal boost). When the first Zionists landed in the 1880's, Hebrew was a language reserved for prayer. It had not been used for ordinary "pass the sugar" family conversation for 2,000 years. The revival is the stubborn creation of one man, Eliezer Ben Yehuda who, vowing his son would be the first modern man to speak Hebrew from the cradle, isolated the child from everyone but Hebrew-speaking adults. The boy did not utter one word until he was three, but no Israeli has stopped talking ever since.

Hebrew was an archaic language written without vowels (as though "dg" were the English for dog, dig, dug, and Doug) and lacking words for hundreds of everyday concepts. Yet, how else could Jews from 100 countries communicate except by learning a new language together? If English or German had been adopted, certain immigrants would have had more linguistic clout. Many of the pioneers knew Yiddish, but this was vetoed as a language of bondage. Only recently has it been judged part of the total heritage and awarded its own literature department at Hebrew University.

The absorption of new immigrants places a great economic and psychological strain on the country, yet their greatest need is for more people. In any country tourists are invited to come back. Here you will find yourself being asked to stay. Perhaps you have no particular urge to make an *aliyah*—to "go up" to Israel. You will never succeed in explaining this to an Israeli. Your only conversational out is to say, "Maybe I will" and then to change the subject, *if* you can.

New land, new language, new climate, new occupations—a whole new style of life to be created and then introduced to the next wave of immigrants. Despite the pioneers' emphasis on farming, about 31 percent of the Israelis live in three large cities, with 51 percent making their homes in towns and urban areas. Only 3.5 percent live on *kibbutzim,* communal farms originated in 1909 so that members could jointly till the soil, without private property or monetary compensation. Traditionally, adults are given private sleeping quarters, but they eat in a community dining room. The children live in special children's houses and are raised by full-time teacher-house-mothers, not by their parents. They visit with their parents for several hours in the afternoon. Thus, women are freed to share in the daily physical work of the kibbutz. Most of the first kibbutzniks were middle-class city dwellers who knew nothing about farming but who nevertheless managed to forge a new form of society, often working under conditions of virtual military siege. As farmers, socialists, pioneers, soldiers, and culture heroes, they achieved extraordinary success. Today despite their small numbers and lack of material wealth, their political influence in Israel is enormous. The kibbutzim are the suppliers of the nation's movers and shakers. Some kibbutzniks commute to their seats in the Cabinet or the Knesset, Israel's Parliament; others work in government or in the arts while retaining their kibbutz membership. Whatever they earn outside goes into the kibbutz treasury.

The cooperative ideal still flourishes alongside capitalism and government-owned enterprises. Only 84,000 people lived on kibbutzim in 1969, but over 127,000 lived on *moshavim,* which are essentially communities in which families have their own houses and raise their own children but pool some of their economic functions—perhaps just the marketing or even the work itself.

A new kind of settlement is the *nahal,* formed by young people while they are still in military service, which serves as both an outpost in a strategic area and the nucleus of their future working lives.

Marketing and crafts cooperatives are also part of the Israeli scene. Nine-tenths of the land is publicly owned. Moshav and kibbutz food products are marketed through Tnuva or the citrus group or other mechanisms. Many of these interlock with Histadrut, the national confederation of unions.

Nowadays most moshavim and kibbutzim are involved in industry as well as farming in order to provide year-round work for all their members, particularly the older ones. Fortunately for tourists, one popular industry is the operation of guesthouses. Some 22 provide excellent resort accommodations right on their own grounds.

Every tourist should stay for at least a brief time at a kibbutz (or moshav) guesthouse. It is easily arranged, reasonable, comfortable, enlightening, and fun.

For a "Jewish" country, Israel has always had a sizable non-Jewish population. Many Arabs remained after 1948, in towns like Acre and Nazareth, in peaceful neighborly integration with the Israelis. There are also several small, but important minorities, chiefly the nomadic Bedouin, who have settled down to the extent of letting their children go to school, and the Druses, who are Arabs, but not Moslems. They have their secret religion and tend to live in their own prosperous farming communities. The Druses are full Israeli citizens, with a fine record of service in the Israeli army. The population also includes Circassians, who are Moslem Slavs from the Black Sea area; Samaritans, whose ancestors inhabited ancient Samaria and accepted parts of Jewish law; and Bahais, who have made Haifa the center of their century-old international faith.

Counting East Jerusalem and the administered territories, the number of Moslem residents soared past 900,000 after 1967. There are also over 30,000 permanent Christian residents in Israel.

To walk the streets of Jerusalem is to participate in a cosmopolitan pageant matched only by a fully costumed assemblage at the United Nations. Excluding the tourists, colorfully arrayed themselves, one sees Ethiopian priests, Greek Orthodox monks, khaki-clad kibbutzniks, dashiki-clad African exchange students,

That's a *koveh tembel* ("fool's hat")
this kibbutz goatherd is wearing.
Courtesy Israel Government Tourist Office

evangelical Christian ministers, soldiers, rabbis with and without earlocks, Arab porters carrying trays of sesame rolls on their heads or sacks of flour on their backs, French nuns in midi-habits, Israeli policewomen in mini-skirts, Hasidic children swathed head to toe in heavy clothing despite the heat, Italian-speaking Franciscans, German-speaking Benedictines, veiled Moslem women—the only sight you are unlikely to see is a man in a conventional business suit and necktie.

Informality is not merely an Israeli custom, it is an article of belief. Women can indulge in fashions and fads (provided they are not too new; girl soldiers were forbidden to mini-fy their skirts until 1970). Men, however, wear short-sleeved sport shirts and slacks most places, most times of the day or year. In the country or during the hottest weather, they might wear short shorts, but never Bermudas. Male or female, sandals are the favored footwear, usually *sans* socks. Particularly in the countryside, the standard headgear is the *koveh tembel,* which means "fool's hat." Actually it is like a sailor's hat, with the brim turned down. Hardly a tourist resists buying one.

Israelis are not neat. What must have been most surprising to the world military establishment is that such sloppy, dusty-shoed soldiers could win three wars. Judaism puts a lot of emphasis on cleanliness, which for the Israelis is largely ritual. I rarely encountered a clean glass or a pressed suit. The scorn for rigidity extends to table manners as well. Israelis assault a table as though a meal were a race against time and a competition against their table mates. They do indeed enjoy food, and eating is a perpetual activity, often combined with walking, moviegoing, or bus riding. Fruit, ice cream, sandwiches, corn on the cob—if it is in season, a snack bar or street vendor is selling it, successfully.

Israelis are big for oral gratification in all forms, except one: they do not drink. They consume oceans of fruit juice, pop and sodas, and even a brooklet of beer, but if wines and hard liquors were removed from the country's shelves tomorrow, no one would notice for months, not even the tourists. In Israel's only golf club, whose very existence is a symbol of sinful self-indulgence, the bar stock consists of exactly 11 bottles, most of them unopened. Israeli wines are adequate and their brandies are quite good, but these are two industries that the usually hyperpatriotic locals forget to support.

Many Israelis are equally restrained about religion. The truly Orthodox constitute a small, but politically powerful, minority. Rabbinical courts handle all questions of personal status—marriage, divorce, parenthood. Reform and Conservative synagogues are a new and small element. "Religious" in Israel invariably means Orthodox, and the only question is "how Orthodox." American Jews tend to be horrified by the status of Judaism in Israel, some because the religious apparatus is an entrenched part of the state, but most because the average Israeli is even less observant than those outside the Holy Land. Observant or not, the Israelis are totally at home with the Bible. "It is our history and geography book," says one sabra.

Most Israeli women work outside their homes, although many take a brief respite while their children are very young. Israeli youngsters are taught early to be independent; a three-year-old is expected to get himself around the corner to nursery school. A high schooler is deemed capable of going off for a weekend hike with other students, male or female. Neither parents nor youngsters seem to worry much about sex, although the puritanism of former days is fading fast. Now, an Israeli will be mildly shocked if a teen-ager tells him a dirty joke, but if the teen-ager is a kibbutznik, he will be horrified!

Considering the pressures and problems of Israeli life, it is astounding to find the country so populated by optimists. Everything and everyone is going to get better—if not tomorrow, next week, next year, or a generation from now. "Now we need housing. The next generation will have time to create architecture." "When we get our new hotels, we'll stop having to overbook tourists." "When we have peace, we'll have nicer manners."

Americans might not recognize all this as an affectionate tribute to my three million best friends. Israelis would. They do not take to flattery. Individually or collectively, they have a vast amount of self-esteem, yet they are more concerned with their flaws than their virtues. Israelis accept no nonsense from anyone, including themselves. There are times when the bluntness is aggravating, but, on balance, it is what makes returning visitors list "the people" as Israel's chief attraction.

Foreigners—particularly American Jews—take Israel much too seriously. The country's present inhabitants do not get misty-eyed about Zionism. They are in Zion, getting misty-eyed from the smog. The tourists enthuse about Jewish cabinet ministers and Jewish policemen. The Israelis know those Jewish cops are out there ticketing Jewish cars instead of getting Jewish prostitutes and Jewish pickpockets into Jewish prisons.

> *"The Promised Land turned out
> to be a nice piece of waterfront
> real estate, but heavens, that is a
> lot of beach."*
>
> —RECENT IMMIGRANT

4

The Country—What It's Like and How It Got That Way

It is the biggest little country in the world, with thousands of miles of "seeable" sights in an area that is about 500 miles long and less than 40 miles across. The Israel that came into being in May 1948 contained an area about the size of New Jersey. Even with the addition of those sections that became Administered Territories after the Six Day War, the area is smaller than that of Indiana.

Within this speck, Israel embraces the lowest point on earth, Sodom on the Dead Sea, which is 1,286 feet below sea level. The country also includes many large hills and small mountains, although Santa Caterina in the Sinai, which is over 8,700 feet high, is unusually large. What there is most of is desert, not Sahara-like sand desert, but more often rock desert like that found in our Southwest.

Don't let the talk of desert create the notion of weather that is uniformly dry and hot. From April to October, the temperature in most places soars into the 90's during the day, and rain is virtually unknown. Yet Tel Aviv has a humidity that rivals that of New York or Washington for sheer misery; often it is in the 60 percent range. On summer nights Tel Aviv stays hot, whether or not there is a sea breeze. Jerusalem, which has a higher altitude (2,741 feet at its highest point) and a drier climate, gets chilly enough for a light topcoat after dark. So does Safad, which is about 3,000 feet high. Dry heat and frequent winds keep the desert areas more comfortable than their normal temperatures would indicate. Far worse than the Negev is the Galilee town of Tiberias, which is 682 feet below sea level and perpetually moist.

The rainy season usually runs from October to April, and

17

then even the desert has its flash floods. Do not, however, visualize a six-month-long monsoon. "Rain" can be a few drops or a few hours' worth or maybe a run of three or four really damp days, usually in December, January, or February, followed by weak sun. In winter heavy coats and heating are needed in most of the country. Jerusalem, in particular, gets chilly enough to shorten the sightseer's durability.

The landscape of Israel is overwhelming in its variety and beauty, but what Israel looks like is much less interesting than what it has been, and what it is becoming.

Jews have lived on what is now Israeli soil since Abraham led his nomads there 2,000 years before Christ. Dispersion and recovery are themes repeated throughout the centuries. Moses led the Children of Israel back from captivity in Egypt—perhaps the year was 1,350 B.C.. In 586 B.C. Cyrus permitted the Jews to return from captivity in Babylon, to rebuild the Temple and resume their life. During the second century B.C., the Maccabees revolted and reclaimed the Temple from Hellenic kings.

Rebellion against Rome had begun around the time that Jesus Christ began preaching in the Galilee. In 29 A.D. Christ was crucified not far from the Temple. Despite the two revolts that culminated in the heroic resistance at Masada, the Jews began the dispersion that kept the majority in exile for 2,000 years. Those who remained around the rim of the Mediterranean became today's Sephardic Jews. Those who headed north and eventually settled in eastern and central Europe became the Ashkenazic Jews, the speakers of Yiddish, the inhabitants of communities known as *shtetls,* whose lives created the patterns we in America think of as "Jewish."

After the destruction of the Temple, and throughout the twenty centuries of dispersion, small groups of Jews continued to return to Israel. There were Jewish communities during the era of the Byzantine emperors, the first period of Islamic rule, the two centuries when the Crusaders held sway, the era of the Mamelukes, and the long sleepy period of Turkish domination. It was during the Turkish era that serious, organized migration began. The first agricultural settlements were set up in the 1880's. In 1895 a Viennese journalist named Theodor Herzl published *The Jewish State,* thereby launching Zionism as the international political ideal of many Jews.

In 1917 the British took Palestine from the Turks and announced, via the Balfour Declaration, their intention to "facilitate" the establishment of "a national home for the Jewish people." During the next three decades, the British facilitated with the same merciful foresight with which they facilitated events around Philadelphia and Boston in 1775. The threat of Hitler made the need for Jewish settlement a matter of life and death. With little help from anyone but other Jews, Zionist groups bought, acre by acre, dollar by dollar, land, much of which appeared to be untillable, but which nevertheless cost huge sums. Swamps were drained, deserts were irrigated, and a shadow government, complete with a not-so-shadowy army, took form. It became apparent that Hitler really intended to destroy the Jews of Europe, but no nation—not even England or the United States—allowed anyone to rescue any sizable numbers.

During World War II, the Jews of Palestine actively participated in the battles of the British army, while preparing to fight for a Jewish State. Peace brought no reward, no step toward independence or even self-protection, no permission to give shelter to those who had survived the death camps. The survivors were brought in anyway, by illegal ships that were forced to run an English blockade. Some sank. Some were turned back, and the passengers were put into new concentration camps.

Meanwhile Jewish spokesmen cajoled, and Jewish guerrillas harassed the British. In 1947 the United Nations took over and set up two independent Palestines, one Arab and one Jewish. On May 14, 1948, the British packed up and left, putting some of their key fortresses into Arab hands. That day David Ben-Gurion declared the independence of the State of Israel. The very next day Arab armies crossed the borders the United Nations had chosen for Israel and advanced to within 20 miles of Tel Aviv. The Old City of Jerusalem fell to Arab forces. Israel seemed doomed at birth, but six months later an armistice was signed. Despite deprivations and harassment, the new country was very much alive.

Israel is a parliamentary democracy, based mainly on the English model. The President is a prestigious ceremonial personage, elected by the Knesset, the one-house Parliament. The Prime Minister is the head of the government, the head of the

Cabinet, and usually the leader of the strongest party or coalition of parties. Knesset members are elected by proportional representation. Their constituencies are parties, rather than geographic districts. The writing of a constitution has been postponed, largely to delay decisions on issues like separation between church and state.

A diagram of the legislative, executive, and judicial branches does not really explain how Israel runs itself. One must also be aware of the Jewish Agency, which is the bridge between the World Zionist Organization and the State of Israel. By means of this bridge, one and one quarter million immigrants have come to Israel since 1948. The agency recruits, trains, delivers, and supports the flood of newcomers that Israel so badly needs. It is the Jewish Agency, not the Ministry of Tourism, that organizes and subsidizes vacation trips for students. The students are regarded as the best potential immigrants. The agency gets its money from Keren Hayesod, the United Israel Appeal, of which the United Jewish Appeal is the American branch. Another major institution is Keren Kayemet L'Israel, the Jewish National Fund which, in pre-Independence days, was charged with acquiring land and is now responsible for developing it. JNF is, in effect, the landlord of most kibbutzim and other farms.

The Histadrut is Israel's confederation of unions and far more. It is a major employer, part owner of El Al and of Arkia, the inland airline. There is a huge private sector to the economy, but the public and quasi-public sectors are strongly visible. Most tour and city buses belong to Egged, the bus drivers' co-op, or a smaller cooperative, Dan. The Ministry of Tourism gets into the actual development of facilities by operating the Israel Government Tourist Corporation, creators of such attractions as Old Jaffa. Only 8 percent of Israeli land is privately owned.

Tourism is the country's second biggest industry, overshadowed only by diamond finishing. Citrus fruit now ranks third. Israel still must import about twice as much as it exports. Because of the continued threat of invasion, more money is spent for security than for anything else, roughly 27 percent of the Gross National Product (America's security uses 10 percent of its GNP).

Only eight years after the War of Independence, Israel had

to face its second great military test. The Sinai Campaign was a preemptive strike against Egypt, launched together with the British and the French. The United States and Russia made the campaigners pull back.

Hassles and harassments continued, reaching a peak in 1967 when Gamal Abdal Nasser and his Arab allies announced they were going to drive the Israelis into the sea. The Arab countries represented over 100 million people. Israel had about two and one half million. Nasser demanded that the United Nations' forces pull out of the Gaza Strip and the Straits of Tiran, which guard Israel's access to the Red Sea. The United Nations complied, and Israel seemed doomed again. Thus was born Israel's third impossible victory. First its planes destroyed the Egyptian air force on the ground. The Old City of Jerusalem was retaken from Jordan. The Syrians were forced out of the Golan Heights. Incredibly, the war lasted only six days, but the arrival of genuine peace was delayed by terrorist attacks across Israel's borders. The cease-fire of August 1970 cooled things considerably. The quiet brought a new invasion—an unprecedented number of tourists. This invasion has proved harder to handle.

"You must have a room for me. I've given thousands to the UJA."

—AMERICAN TOURIST

5

The Tourist's Life

The first guided tour to Israel wandered in the desert, ran out of food, lost its leader, and arrived 40 years late. In 3,300 years things have not gotten much better. Americans expect to feel right at home in Israel, particularly if they are visiting relatives or can read Hebrew. What a shock it is for them when they arrive and find themselves in a foreign country.

For many, the trip to Israel is their first vacation outside the United States. People who already know Europe have an easier time. In manners, customs, and economic organization, Israel closely resembles the Continent. Actually, the best pretrip training is to ride the New York subways at rush hour. The only tourist who is doomed is one who cannot assert his rights.

FIGHT! FINAGLE! ASK!

Consider what you have heard about The Great Tourist Glut of 1971. Hotels were overbooked; tours were overbooked; even the kibbutzim accepted more volunteer apple pickers than they had room for. People paid for luxury hotels and ended up sleeping in their saunas. Some who had dreamed of being in Jerusalem for Passover found themselves crying into their Haggadahs in Beersheba. Others had to buy days of extra sightseeing they did not want before their hometown travel agent would give them bookings. The trouble was created by sharp dealing and overenthusiastic salesmanship on both sides of the ocean. Overbooking is a universal travel industry practice because everyone knows that a certain percentage of reservation holders never show up. In Israel in 1971, they all showed up. And stayed. Perhaps in a nice, calm country like Switzerland, hotelmen could have defused their irate guests. In

22

ever-earnest Israel, they yelled right back. I think thousands of tourists got halfway through their vacations before they realized that, despite the snafus, they *were* having a wonderful time. Even if all the causes of the 1971 debacle were to disappear— in Israel, miracles often happen—the war between The Tourists and The Tourism Establishment is not yet over. Don't worry about it. If Israel were the kind of place that produced superb waiters and receptionists, none of us would want to go there.

To truly enjoy your visit, you must get yourself into the right frame of mind. Reconcile yourself to slow service, ugly hotels, and tourist food specially processed to remove all nutritional and aesthetic value (only the calories are allowed to remain). Largely for your own sake, not because it will win concessions of service, I urge you, Don't Yell Back. Find a Christian and observe how to turn the other cheek. If you are a Christian, turn it.

Once, Israeli guides were endearing fountains of fact. Now, the tourist must ask, "Whose tomb are we visiting?" and settle for "A famous rabbi's. He wrote a book." (This, at the colorful shrine of Rabbi Simon ben Yohai, whose book, *The Zohar,* was the foundation of Cabala.)

Brace yourself for the sheer volume of noise and dirt. Ritual cleanliness might still rate high, but not sanitation. Streets are garbage dumps. Litter baskets are ignored. Public toilets tend to be filthy, even in lavish hotels. The farther you get from the tourist hotels and restaurants, the more perilous the plumbing becomes. You will encounter Turkish toilets which consist of a hole in the ground and a footprint on each side to indicate proper placement. Far more offensive are the toilets that were designed to flush, but don't. Always carry tissues and wash-and-dry towelettes.

And yet, Israel is a country devoted to building parks, creating forests, filling homes with paintings and fresh flowers. In Israeli hotels the greenery is all genuine. Above all, the Israelis are dazzlingly, endearingly *real*. The basic law of Israel tourism is: people are helpful in inverse ratio to their responsibility for you. Hotel clerks, waiters, tour sellers, guides—they won't even listen to your problems. But a housewife bound for the supermarket, a farmer en route to a funeral, a soldier scurrying back to camp—people who are not being paid to look after you—they are the very ones who take you by the arm and walk you to the right entrance, pointing out places of historic interest as you go. This principle goes into effect the moment you take your first step toward Israel. Walk into the New York office of the Ministry of Tourism. The reception area is big enough to hold you and one sweater-clad young man. Announce that you want to go to Israel and he says, "So?" Actually the "So?" smoothly acknowledges that you are in the right place and moves you along to specifics, although "wonderful" might sound nicer to a prospective guest. One school of thought is that Israelis are consciously testing the visitor's determination.

AS ISRAELIS SEE US

The Israelis, for their part, say that some of their best friends are tourists. However, with typical Israeli generosity, they suggest means of self-improvement—*our* self-improvement. The ten most frequent suggestions:

1. Thanks for contributing all that money, but please stop talking about it. Israelis also gave money—and blood.
2. Don't be a sucker and always choose the most expensive item. Count your change. Check the bill. Tell the cab driver to turn on the meter.
3. Do some homework. Many tourists have no idea of where they are or why.
4. Don't spend so much time in Tel Aviv. See the whole country.
5. Don't stick to tour buses and luxury hotels. Get out and do what Israelis do—walk, swim, sit at a cafe.
6. Don't rush around so much. Digest what you are seeing. Meet some Israelis outside the tourist industry.
7. Don't expect things to be exactly like home. If you want every place to be alike, why travel?
8. Being Jewish and/or American doesn't give you the right to run their country. Immigrate or act like a foreign guest.
9. Don't shout at an underling and then walk away. If something is amiss, consider your fellow tourists and take the time to register a proper complaint with the proper person.
10. Don't get upset about little things. Small rooms, cold soup, and rude waiters are rather minor inconveniences.

ONLY FOR NON-JEWS

Non-Jews should have no fears about being treated like outsiders. In this most cosmopolitan of countries, non-Jews are welcomed with enthusiasm ("After all, *they* don't *have* to come") and a genuine understanding of their interests. During some years, non-Jewish visitors outnumber Jewish guests.

Christians and Moslems will be relieved to find their holy places in excellent condition, probably more accessible and better protected than ever before. Non-Kosher food is readily available. The prevalence of Jewish customs does not interfere with other modes. Christians often arrive as pilgrims but then, as weary American newspaper readers, become enchanted with finding a new country where things seem to be going right.

PATTERNS

Most Americans visit Israel for 7, 10 or 14 days, unless they are making long visits with relatives. Because one cannot drive around to neighboring countries, there are no today-is-Tuesday-this-must-be-Belgium bus safaris. About 90 percent of the visitors arrive by air. Zim Lines no longer operates New York–Haifa, although ship lovers can sail or fly across the Atlantic and join the many European visitors who sail over from Marseilles or Venice. Mostly the tourists cram in at Passover, Christmas, July and August, creating a seven-month high season that is the envy of other tourist nations. First-timers are likely to come with an itinerary that has been preset, prebooked, and prepaid. Whether they come individually or with organizations, they spend most of their time circuiting Israel in tour buses.

The typical itinerary will call for a certain number of nights in Tel Aviv and Jerusalem, possibly with added overnight stops at a Galilee Kibbutz, Haifa, Elat, Arad, Beersheba, or Herzliya. In Jerusalem or Tel Aviv, the bus usually starts out each morning and returns to the hotel before dinner. Sabbaths and occasional half-days are reserved for "independent activity"—shopping, visiting relatives, swimming, strolling. When the bus leaves the major cities, it goes into orbit, arriving at a different city each evening. You might not get your hands on your suit-case every night, but have to live out of a tote instead. Sights are seen on the way in and out of town. There is little time to browse through town.

This is not the only possible life style. *You can go wherever you like.* At this writing, the only place in Israel you cannot go alone is the Sinai desert. Because of the Sinai sands and security problems, you must go on a tour bus, organized jeep trip, or plane.

Israel is ideal for the antitourist tourist. A visitor can trans-form himself into a kibbutz volunteer or a student (a minimum of one month), a camper (no minimum), or an amateur ar-chaeologist (one day to one month). Or go to Elat to skin-dive or to Caesarea for golf.

WHY IT'S SAFE

Americans sometimes worry about their safety in the Middle East, but they worry from the wrong angles. There is little risk from infiltrators, despite stray headlines. You are safer walking down a street in Jerusalem or Haifa than in Boston or New York. Of course, if you walk across the street or drive around town, you are courting true danger. Israelis have the world's highest auto accident rate. They are terrible drivers and worse pedestrians. Don't let this discourage you from taking the wheel, however. Just bear it in mind as you travel, lest you begin to think it is normal to pass on a blind curve.

Save another smidgen of caution for money transactions. Don't pay your bill until you have added up the items and checked the service and tax charges. Keep your receipts. "Re-mind" the taxi driver to turn on his meter or bargain with him until you get a firm price before starting out. Don't change money on street corners or promise to deliver packages to peo-ple you do not know. If something seems wrong, say, "Let's ask a policeman." I would hate to scare you away from talking to strangers. The casual acquaintances you make along the way are often the highlights of your trip. In the past few seasons a small crop of con men, gigolos, and freeloaders has sprung up to take advantage of Israel's tradition of spontaneous friendships. Go ahead and talk to the nice fellow, but mind your wallet and your common sense. Would the Ten Commandments have been given to a people who needed no "Thou shalt not's"?

The Ministry of Tourism helps by bestowing its symbol of approval on restaurants, shops, hotels, and guides that meet minimal standards and have avoided accusations from tourists. The symbol, usually in red, is of two men in biblical dress carrying grapes. They represent the spies Moses sent to scout the Promised Land. They came back bearing the grapes to show how rich the land was. (It's fun to have a Bible handy, so you can look up the passages pertaining to your daily rounds.)

Incidentally, there is no need to be suspicious of the flowery speech of Israel's Arab residents (yes, you will meet Arabs). It is their way. After a barrage of Israeli "so's" a few effusive "welcomes" and unnecessary bows are extremely pleasant.

Particularly in the Old City of Jerusalem, hotels, restaurants, and shops run by Arabs are patronized by all tourists for the most ecumenical of reasons—they are good. Throughout the Land of the Bible, Arabs and their culture have blossomed for centuries. Their holy places are intermingled with those of the other religions. Moses, Abraham, and Jesus are sacred to Moslems, too.

AND AT NIGHT

High life is minimal, but each city has several possible places to dance, usually at the large hotels. Israelis stroll, cafe-sit, visit friends, or go to concerts, plays and, above all, movies. For tourists, special folklore performances are held weekly in the cities, and these are fun. Plays are done in Hebrew, although sometimes Yiddish- or foreign-language companies perform. The Habimah Theatre in Tel Aviv provides earphones with simultaneous translation, so English-speakers have at least one bright prospect. Movies are simpler because English-language films are shown undubbed. Sometimes European films have English subtitles (not always). Israel's two dance companies, Batsheeva and Bat Dor, also provide entertaining routes around the language barrier. Movies are shown at fixed hours, usually 7:00 and 9:00 P.M. Tickets must be bought in advance for the Sabbath or for very popular films. Orchestra seats are the least expensive; front row mezzanine the most.

For concerts and plays, the orchestra seats are the most expensive—if you can get them, through the boxoffice, ticket agent, or hotel. You pay extra for programs in Israel, but you do one have to tip ushers.

After a 12-hour day on the tour bus, most visitors settle for dinner and a peek at the hotel lobby program, live or on TV.

AFTER YOU LAND—MISCELLANY
TO BEAR IN MIND

1. Avert identity crises. If you booked your trip through Hometown Travel, which bought you a tour operated, for example, by Four Stars, which is represented in Israel by Global of London–Albany, when someone asks who booked you, the answer is not "Hometown," but "Global," since that is who is on the scene.

2. Mysterious charges? Unarguable complaints? Complain at the local tourist office, but don't expect instant aid. Pay, get receipts, and get the name of your opponent in block letters, not his signature, and present to your hometown agent.

3. Reconfirm all airline reservations 72 hours in advance for flights around or out of the country. "Reconfirm your homeward flight when you land at Lod" is the timesaving suggestion of TWA's Jerusalem chief, David Roudner.

4. Looking for a chiropodist or podiatrist? Seek a sign reading "Pedicure."

5. Public phones are considerably cheaper than calling from your hotel, but—for automatic phones, you first buy tokens at the post office.

On long-distance calls the tokens are consumed rapidly, and if you run out, you are cut off without warning. "Public" phones can be ordinary-looking phones in public places; usually you pay 50 agorot, and are honor-bound not to direct-dial another city. Phone before 8:00 A.M.; after that, the country's line is busy. As soon as you hear a voice, yell something quick or the party will hang up. Dial 14 and you get an information operator who, if she does not speak English, will grasp the problem and switch you to another operator. Area codes are used for long-distance calls.

6. You probably won't find a TV set in your room, but there will be one someplace in the hotel, receiving the Israeli station (Hebrew and Arabic) and one or more of the neighbors (Arabic). However, American and English programs are shown undubbed.

7. The Voice of Israel has English radio newscasts on several stations simultaneously at 7:00 A.M., 1:00 P.M., and 8:30 P.M. With a good transistor, you can get the BBC English news at 7:00 P.M. and the American Forces Network at 10:00 P.M.

8. The *Jerusalem Post* is an excellent English-language paper that will get you properly enmeshed in local issues and theater schedules while reassuring you that the United States is still in business. Its weekend edition comes out on Friday and is as valuable as the Sunday *New York Times*.

9. International editions of *Time* and *Newsweek* magazines reach the big cities around Thursday. The *International Herald Tribune* is widely available, one day late.

10.   Don't be thrown by nightclub prices; the admission includes one drink, and who in Israel orders a second?

11.   Hotel laundry is sometimes fast and sometimes cheap. It varies. Ask.

12.   The Bible is overrated as a practical guide to Israel, but try reading up *in advance.* By all means, bring an edition along. (Few hotels in the Holy Land have Bibles in their bedrooms.) It is particularly handy in the Galilee, Jerusalem, and the Sinai—and after you get back home.

13.   Tut-tut—that sucking sound Middle Easterners make to express sympathy, helplessness, and noncommitment is the only workable response when they are bragging, urging you to immigrate, or revealing a tragic personal history.

*"It's only a four-star hotel. I'm
not going to unpack."*
—AMERICAN ENTERING HOTEL BASEL,
ISRAEL'S BEST-RUN HOTEL

6
Hotels

Israel has over 300 hotels that have been deemed suitable for
tourists by the Ministry of Tourism and the Israel Hotel Association. The kibbutz and moshav guesthouses that accommodate
tourists are also included. I visited most of the existing hotels,
guesthouses, and camping sites, plus several hostels and hospices. All over, I found many that were comfortable, but few
that were impressive or charming or even laudably clean.

ROOMS

When the 1970's started, the Hotel Association offered fewer
than 16,000 rooms. Before the decade ends, government loans,
subsidies, and persuasion will have boosted the number to
25,000 rooms, which is still fewer than for the State of Colo-
rado. For a country that entertains 600,000 tourists a year, it
is not enough, and therein is the crux of Israel's tourist problem. During July and August, they could use that many rooms
in the first-class hotels alone.

Most of the rooms being added will be in the highest price
range. "Luxury" is a relative term and, sometimes, here, it is
merely an honorary title. In no country does it pay to be daz-
zled by the number of stars a hotel brandishes. In Israel the
stars are less communicative than usual. Five star is the highest rating, but few five-star hotels are palatial; some are not
even decently run. As in other countries, there are fine little
hotels that the bureaucrats have mysteriously pigeonholed as
three-, two-, or even one-star houses. Actually, here, the two-
and three-star standards are virtually interchangeable.

There is a standard-average-normal All-Israel double hotel
room—about 9 feet by 12 feet, furnished with two hard, nar-

row beds, a table, spartan chairs, night tables and shelves, two ruglets, and a floor of marbleized tile. What seems to be a closet contains the toilet, washbasin, and shower, scrunched together so that simply activating one appliance could flood the whole cubicle. Instead of an American-type chest and wall closet, there is usually a European-type wardrobe closet sitting against the wall. Behind its doors are both shelves and hanging space. The All-Israel single room is similar, but much narrower. The Potential Triple has a sofa that makes up into a cot.

Plush hotels have the same "plain Jane" furnishings (and hard beds), plus a special nook with table and chairs, and perhaps some carpeting. There might be a painting or photographs on the walls, but bold colors are rare. Israelis usually omit bedspreads, although they sometimes employ a festive coverlet. Everything else tends to be colored gray-beige, like yesterday's noodles, except for the ruglets, which are Oriental-patterned red. Score a plus for Israel: almost every bed comes with a reading light.

The sink might be in the bathroom or in the room proper. Stall showers are prevalent, while a full-sized bathtub is hard to find. Travel agents and hotel clerks use the phrase "room with bath" out of habit. Your "bath" might be a miniature sitz bath or just a shower made by affixing a shower head to one wall, with a drainage hole in some distant patch of floor. Your shower might also be a handspray attached to the bathtub faucets (actually, very convenient for hair and feet). The hot water faucet usually bears a red dot and the cold water faucet a blue one. Don't assume the letter "c" signifies cold water. The plumbing might have been manufactured in France or Italy where "c" signifies hot.

In the unlikely circumstance that you will share plumbing facilities, the toilet will be in a small room in the hall, indicated either by WC, for the British "water closet," or by two zeros: 00. The double zero is used in restaurants and other public places. Turkish toilets are rare in hotels.

In French-influenced hotels your room might have a bidet, which is a low, pear-shaped sink designed for washing the lower body. You sit down on it, facing the wall, and turn on the faucets.

Unlike their European counterparts, Israeli hotels provide

soap, but no washcloths. They are beginning to provide clothes-lines and hooks for drip-drys.

Large old hotels are particularly prone to having several classes of rooms, the best of which are usually called "belle-vista." Don't count on getting one, but don't expect to get the "economy" room either. Some hotels won't book their cheaper rooms to individuals.

PRICES

In the chapters on various cities, estimates of future hotel prices are divided into brackets to guide your planning. The prices are my own estimates (not the hotels') for room and bath, double occupancy, bed and breakfast, individual summer rate, per person. Many four- and five-star hotels now require guests to take Modified American Plan during the busy season.

Somewhere in your room, and also in the hotel lobby, there will be a sign specifying the maximum price for your accom-modation. If it seems to be less than you are paying, look again. Unlike Europe, the quoted price probably does not include all taxes and service charges. If you are on a group tour, you are probably paying less than the prescribed maximum.

Single occupancy of a double room might cost virtually the same as double occupancy. Lately most hotels include an Israeli smorgasbord breakfast in their prices. In cities as well as in resort areas, particularly those favored by Israelis, the ho-tels are insisting that guests pay for half board (that is, either lunch or dinner) or even full board.

Nationwide maximum prices are set by the hotelmen in agreement with the Ministry of Tourism and usually are bind-ing for 12 months beginning the following March. Season also determines price, and locality determines season. Tiberias, Elat, and En Bokek are primarily winter resorts, so their highest charges go into effect around October. Elsewhere, the regula-tions vary, but common sense applies: the heavier the traffic, the more it is asked to bear. In Tel Aviv, Beersheba, and Herzliya, high season consists of April and May, regular season is March and the June through October stretch. In Jerusalem, Haifa, and Arad, there are only two seasons—high (March

through October) and low (November through February). The
seasonal differential can be 10 to 25 percent.

Here is a rough yardstick, the approximate price ranges as
announced for 1972, per person but based on double occupancy, bed and breakfast, at the most expensive time of year, in
Jerusalem and Tel Aviv.

FIVE-STAR	$11–19
FOUR-STAR	6–12
THREE-STAR	5–9
TWO-STAR	3–7
ONE-STAR	2–6

Category, designated by the number of stars, is determined
by the hotelmen and the Ministry. For each category there are
minimum standards and maximum prices. Even a one-star hotel
needs at least an employee conversant in English or French
on the desk staff and private showers in one third of its rooms. A
five-star hotel must have "spacious lobbies, furnished in exquisite taste," radios, telephones, air conditioning. A four-star
can squeak through with units in only one third of its rooms.
What is "exquisite taste"? The code does not specify.

In 1972 the standard service charge rose from 10 percent
to 15 percent. This money does not go to the owners, but to
their employees according to a formula they helped create. A
service charge is, in effect, your involuntary tip, payable whether
you consider the service good or bad. If the service is a special
one—sewing on buttons, picking up packages, carrying bags—
you will be expected to dole out small additional tips. This
seems bizarre to Americans, but is universal procedure in
Europe and Latin America.

Happily, extra tips are not customary for Israeli waiters, bar-
tenders, taxi drivers, or hotel personnel—unless the service is
exceptional and/or part of an extravagant occasion. Remember, in or out of a hotel, hairdressers, rest room attendants, and
bag carriers are tipped. For luggage, figure one Israeli pound
for each piece.

Unhappily, only a few Israeli hotels have a European-style
concierge, that all-powerful gentleman who dispenses keys,
messages, and advice, obtains theater and airline tickets, and
generally fulfills the role of a well-connected angel. These
functions are performed, instead, by the reception staff.

IS THIS ELEVATOR KOSHER?

Many, but not all, of Israel's hotels are Kosher, in the familiar sense that they prepare and serve food according to Judaism's traditional laws of *Kashruth*—no pork, no shellfish, no mixing of meat and milk, among other rules. They have a *mashgiach*—a religious supervisor—on hand to make sure that every rule is observed.

But wait—a hotel can follow the laws impeccably and still be declared non-Kosher. This is particularly likely to happen in Jerusalem.

Don't panic. It is up to the local rabbinate to bestow the *hechshers,* the seals of Kashruth. In Jerusalem, the rabbinate has decreed as non-Kosher any hotel that on the Sabbath allows guests to check in and out or permits its elevator to be operated by human hands. In the rabbinate's eyes a hotel manager who would cash a traveler's check or turn on a hotel light on the seventh day cannot be trusted not to slip creamed pork into the goulash. The hotel people have been battling this for years, with the aid and encouragement of the Ministry of Tourism.

Some hotel people have decided they would rather use what they consider common sense than have the blessings of a seal. So, they follow all the laws pertaining to food, listen to the *mashgiach,* and let the elevator run as needed.

These days, even Kosher establishments can provide coffee cream and ice cream with a meat meal, by serving products with artificial ingredients, like our Preem.

If you would like to avoid staying in a Kosher, much less a Kosher-plus, hotel, your alternatives are obvious: go to East Jerusalem or seek out the places Israelis themselves stay, particularly in Tel Aviv, Netanya, Ashkelon, and Elat.

Extremely religious hotel keepers expect their guests to be totally decorous on holidays and Sabbaths, starting late the preceding afternoons. Guests are expected not to turn lights on or off themselves; usually, they are on an automatic timer. Elevators are switched to automatic operation, stopping at every floor whether anyone is aboard or not. This saves the passengers from doing the work of pushing their floor buttons. Meals and beverages can be paid for in advance, if necessary.

Television and telephones are not operated. Singing of traditional songs is not only permitted, but encouraged. All guests
are invited to join in the singing and prayers and the kindling
of the Sabbath candles.

ASSORTED ODDITIES

If you have fewer than four flights to ascend, walk. The
elevators in Israeli hotels are totally inadequate to the traffic.
. . . The quietest spot in a hotel is likely to be the bar, if not
the nightclub. When surrounded by Israelis, even tourists lose
their inclination to drink. It is often more pleasant to have
coffee or other drinks served to you in the lobby. . . . The
most festive spot is likely to be the pool. Four- and five-star
hotels (except in Tel Aviv), even kibbutz guesthouses, feature
big swimming pools, surrounded by terraces and lawns. At the
large hotels expect to pay extra for the beach chair, mat, pillow,
umbrella, and so on. . . . Despite the climate, the latest
prestige item for a hotel is a sauna. . . . Rooms that face a
courtyard might be quieter, if less scenic, than those facing the
street. . . . Suburban hotels usually provide free or inexpensive shuttle service, but at scattered hours. . . . TV in
guest rooms are rare. . . . Locate the hotel's bulletin board
and study it often. Groupers' schedules are posted there, along
with announcements about opera, theater, concerts, religious
services, and other special events. . . . If you cannot unlock
your door, try pushing the key in only halfway and turning
to the right instead of to the good old American left. . . .
When you check out, there are bound to be extras to pay, no
matter how all-inclusive your tour. The tab might be for after-
dinner coffee or tea (rarely included in meals), stamps, laundry,
phone calls. Check, but be prepared to pay. If you leave before
7 A.M., ask for your bill the night before. Pay in dollars if it's
convenient; it only costs about 25¢ more.

THE LOBBY AS BATTLEGROUND

Hell is a hotel lobby in Israel at 4:30 P.M. when two busloads of overstimulated camera toters launch a massive attack
against the desk clerk. Keys they want, and telephone messages,

and travelers checks cashed, and instructions for getting to Herzl Street. And explanations of why the air conditioner is so noisy. The desk clerk waits on his side of the barricade, ready to counterattack. Questions he ignores. Complaints he disposes off with an irate, "You must be mistaken." Should the complainer persist, the clerk escalates to statements like "If I had to answer everybody's complaint, I'd be here all day" or "Who said you should come to this hotel?"

In Israel, the spirit of guerrilla theater involves all. Maybe the afternoon's combat is sparked by an overbooking problem —a half-dozen people, or even a whole busload, that the management is obligated to dispose of, preferably by nonviolent means. Remember that if you or your group arrive with confirmed reservations and vouchers or letters to prove it, the management must find beds *someplace* and compensate for any discrepancy between quality and payment.

Of course some of the most self-righteous yellers are visitors who know they do not have firm reservations but have come on a waiting-list basis and are trying to force their way in. Good luck, but you can't outbrazen an Israeli. Instead, try sobbing, smiling bravely, and whispering "Please help." Shock tactics might work.

Stay in an Arab hotel, and you will miss all this fun. If there is a shadow of a possibility of a mistake, they will act as if it is their fault.

Americans tend to judge the service of a hotel by the quickness of the telephone operators and the desk clerks. By anybody's standards, Israeli hotel service is dreadful, but by American criteria, it is hopeless. Make up your mind that it is going to be unpleasant, but of marginal importance.

CHOOSING HOTELS

If you end up buying a packaged tour, as most visitors do, you won't have to make the final choices yourself. You choose a price range, and the tour operator makes the arrangements from his list of hotels that he deems acceptable or attainable.

In any tourist mecca there are hotels that specialize in groups. Often these are old hotels that have had to abandon their once-proud standards. Your hopes are high when you see a famous name, but wait. There is not a hotel in the world, much less in this pressured corner of it, that can maintain its style and grace while churning out assembly-line service for tour groups. The fallen dowagers can be even worse than some of the new hotel-factories, which were at least designed for minimal service and maximal wear.

If you are not traveling as part of a group, your most important safeguard is to seek out hotels that do not cater to tours. In Israel they are relatively scarce. Look for hotels with only 20 or 30 rooms, too small to accommodate a 40-passenger bus battalion. If you like quiet and do not mind commuting, consider a suburban hotel. Consider each accommodation in light of location, category, atmosphere, and most of all, its suitability for your style of trip.

Advance reservations are essential during the summer and the holidays. Do not count on just gypsying around. You will spend most of your time searching for a place to lay your head and will end up with accommodations that are either too expensive or too uncomfortable for your taste.

Working with a travel agent is the most efficient approach. If not, you must write to several different hotels, indicating when, how many, what, and how much. Enclose an international postal reply coupon (no American stamps). When you get the right nibble, send an immediate deposit and ask for a letter of confirmation. Bring it with you. You will bolster your luck if you write to a chain and ask for rooms in their various hotels.

Problems? Consider an apartment, hostel, campsite, kibbutz, or room in a private house. Once you get to Israel, the Ministry of Tourism booth at the airport will try to help and so will their branch offices, but they will find you a room only for one night. One private outfit has been performing miracles, helping desperate tourists in order to spread good will; it is a new travel agency: Promised Land, Ltd., 12 Hillel Street, Jerusalem (03) 2 72 25.

KIBBUTZ GUESTHOUSES

The guesthouse on a kibbutz or moshav looks like a small motel with a gigantic garden. In fact, that is what the kibbutz itself usually looks like, although neither the members' "motel rows" nor the dining rooms are as pretty as the tourists'. You have to stay for several nights in order to get to know the people and a little about kibbutz life, but something beats nothing. Even an overnight gives you a chance to talk with genuine kibbutzniks around their swimming pool. One member will, no doubt, present an after-dinner slide lecture and, probably, show you around the workshops, nursery, and houses before you leave the next day.

The guests' dining room usually has a bar, sitting room, TV room, and ample porches and lawns. Sometimes, there are films, entertainment, Ping-Pong, or even tennis courts. Rooms are often comfortable, and the food outshines the cuisine of Israel's best hotels, admittedly an easy task. Most of the guesthouses rate as three-star hotels. The most famous among them, Ayelet Hashahar, is a four-star hotel, and so is the runner-up, Nof Ginossar. Guesthouse prices tend to be lower than those at big city hotels.

Particularly good as base camps for individual travelers are the Galilee kibbutzim, the trio near Jerusalem—Shoresh, Ma'-ale Hahamisha, and Kiryat Anavim—plus Bet Oren near Haifa and Bet Chava and Gesher Haziv near Nahariya.

The kibbutzim run a simpler type of operation known as holiday villages, which are more like campsites and usually near the sea. Hof Dor, Neve Yam, and Kayit Ve'Shayit are in this category. These are organized for Israeli tourists to an even greater extent than are guesthouses. Amirim is still another special case: a moshav in the Upper Galilee devoted to organic farming and vegetarianism, it also takes in tourists as guests in individual homes.

You can make reservations by contacting the Association of Kibbutz Guesthouses, 100 Allenby Street, Tel Aviv, or via travel agents. Eastours, Inc., 1140 Avenue of the Americas, New York, N.Y. 10019 (212) 490–2040, packages a go-it-alone kit, kibbutz reservations, and a bus ticket along with summer-long kibbutz visits for senior citizens.

CAMPING

You do not need to bring tents or sleeping bags to utilize the 16 well-organized campsites that are part of the Camping

Union. There are also some nonmember areas on farms, communal and private, that exist pretty much for Israeli families and which do require you to bring your own gear. The camping craze hit the country late, in 1962, so gear is still hard to rent or even buy, but a nationwide network of campsites is already flourishing.

Before leaving home, the would-be camper buys *Israel on $2.00,* a deal which gives him an unlimited Egged bus ticket and vouchers for 14 nights, each good for one continental breakfast and one bed in a tent, plus fresh sheets, electricity, and use of washrooms. Cooking gas and food are available at low cost. Most campers get around by hitchhiking or using their bus ticket, but it is perfectly legal to travel by rental car. Advance reservations are recommended. The voucher books are sold by travel agents, although they get no commission. "It is group travel prices for antigroupers," says Gershon de Haas, who runs the operation.

You can, of course, use the campsites without enlisting in this program. Paying by the night costs just a trifle more, providing you can snare one of the available cots.

Along the Mediterranean coast or in the Galilee, there is a good choice of locations. Many are in or near national parks, with important landmarks and recreational facilities right at hand. An innovation is a campsite near the airport at Lod, designed for first and last nights in the country. From the airport, dial 97 and a car will pick you up. Other strategic spots: outside Jerusalem, Elat, and on the Dead Sea.

For maps and detailed instructions, contact Israel Camping Union, 43 Ha'atzmaut, Haifa (04) 52 09 07, or the Union's American sales representative, Eastours, Inc.

Those who like living informally, but not heroically, should consider the various holiday villages run by private organizations as well as kibbutzim. The prizewinner is the Club Méditerranée at Achziv, on the Mediterreanean Sea, which has the best food in Israel and certainly the most oo-la-la. Non-Kosher, it is designed mostly for French visitors, so you will have more fun if you speak the language. The Club Ashkelon, also on the sea, and also French, offers more physical comfort, if less pizzaz. Other candidates for your attention will be mentioned where geographically relevant.

YOUTH HOSTELS

You do not have to be an "official" youth in order to stay at a hostel, but you do need a membership card from a national hostel organization or something to show that you are a kibbutznik, new immigrant, or member of an organization like the Nature Protection Society. For information and a directory, contact the Israel Youth Hostels Association, 3 Dorot Rishonim Street, Jerusalem (02) 22 20 73. Regardless of age, Americans can join for about $5. The country's 28 hostels, featuring bunk beds, usually are divided into girls' and boys' dorms. Organized meals are served only to groups that have paid in advance. Otherwise, you cook and clean up later.

Most hostels charge a top rate of about $1 for adult nonmembers. Members under 18 might pay only 50¢ a night. Mattresses and pillows are provided free, but there is a small charge for sheets. There are also small charges for meals or the use of kitchens.

Some hostels are in the heart of tourist country or in residential quarters of big cities. I visited several and was very impressed. Many are more like college dorms than like the barn lofts and chicken houses often found in America.

You must check in before 9 P.M. (final gate-closing is usually 10:30) and have your bed empty and cleaned up by 8 A.M.

Christian hospices are much like hostels, operated for all travelers, not only those of the same faith (which usually is Catholic). Accommodations vary from dorms to private rooms, from simple to austere. For a current list, contact the Israel Pilgrimage Committee, P.O. Box 1018, Jerusalem.

The Israel Youth Hostels Association also runs a travel bureau that helps individuals and groups plan special activities. This is one place to write if you want to live and work at an archaeological dig. Hostelers get discounts at national parks, as well.

APARTMENTS, PENSIONS, PRIVATE ROOMS

Pensions, Europe's small boardinghouses purveying inexpensive rooms and meals, are not an Israeli specialty. There are places called pensions, but they are more like small hotels and will be considered as such in the hotel rankings that appear in the chapter on each region.

Rooms in private homes are becoming available through organized channels for $3 a night. It is now possible to contact the Ministry of Tourism before you leave home, but do not count on getting fixed reservations this way. The room renters are not professional hotelmen. After you arrive, the representatives of the Ministry in various towns and at the airport can also direct you to the available rooms. Another bet: Atlas Travel, 57 Ben Yehuda, Tel Aviv (03) 22 79 15, is an agency that locates private rooms for tourists. Bear in mind that most Israeli homes are small and multiple bathrooms are rare.

Furnished apartments are now a realistic alternative, particularly for those wanting to stay in Jerusalem and remain at least a month. Contact the agencies specializing in short-term sublets. If you decide to try for an apartment after you get to Israel, check out the agencies and the newspaper ads. The *Jerusalem Post* is good, but the Hebrew newspapers might be better. Prices are high—until you compare them with the hotel prices.

At Home Abroad, Inc., the American outfit that finds vacation homes and apartments all over the world, has begun to operate in Israel. From this side of the ocean, you can contact them for houses in Jerusalem or luxury apartments in Herzlia Heights, outside Tel Aviv. In summer, a one-bedroom apartment might cost $200 a week. Contact them via travel agents or directly, at 136 East 57 Street, New York, N.Y. 10022 (212) 421–9165.

The biggest wheel in short-term rentals bears a name that would be scandalous in Boston, but which is normal in Israel: Anglo-Saxon Realty. In Tel Aviv the main office is at 14 Frishman (03) 24 11 55, and in Jerusalem it is 2 Hassoreg (02) 52 65 54.

Anglo-Saxon says that most of its sublets are for the summer months and are put on the market after Passover. Prices run $200–$250 a month for a one-bedroom apartment big enough for a couple. A two-bedroom apartment might be $350 a month, and a one-family house, $500–$600. Gas, electricity, water, and utensils are included, but not a telephone. Anglo-Saxon does not usually book through travel agents. A washing machine might be included, but a dishwasher is rare. If you want to maintain a Kosher home, specify. Some homeowners will only rent to families that are accustomed to keeping Kosher.

Three more agencies recommended by the Ministry of Tourism, all in Jerusalem, but possibly having apartments elsewhere, too, are: Carmi Ora, 5 Hama'alot (02) 23 30 30; Or, 3 Ben Yehuda (02) 23 48 62; Universal, 60 Jaffa Road (02) 22 56 74.

Beach lovers and families that include young children should investigate the car-and-cottage deals organized by Shartours, 6 Shemuel Hanatziv Street, Netanya (053) 2 22 54.

This agency will bring your car and new landlord to meet you at the airport and then escort you to your home, anything from a one-room apartment to a house, probably in Netanya or one of its rural suburbs and within ten minutes of the sea. The minimum stay is two weeks. The summertime rate for lodging and rental car runs from $100 for a studio to $500 for a place big enough for four and might zoom toward $1,000 for a seaside villa. Housecleaning is not included, but gas and electricity and housekeeping gear are. If you don't want the car, you can substitute sightseeing tours. Shartours works with travel agents, for the customary commissions.

7

Food and Drink

It is not what you expect. Red Sea shrimp, Chinese egg rolls, ham and eggs—Israeli food is not necessarily Kosher nor is it necessarily bad, although hotel meals served to tourists are usually both. An Israeli cuisine has begun to evolve, but it has gotten no farther than breakfast, which is a major contribution to culture. Someday, there will also be an Israeli lunch and an Israeli dinner that will be more Mideastern than East European, but so far the main meals are a high-calorie chaos of Turkish shashlik, Greek moussaka, Russian blintzes, German roast goose, and Wiener schnitzel. Of course, the schnitzel is usually turkey rather than veal because the cookery is based on what is available, and the most available foods in Israel appear to have wings. Other meats tend to be imported, tough, and served in minute portions. Chicken and turkey are in over-supply. Meals are fattening, heavy, and bland, except for an inordinate use of pepper.

What makes Israeli food bearable is the prevalence of fresh fruits, vegetables, and fish. It gets tiresome eating tomatoes three times a day, until you reflect on the lusciousness of the tomatoes and their sky-high prices back home. Kosher or non-Kosher, if you eat out, you can find varied, interesting meals. Non-Kosher restaurants operate openly. They just don't have a "Kosher" sign. If you are committed to set-menu hotel meals, you can compensate by adventurous snacking.

ISRAELI, BUT EDIBLE

Chief among the stateside "Jewish" specialties which are virtually nonexistent are cold cuts. The Hilton has pastrami flown

44

in from the States. Feferberg in Jerusalem serves a corned beef that might fool a Baptist. Otherwise, nothing. Abandon all hope of bagels and lox. Smoked salmon appears here only as a hideously expensive appetizer in fancy restaurants. Our plump, toastable, sandwich-capable bagels cannot be had. The Israeli *bagele* is a thin, salty twist to be munched like a pretzel, so unbagel-like that at first glance I thought it was an Arab specialty. Even the cream cheese is not right.

Milk, cottage cheese, tuna, pickles, and cheesecake are among the many foods that have been Israeli-ized beyond recognition. With the growth of fish-pond farming, gefilte fish has become the Israel hamburger. It makes a refreshing cold lunch. Borsht usually comes in a glass, with sour cream or imitation nondairy cream added only at extra cost. Served this way, it is a lunchtime beverage more than a soup. The *cheeps* that accompany virtually every meat dish turn out to be French fried potatoes, referred to by their British name, "chips." The word "salad" with no further description is usually chopped cucumbers and tomatoes without dressing or herbs. Mixed green salad, American style, is rare. A "cheese toast" is that European pastry shop specialty, the grilled cheese sandwich. Breakfast toast is uncommon, as are diet sodas, cornflakes, and poached or fried eggs. Menus sometimes use Europeanisms: "marrow" is squash, "aubergine" is eggplant, "maize" is corn (corn on the cob is sold on street corners, rarely is it served in restaurants).

Street corner vendors and snack bars purvey the country's tastiest treats.

Felafel is the king of the street foods. It is made of mashed chickpeas, seasoned, deep fried, then poked into a pocket made of *pita*, the flat Oriental bread served all over Israel. Poked in with it are pickles and tomatoes, and it is sprinkled with *tahina,* a sauce made of ground sesame seeds. A half felafel is a snack; a whole one is lunch.

The word "pickles" barely describes the array of vegetables that are pickled and offered in adornment of many dishes; cauliflower, carrots, onions, and olives are mixed in with the cucumbers.

Shwarma is the new rival to king felafel, and people who know New York and Athens will understand why when they recognize that the giant pieces of lamb revolving on special rotisseries are the same thing as Greek *gyros*. The lamb is sliced to your order and poked inside a pita with tomato, parsley, and pickle.

Other vendors' wares include: nuts, corn on the cob, pumpkin seeds, chocolate, poppy seed buns, bagele, ice cream (on sticks, in cones, in sandwiches, with or without syrup, hard or soft), coffee, tea, soft drinks, quasi hot dogs, pseudo hamburgers (the Wimpy chain's burgers are skinny, but good; also Kosher), and—strike up *Hatkvah*—cold sabras, fruit of the cactus, which is delicious, particularly when cut open and handed to you juicy and cold, wrapped in the peel.

Your culinary range will be most satisfied at an "Oriental" —i.e., Arabic—restaurant or a *steakiyot,* a simpler spot specializing in the grilled portion of the Oriental repertory. Kosher steakiyot and Oriental restaurants are as easy to find as their non-Kosher counterparts.

Pita is the basic breadstuff of these restaurants. Served cold or hot, and unbuttered, you tear off a piece and use it to scoop up other foods. These might include:

Tahina—a paste of sesame seeds used as a sauce or as a first course, with parsley or other seasoning.

Humus—ground up chickpeas served as a cold first course, with tahina or olive oil and lemon.

Eggplant salad—a creamy white mishmash of eggplant.

Shashlik—skewered beef, fish, pork, or chicken, but usually lamb; what we tend to call shish kebab. In Oriental restaurants, onions, tomatoes, and peppers are rarely served on the skewers.

Kebab—spiced chopped meat, grilled with garlic and parsley.

Snia—mincemeat, with onions and tahina or tomato sauce.

Stuffed pigeon—pigeon, with pine seeds and rice (this treatment is often applied to chicken).

Kubeh—chopped lamb and onion croquettes.

Mansaf—a bland mix of chopped lamb, rice, and sour milk.

Baklava—a generic name for the myriad supersweet pastries that combine honey, coconut, and nuts.

Grilled chicken and peppery grilled fish sound tame, but they are the stars of the Oriental kitchen. The best first course, if there are at least two of you, is a medley of salads—humus, tahina, Arabic salad (tomatoes, cucumbers, onions, olives, herbs), Turkish salad (featuring peppery tomatoes), and eggplant salad.

When a restaurant advertises itself as "European," it can mean a particular section of Europe from which its proprietor or chef came, or a mythical continent composed largely of Jews in Central and Eastern European countries. If the proprietor wishes to convey a sophisticated French–Italian–Swiss background, the restaurant will be called "Continental." Israelis are partial to some Continental and European dishes that are not widely known in the States. Be on the lookout for:

Goulash soup—a thick soup with little meatballs or large chunks of meat.

Veal Cordon Bleu—veal cutlets with cheese.

Swedish plate—a cold platter with a smorgasbordlike array of whatever salads, cold meats, and garnishes are available; a great hot weather lunch or light dinner.

WHAT KOSHER MEANS

Warning: Chopped liver on the menu is not the same as a seal of Kashruth.

What is Kosher, (or *Kasher,* in Hebrew) and what is not is specified in the Bible, in Leviticus, Chapter 11, and Deuteronomy, Chapter 14. Among the items that now seem mysterious are those that represent a far-sighted attempt at a pure food law. Nowadays Orthodox Jews follow every twist and turn of the code and its subsequent interpretations. Non-Orthodox Jews adapt their own interpretations, sometimes ignoring the code, sometimes paying homage to tradition. Basically, only animals that chew their cud and have divided horns *and* cloven hoofs are Kosher, as are only those fish with fins and scales. That eliminates pigs, camels, oysters, lobsters, clams, crabs, and shrimp. Moreover, animals must be slaughtered with one swift blow and washed and salted so that all blood is removed. The hind quarters are forbidden. (Now do you understand why Kosher meat is so tough?) Another major complication is that dairy foods can be eaten before meat foods, but not simultaneously or immediately after. Hotels and homes must have two sets of dishes, and two more to be used during Passover week, when, in imitation of the hurried departure from Egypt, no leavened bread can be eaten.

The milk-without-meat dictum has inspired the dairy or vegetarian restaurant and a magnificent array of dairy and fish

dishes (fish, considered either as milk or meat, belongs to the
neutral category of *pareveh* dishes). On a hot day seek out a
dairy restaurant for a revivifying lunch of *blintzes* (pancakes
filled with cottage cheese; accept no light Czechoslovakian sub-
stitutes, but hold out for a properly klunky Russian version)
or potato *latkes* (pancakes). Or choose an array of vegetable
salads, garnished with *leben* or *eshel*, which are like yogurt, or
shemenet, which is Israeli sour cream. With such dishes, drink
borsht, a soup-drink made of beets, or cold fruit soup.

HOTEL FOOD

Having let the sunshine in, I now take you back to the
subject of the meals that hotels dispense to their guests, but even
here the news is one-third good. The Israeli breakfast was born
as a midmorning spread for kibbutzniks, utilizing whatever was
on hand that could be consumed in a dining room or in the
fields. As now served in a tourist hotel, it is a smorgasbord at
which guests help themselves to orange juice, boiled eggs,
herring, sardines, grated carrots, quartered tomatoes, chunked
cucumbers, black olives, green olives, peppers, slices of yellow
cheese (resembling Edam or Gouda), mounds of cream cheese
with or without pimentos and other garnishings, dishes of
cottage cheese, pitchers of yogurt, crackers, rolls, butter, and
jam. Coffee or tea are brought to your place, once you file an
application with the appropriate waiter. Everything has been
thought of, except—guess what—milk and honey.

At most, but not all, hotels with at least three stars, it is also
possible to get scrambled eggs. A few provide the eggs or pancakes only for an extra charge. Ham and bacon are usually available only in Arab hotels (Moslems are not supposed to eat pork
either, but they freely serve it to their guests). At kibbutz guesthouses a bag of fresh fruit is presented to help you survive until
lunch. Remember, some hostels, campsites, and very simple
spots serve a Continental breakfast of bread, butter, and coffee.
At hotels in the one- to three-star ranges, a stripped-down
version of the Israeli breakfast might be served. *Challah*, the
eggy Jewish Sabbath bread, customarily appears on Saturday
morning.

Breakfast is usually served from 7:00 to 9:00 A.M., sometimes earlier; lunch is from 1:00 to 3:00 and dinner is 7:00 until 8:00 or 9:00 P.M. Hotel lunches and dinners relentlessly pursue a cholesterol-strewn course from appetizer (chopped liver, moussaka, fruit cup) to soup, and on to a main course of meat or fish with vegetables, then dessert (compote, ice cream, Bavarian cream, chocolate mousse). The afternoon meal is usually a bit larger, because that is what Israelis and Europeans like, but the evening meal is also gigantic, in deference to American tastes. In four-star and five-star hotels, choices may be offered for each course. At lesser places there might be a choice of appetizer or dessert. You can sometimes negotiate a substitute for any dish, but you will usually have to pay extra. There will be a printed menu on your table or on the dining room door, but it might be part-fiction. Before you skip any courses, check.

Because this parade of dishes is too long to impress many modern-day clients, hotels often have à la carte restaurants where, in effect, you pay more to eat less. Outsiders can usually arrange to eat the regular menu in the hotel's main dining room.

Kosher hotels often maintain an independent dining room, for dairy dishes which house guests or outsiders can elect instead of the meat meal.

POSTSCRIPT ON ALCOHOL

You want a drink? Have a drink. It might not be up to your hometown standard and might cost the better part of two dollars, but no one will be offended by such an un-Israeli action. In fact they will be offended if you make a show of passing up a drink. Be aware that unless you order by brand name, "whiskey" will be assumed to mean Scotch. Bourbon and blended whiskeys are available at the big, American-oriented hotels, but Scotch is more common. Ask for a martini, and what you are likely to get is a glass of Martini-brand vermouth. As a matter of fact, if you are a real martini nut, the only way to avoid disappointment is to order something else.

If an Israeli invites you to his house for a drink or issues an invitation to go out for a drink, he does not mean a "hard" drink. He means a Coke or a coffee.

These are the people who invented the world's nicest toast, *L'chayim*—"to Life!"

EATING OUT

In the three big cities and Elat, eating out is more interesting than eating in, and not necessarily more expensive. In observance of the Sabbath, many restaurants close down after lunch on Friday and do not reopen until Saturday dinner. This also happens on holidays. In Tel Aviv, Haifa, and Jerusalem, there will always be something open, but in many cases a hotel dining room is the only feasible alternative. Of course, it does not have to be *your* hotel's dining room. You can get a feeling of variety by going to another hotel, but better ask about payment and reservations before the Sabbath descends.

Most "fancy" Israeli restaurants are strictly à la carte. Haifa, which lives by its own rules of reason, is the one spot where many restaurants offer a complete dinner at fixed prices.

Every restaurant posts its menu outside so that you can analyze the fare and price scale before committing yourself. The menu is composed in Hebrew and, 80 percent of the time, paralleled by an English translation. Because it originated as something to be read from right to left, the English version will seem to lead off with desserts and end up with appetizers.

To every check, 15 percent will be added for service. Whether or not you are Israeli, you might also have to pay the extra 10 percent of local taxes.

Be warned that pickles and bread often cost extra, even though the waiter brought them without asking. Some restaurants even charge additional for vegetables that appear to be natural accompaniments to the main course. Whenever wine is placed on your table unordered, demand that it be removed immediately and remove yourself as soon as feasible. Unordered wine is not a quaint local custom, but the international symbol of clip joints.

As in hotels, wine, beer, coffee, tea, or soft drinks cost extra. Plain tap water is free, but you will usually have to ask for it.

With their meals, Israelis prefer the same beverages that they like before their meals: cola, soda, juice, beer, coffee, tea. The best thing I can say about Israeli beer is that it is not sweet, virtually the only beverage in the country that isn't.

I suggest you try the grapefruit juice; in Hebrew, *mits ehskoliat.* It is sweetened, but more sour than the orange juice (*mits tepus*) and a good refresher. Another good bet is Tempo Lavon, white Tempo, white signifying that it is a colorless lemon-lime soda and Tempo being the brand name.

Israeli wine is reasonably priced and well worth trying. Among the dry reds, try Benyamina, Adom Attik, Ashkelon Red, and Avdat Red. Among the relatively dry whites are Carmel Hock and Ashkelon.

Ask for tea anyplace in Israel, and you will be served a totally adequate cup of boiled water flanked by a tea bag (usually, with an aluminum tab rather than a string) and a slice of lemon. Ask for coffee, and anything can happen. Turkish coffee, the customary coffee in Oriental restaurants, is often available elsewhere. Thick and sweet, it comes in a cuplet whose lower half is occupied by muddy grounds. Espresso, made in an Italian-style machine, is doled out in strong, bitter portions. This is a favorite at snack bars and places that consider themselves sophisticated. Regular Israeli coffee is usually stronger and more bitter than American coffee, but somehow it can also be much more watery. Nowadays coffee comes with a cream substitute that is Kosher. (So far, despite the acceptability of margarine, you will be expected to eat dry bread with a meat meal.)

In restaurants and hotels, neither coffee nor tea is included in the price of the meal, except at breakfast.

Iced coffee is widely available but, if it is just coffee, it is probably presweetened. Ask for iced coffee and what you are more likely to get is coffee with ice cream blended into it, as is customary in Germany and Switzerland. If you want iced *coffee,* first hold exploratory discussions.

Iced tea is harder to find and it too usually arrives pretreated with sugar and lemon.

*"The scientists live on the right
and work on the left."*
—GUIDE'S EXPLANATION OF
WEIZMANN INSTITUTE

8
Getting Around

Maybe you never go to museums at home. Perhaps you hated history in school. Could be you don't like getting up at 6:00 A.M. to see sights that someone else has chosen for you. So don't. Tell your guide you won't be joining the group. He will argue and threaten like an abandoned lover. Be stalwart. On the other hand, don't outsmart yourself. What bored you as a child might fascinate you now. On the spot, you can discover a lot of things about the past, including the fact that it genuinely interests you.

GETTING STARTED

When you arrive at a new spot, step one is to obtain a street map and a current brochure or a newspaper. Also, get the current copy of *This Week in Israel,* an advertising giveaway that is not as helpful as its Mexican or Parisian counterparts, but still worth looking through. You should be able to get these from your hotel. Better yet, go to the nearest office of the Ministry of Tourism. Weekdays, they stay open from 8:00 A.M. to 6:00 P.M. in Tel Aviv and Jerusalem, but close for lunch and keep shorter hours elsewhere. Sometimes, as in Tel Aviv and Jerusalem, there are also municipal Tourist Information offices which are equally good and might be closer to your hotel. They have literature covering the whole country. Their well-informed staffers can help you plan your morning, or your entire vacation. They give emergency help in locating rooms, information about trains and buses, advice on entertainment, restaurants, shops, tipping, tours, guides—the works. If anything goes amiss and neither your guide nor hotel seems to be able to help, the Tourist Information Office is where you should bring your question or complaint.

In large Tel Aviv and Jerusalem hotels, local volunteers materialize each evening in the lobby to perform the same range of good deeds.

No matter how or where you travel within Israel, it helps to carry a local map; a national map; your own itinerary; the name, address, and telephone number of your current hotel; the name of your guide; the name of your travel agent's Israeli correspondent; and the tour operator's local telephone number.

FINDING A GUIDE

Most visitors to Israel get their guides the way their ancestors got spouses, unseen and unchosen. It is just as well because it is harder to prejudge a guide than a spouse. What counts is performance.

Israel has over 1,700 guides who have survived intensive training that usually lasts a full year. A license holder is easy to recognize. He—it is usually a he, although there are some women—wears a small bronze badge. No badge? No license. Someone peddling his services at a church or monument might say he left his badge home. Don't you believe it.

Tourism is now big business, and the guide corps has expanded accordingly. Back in the 1950's and 1960's, guides considered themselves their nation's salesmen and ambassadors; they tackled their responsibilities with gusto. Now, being a guide is just a job. Many are teachers or advanced students who only work during the summer months. They tend to be less jaded, if less experienced, than the veteran year-rounder. How many times can you take a bus through the Weizmann Institute and still sound thrilled by it? Since European and South American tourists began pouring in around the 1960's, guides often have to conduct each tour in several languages. Few are equally skilled in all their "official" tongues. A surprisingly high percentage of the current corps cannot speak English clearly or accurately. Sometimes the problem is not linguistic: the guide has nothing to say in any language. Your only hope is to keep asking questions.

To get around by yourself, your alternatives are tour bus, chartered bus, plane, plane-bus, ordinary nontourist bus, train, and hitchhiking.

TOUR BUS

Egged is the name of the bus driver's cooperative, which is Israel's Greyhound, Grey Lines, and all its municipal bus systems combined. Egged controls all regular intercity and intracity buses, except for some lines within Tel Aviv, which are controlled by a rival cooperative, Dan.

For sightseers, Egged Tours is the division that operates 3,000 sightseeing buses and conducts more than 50 regularly scheduled guided tours from Jerusalem, Tel Aviv, and Haifa. It also charters these buses to various travel agencies and tour operators, so that the bus you board might be a blue-and-yellow Egged vehicle no matter whom you booked through.

Egged's biggest rival in the tour field is United Tours, on whose buses you can take exactly the same 50-plus tours, seeing the same sights, paying the same prices and, probably, hearing the same jokes.

If all your traveling is done with the same group, you will be provided your own bus, guide, and driver each afternoon. If you arranged your sightseeing excursion yourself, either via your hometown travel agent or on the spot in Israel, sit in your hotel lobby at the appointed time and wait until the guide arrives and reads out your name. Do not fret if you were told you would be picked up at 1:30. It might be closer to 2:00 by the time they reach your hotel. If you are not staying at one of the larger hotels, you might have to transport yourself to the bus company's office or other designated starting point. Check. If you are staying outside the main tourist centers, there might be a special tour and pickup schedule benefiting you or a local company specializing in doorstep-to-doorstep tours.

Booking a tour after you arrive in Israel is simple. In a large hotel there is a staffer at the front desk or else a complete travel agency office that can handle the booking. Because morning tours start out so early, you should book a day ahead. For popular multiday trips to the Galilee or the south, sign up as early as possible. There is such a thing as a tour being completely sold out. In addition, not every tour operates every day.

Incidentally, if you are having a problem with hotel reservations, the easy way out is to book yourself onto a two- or three-day tour.

Each tour company has a brochure or listing of its offerings giving the starting time, duration, operative days, price, and points seen; *accept the fact that every itinerary includes places you don't want to see.* Not at every place are you promised an actual visit—dismounting from the bus and entering the site. Read the literature carefully lest you be broken-hearted when the guide points backward through the window and says, "There they were, folks, King Solomon's Pools." Also check the literature to see where you should bring along a head covering, low-heeled shoes, a bathing suit, and refreshments.

As a matter of fact, every tripper should carry a small tote or large handbag to hold bathing things, toilet paper, towelettes, emergency rations, and a head covering at the ready. As for low-heeled shoes, before boarding, they should be placed on the feet. Not even a passport is more essential to an eventual safe return.

On full-day trips the individual passenger often has the option of prepaying lunch or not. My advice is: skip the prepaid meal and bring a picnic lunch. You can always eat in the bus, but will probably have the chance to picnic in a field or at a beach. Meanwhile the lunch buyers will use up a minimum of 60 minutes sitting indoors, being served a hot and heavy hotel lunch. It might be the best available locally, but chances are it is not very good.

Typically, the cost for a half-day tour is $5–$8. For a full-day trip without lunch, the tab is $7–$13; lunch might add $2–$3. A two-day trip from Tel Aviv to Jersusalem, including all meals, will cost $35–$45 in a second-class hotel, $40–$50 in a top house. A two-day trip to the Galilee and the Golan Heights runs about $40 in a second-class hotel, $50 in a first-class house. Admissions, entrance fees, and fees for special local guides are included in the tour cost. Special sidebars, like skin diving at Elat, might cost extra. Refreshments always are additional. Tips are not mandatory. They have come into fashion, however. Do not feel obligated to tip one cent, but do tip 5–15 percent if your guide and driver have been special.

Families or friends traveling together can find freedom by

renting their own full-sized air-conditioned bus and hiring a guide. Even with only 12 passengers, they still save money. Rates start around $125 per ten-hour day.

Individual students and those young enough to pass as students can join the special summer tours known as Operation Joshua, run under the aegis of the United Jewish Appeal. Instead of seeing "sights," the group visits border settlements and absorption centers, meets Knesset members and Arab students. Day trips from Jerusalem or Tel Aviv used to cost $3, including lunch.

SMALL, BUT SPECIAL

The antigrouper who lacks the budget for a private car has a good compromise in the mini-bus tour. Some companies organize regular Volkswagen bus trips, with driver-guide, to the standard destinations. A seat might cost $10–$15, higher than for a tour bus, but the trip is more educational. Mini-buses will also take you wherever you choose. Depending on distance covered and the number of passengers, a custom trip tab can be $8–$20 per person per day. The hirer must also pay for meals and overnight expenses for the guide.

A good mini-bus specialist in Tel Aviv is Hemed Tours, 118 Hayarko Street (03) 24 30 77. Kopel Tours, 6 Tchernichovsky Street, Tel Aviv (03) 5 05 55, has branches in Jerusalem and Haifa. In Tiberias try Galilee Tours, 10 Hayarden Street (067) 2 03 30.

For jeep trips into the desert, the name to know is Johnny Desert Tours, Commercial Center, Elat (059) 26 08. Johnny operates day trips in the fascinating environs of Elat. Johnny, together with Neot Hakikar, also organizes more ambitious trips into the Negev and the Sinai, which involve camping out. So does Rekhasim, P. O. Box 3355, Jerusalem (02) 6 86 76. You can arrange to rent the equipment.

For desert camping tours consisting of guided groups of large jeeplike army vehicles known as command cars, the specialist is Neot Hakikar, which sometimes advertises itself in English as

Blue Line Tours. Their Elat base is Neot Hakikar, Commercial Center, Elat (059) 2 29 33; their Tel Aviv representative is Canaan Tours, 113 Ben Yehuda Street (03) 22 91 25.

To see the Galilee by boat, you can use the regular services of the Kinneret Sailing Company, P. O. Box 108, Tiberias (067) 2 02 27, or you can hire your own vessel from Blue Beach, Safad Road, Tiberias (067) 2 01 05.

Having a car and guide at your disposal for key days is not prohibitively expensive. For four people, ten hours or 200 kilometers costs about $40—about what a day's bus tour would cost. There is a $2 daily supplement for air conditioning, as well as charges for extra kilometers, hours, or passengers. Driver-guides usually provide Ford, Mercedes, or other big "family" cars, usually white, with the large red emblem of the Tourist Ministry, the two men carrying grapes. Most of these cars are operated by small cooperatives. Some taxis (not all) are owned by licensed guides, so your car might be a big black cab.

You can arrange for a car through your travel agent or, after arrival, through your hotel or a local travel agent or cab company. The Ministry of Tourism can give you a current list of companies and individuals. The rates are standard, nationwide. Taxis are likely to be available for just an hour or two. Rates are higher at night. On day and overnight trips, the hirer must pay for the guide's room and meals. Find out how much this costs. A tip is not necessary, but a 5–10 percent tip would be in order if the guide has been with you for several days or has been particularly good. There is no need to keep one guide throughout the trip. You can get licensed guides in any of the big cities. However, once you get to Beersheba, the Golan, Masada, and so on, your chances of finding a local guide are slight. One veteran guide suggested that people who like a nonstop instructional spiel should hire a guide in addition to the taxi. The driver concentrates on the road, the guide on the scenery.

You can set your own itinerary or plan your route with the aid of the guide or his company, for a half-day or for your entire visit. You go at your own pace, see what you want to see.

WARNINGS: HOW AND HOW NOT

So many Americans are interested in seeing the fruits of their philanthropies that the guide may pause at every baby home or clinic. The taxi driver who volunteers his services as a guide may or may not be qualified. Ask to see a license.

Harder to decree is when to pass up the services of the would-be guides who frequent the religious sites. They may or may not know anything about the place, and, once inside, their English might be inadequate. The volunteers—that is how they try to present themselves, but they expect to be tipped—are often quite young, sometimes mere children. If you think a youngster tagging along will be amusing or if you already have a good idea of what you will see, then strike a bargain and stick to it, and watch your wallet during the tour. Or after. The "volunteer guide bit" is a favorite come-on for souvenir shops in Bethlehem, Nazareth, and parts of Jerusalem.

If you want a professional guide to walk you around—no car, plane, bus, or speedboat—acquire one in advance via your hotel desk, travel agent, tour operator, or an office of the Ministry of Tourism. Agree on price, time, and itinerary before starting. Expect to pay about $2 an hour, plus whatever admissions and refreshments are involved. No tips are necessary.

For East Jerusalem I suggest you try to locate an Arab and/ or Christian guide, who will be more familiar with the Moslem and Christian sites than most of the Jewish guides. Ask at one of the travel agencies in that part of town or at the tourism office inside the Jaffa Gate.

FLYING TOURS

If your time is short, a flying trip is worth the splurge. You can see Elat, Sharm-el Sheikh, or Santa Caterina on a one-day trip only if you fly both ways. The price: about $40 to Elat, $70 to Sharm, and $100-plus to Santa Caterina.

With a little more time and less money, you can get an even closer look via an Arkia–Egged package that flies you one way, buses you the other. Price: $65–$100, with one overnight.

The hurried traveler has the option of doing Masada, the Galilee, and Golan tours by flying most of the way.

For these organized tours the major carrier is Arkia Israel Inland Airlines, whose main office is 88 Hahashmoniam Street, Tel Aviv (03) 26 21 05. Any travel agent can book you on its tours. Arkia uses fairly large jet-prop planes. The air is usually cloud-free, so you truly can see the land you fly over.

Arkia's most popular tours are the Saturday trips to Elat and Sharm-el-Sheikh, the bus-air two-day trip to Elat, and the four-day plane-coach trip to the Sinai.

A tour is very convenient because of the chronic bed shortage south of Beersheba. When buying transportation rather than tours, remember that you *must* reconfirm your flight 72 hours in advance. If you don't, you not only lose your seat, on domestic flights you lose your money. That is the law.

Fans of smaller aircraft can look into the tours operated by United Israel Airlines, University Road, Dov Airport, Tel Aviv (or via travel agents). Its single- and twin-engined craft make day trips to Elat, Santa Caterina, Sharm-el-Sheikh, Masada, or the Galilee.

Chartering small planes is also feasible, and because of the short distances involved, not prohibitive, perhaps $15 to $150 an hour.

ALMOST-FREE TOURS

For individual travelers or groupers, some of the best tours available are free—or almost so. The Municipality of Jerusalem runs low-cost walking tours of the city every Saturday at 10 A.M. They leave from the Municipal Information Office, 34 Jaffa Street. The walk varies from week to week. On Friday afternoon, through the Government Tourist Office, you can join a walking tour of the old synagogues section (a commercial tour covers the same ground). Hebrew University and Hadassah Medical Center offer free tours. In Tel Aviv both Bar-Ilan and Tel Aviv University conduct tours. In Haifa the Technion does.

Tree-planting trips are operated by the Jewish National Fund from principal cities. From Tel Aviv for example, you can be picked up at your hotel at 8:30 A.M. and taken for an interesting drive free to Modi'im, where you plant a tree with your own hands. The tree costs about $3. You are back by 1 P.M. Contact Keren Kayemet L'Israel, 96 Hayarkon Street (03) 23 44 49.

For Hadassah members there are two-hour $2 tours in Jerusalem that start at the Straus Health Center, Straus Street, at 8:30 weekday mornings. The tour's highlights are the visits to the new Hadassah Hospital and to Mount Scopus. In Tel Aviv, if you pay for the taxi, Hadassah will send someone along to show you the Youth Aliyah installations. Mizrachi ladies also have daily tours of their good works.

The Israeli representatives of Hadassah, Mizrachi, WIZO, B'nai B'rith, and other organizations, all join in asking tourists to be realistic about expecting special guide services. People appreciate the interest of visitors, but they have neither the staff nor budget to unroll a red carpet for every supporter. In fact such visits can disrupt the project one has been trying to help. The Golden Rule is never, never try to visit without telephoning first, and accept a turndown with good grace.

Most Christian sites have someone on hand to provide an explanation. On Fridays the Franciscans hold a religious procession along the Way of the Cross, but on other days, there is a guided walk. The Convent of the Sisters of Zion provides tours of its own premises.

National institutions, for example, the Knesset, often have free tours or a resident explainer. Among the national parks, Tel Jericho and the Qumran caves have guide service. At the others, there is also someone on hand to answer questions. Remember, the major archaeological and natural wonders are administered by the National Parks Authority, which provides good signs to direct you to key points and explains them. At any park you can buy a 14-day, 28-park ticket for under $2.

RENTAL CARS

Forget the Israel that used to be—the clogged and winding unmarked roads, and the real possiblity of mines and bullets. Israel still has plenty of clogged and winding roads, particularly near the Galilee and Dead Sea, but the main ones are both adequate and safe. I myself, being a Manhattanite, am not a particularly eager driver, yet at the height of the tourist season, I managed to chalk up 2,000 miles. About 10 percent of that amount was clocked looking for a parking place in Jerusalem (I eventually found it in Bethlehem), but I had no real problems and a lot of fun. I did not have an air-conditioned car, but was reasonably comfortable.

I was constantly lost. Road signs now exist in good quantity, but in bad places (at the actual intersection, after it is too late to turn) and in bad sizes (must "UJA" appear in letters as large as the place name?) or else have bad arrows pointing I know not where, but not in the direction the road is going. Roads are not identified by number. Most, but not all, of the place names appear in Latin letters, as well as in Hebrew print. Place names are almost uniform, but not quite: sometimes you are approaching Belvoir, other times Kochav Hayarden, and sometimes Sachne, but at crucial moments, Gan Hashelosha. International road signs are used to indicate one-way streets, curves, speed limits, and so on, and these are fine.

The easy way to meet Israelis—give soldiers a ride.
Courtesy Israel Government Press Office

There is no point in getting detailed directions in advance because everyone says, "But everybody knows where it is." Arm yourself with good Carta road maps, available in bookstores. Don't rely on the Ministry of Tourism's "freebies."

Better than any road map, however, is an Israeli soldier. Everyone gives lifts to the soldiers, and you should too. Even if they don't speak English, they know their country and they are efficient guides. (Why does the right route always go past their girlfriend's house?)

Warning: Road rules are much like ours—drive on the right-hand side of the road, pass on the left-hand side, and so on—but Israelis are still unaccustomed to driving. They pass on blind curves and hills, or in direct defiance of oncoming cars. They tailgate. They rarely dim their road lights or use their turn signals. They park wherever and however they please. Your best defense is to stay as far away as you can, even it it means letting everyone else pass you.

Despite all of this, I urge you to consider renting a car for at least a part of your trip. Set your own pace. Explore the sights Egged and United usually skip. Stay by the sea or in the country. Kibbutz-hop, try a camping site, a hostel, a luxurious city hotel. You might not be as fact-drenched as the bus passenger being guided along the same road, but you are on your own, dealing with the country and the people. You can still take advantage of group fares since many packages offer rental cars as an alternative land arrangement.

Alas, renting a car costs more than the alternatives and more than renting in most other countries, but split among a family or a few friends, the cost is not exorbitant. If you rent from the big international companies—Hertz, Avis, or National—$8–$10 a day plus 8–10¢ a kilometer (about 6/10's of a mile) is the lowest rate, for the smallest car, a Simca 1000, Ford Escort, Fiat 124, or other stickshift model. For a larger car with automatic shift, the base rate is $12 and 12–14¢ a kilometer. The heaviest car available might be an air-conditioned Ford Torino or Mustang: base rate $24 a day and 24¢ a kilometer. The longer the period for which you rent, the better the base rate. Air conditioning starts at $16 a day and 16¢ a kilometer, but is sometimes hard to get at any price. Smaller, purely local companies have lower rental scales (with or without kilometerage thrown in), but it is only the big three that accept reservations from anyplace in the world, allow you to pick up and drop off the car at a variety of locations, and honor American charge cards.

The rental price includes insurance for public liability and property damage up to $200. You can get full coverage for around $2 more per week if you are 25 years or older. If you pay in foreign currency (traveler's checks, credit cards), you do not pay local taxes. Having a major American credit card absolves you from paying a hefty deposit.

The only other document you need is an American driver's license, or any other license written in English or French, including an International Driving Permit. The license must be at least one year old; the license holder must be twenty-one or older.

Gas is shockingly expensive. You might as well start thinking in terms of Israel's metric system right now. Gas is sold by the liter, which is roughly the same as a quart. It takes about four liters to equal one gallon. Ordinary gas (830 octane) costs about 13¢ a liter, almost 55¢ a gallon. The 94 octane grade costs about 15¢ a liter. Except for large cities, few gas stations are open after dark or on Saturday. Always check gas, oil, tires, and, above all, water on Friday afternoon and before taking off across the desert. Water is used up very fast.

Emergency road service is supplied by the car rental company, so there is no need to join the Automobile and Touring Club of Israel. Bring your AAA card if you are staying a long time, but the A.T.C.I. extends its basic services to short-term visitors for free. If you bring your own car, via ship, you must have special third-party insurance before you are permitted to leave the port. You are not allowed to extend the policy later, so get coverage for your full stay. A Green Card from European countries may or may not be valid for Israel. Check specifically. Does it pay to bring a car you rented in Europe? Not unless you got a spectacularly low long-term rate.

Speed limits are posted in terms of kilometers per hour. On the few four-lane highways the limit is 90 km, not quite 60 miles per hour. On regular roads it is 80 km. Do not count on the usual mileage feats. Traffic is heavy. Roads are limited. Fortunately, so are distances. From the edge of Tel Aviv, one can reach Jerusalem in 80 minutes, Haifa in 70 minutes, Beersheba in two hours. From Tel Aviv it is only 250 miles all the way down to Elat and less than 150 miles to northern border points like Rosh Hanikra.

TRAINS AND BUSES

Trains are cheaper than buses and often less hectic because buses are sometimes faster and more flexible and therefore more popular. Good, if not particularly frequent, service links Jerusalem, Tel Aviv, Haifa, Nahariya, and Beersheba. Stations are often on the edge of town. The engines are Diesels. The coaches are comfortable, without Pullman or First Class, but there usually are buffets on board. Seats can be reserved for a small charge. In any case buy your ticket before you board. Trains do not operate on Friday evenings, Saturdays, or holidays.

To get from city to city, most Israelis take the bus (or *sherut,* see below). Tourists can buy a 15-day ticket for about $15 and a 30-day ticket for $25, good on any regular Egged bus. Service is fast, frequent, and cheap. Service between cities does not operate from sundown Friday to sundown Saturday. Service also stops inside cities, except for Haifa, which simply decided to have bus service on the Sabbath. Elat runs Sabbath buses, too.

For most buses, city or intercity, you pay after you board and are given a ticket (your fare depends on how far you go), which you are supposed to hold on to in case an inspector comes through to check. They rarely do.

Buses do *not* stop at every corner. You might not be able to get off or on for nearly a mile from when you would like to.

A nationwide unlimited Egged ticket costs about $12 for two weeks, under $25 for a full month. Tel Aviv has its own multiride ticket bargain. It is possible to reserve a seat on long-distance buses.

TAXIS, SHERUTS, AND HOPPERS

Taxis are either black or white; the color makes no difference. The same vehicle can operate as what we would call a regular taxi (which is what Israelis call a special taxi) or as a *sherut* or *hopper,* two forms of collective taxi. A special taxi can be summoned by phone, hailed on the street, or found waiting at a taxi stand. It will take you wherever you want to go for a price indicated by the meter or agreed upon between you and the driver in advance. In East Jerusalem, in particular, it is worthwhile to bargain with the driver. Elsewhere, your best deal is the meter. Insist that the driver turn it on, but be prepared for additional charges for after dark or because the fares have been raised too recently for the meters to have been adjusted. Taxis are not cheap: a ride between two central city points will be at least $1. Tips are not necessary.

Sherut is a noun meaning "service." In talking about taxis, a sherut is a collective taxi service, or jitney, supplementing bus service at a slightly higher fare. Intercity sheruts operate between fixed central points, like Zion Square in Jerusalem to the Central Bus Station in Tel Aviv. Unlike buses, they leave whenever the driver decides he has enough passengers to make it worthwhile. For travelers with heavy baggage, a sherut is handier than a bus, even though it goes to approximately the same place. Intercity sheruts operate on Saturdays and holidays. Hail a sherut by holding your arm out at 4 o'clock.

Within big cities a sherut is also a red mini-bus or big taxi that shadows the regular city bus routes, stopping only when flagged down or when a passenger wants to debark. Less crush, more leg room, faster service—for a slightly higher price. City sheruts do not usually operate on the Sabbath.

What operates on the Sabbath is called a hopper, after the Yiddish word meaning "snatcher." A hopper parks at a central location and snatches passengers wherever it can. Conversely, passengers snatch hoppers when they are lucky enough to spot one. Once you *hop* a *hopper,* you *hahndel* (that is, bargain), about the price. On Friday nights in Jerusalem, it is not a buyer's market.

HITCHHIKING

Go right ahead. Everyone does. *Several precautions:* Don't take big heavy suitcases. You will never get a ride. Don't try competing with soldiers. Pick an empty spot. Stand where it is easy and safe for cars to pick you up. Don't wave your thumb; hold up a sign, preferably in Hebrew, saying where you want to go. Israelis don't do this, and so it will give you a competitive advantage. Hitch in pairs and in daylight.

"One hundred is too much. Did
you mean pounds or dollars?"
—NOVICE BARGAINER

9

Shopping—What to Buy, What to Avoid, and How to Haggle

It takes money to save money. The best savings are on big-ticket items like diamonds, furs, gold and precious jewelry, fine leathers, silverware, carpets. Finding something that is reasonable and attractive and typically Israeli is difficult, but not impossible.

One pays a premium for good design. The most interesting work is being done in ceramics, jewelry, and glassware. So is some of the tawdriest commercial work.

Simplify your shopping. The revolution in design was sparked by Maskit, a crafts organization run by Ruth Dayan. The Maskit shops are on the main shopping street of every major tourist center. They have the best examples of each Israeli specialty, at prices close to everyone else's. In comparison, the Wizo craft shops are dull and old-fashioned. In addition to Maskit, good outlets run by and for craftsmen include the Jerusalem House of Quality and Source of Folklore. The craft shops in Old Jaffa, outside Tel Aviv, are fun to visit, but their stock is less sophisticated and more commercial.

Religious articles and books, Christian as well as Jewish, are excellent buys. For all groups Jerusalem is the natural place to shop, but good things are available all over. Copper, Elat stones, paintings, knitwear, embroidered housewares and dresses. There is much that is good, but following Gresham's law, it is overshadowed by the bad.

In approved tourist shops visitors get a special discount on many items by paying in dollars, traveler's checks, or cash. This is actually a dispensation from the sales tax that residents pay on the same merchandise. However, don't count on going straight from Lod to Beged Or for the coat you will wear on the trip. The rules vary by product category; the discount is 15 percent on jewelry, footwear, clothing, carpets, films, and

66

plastics made in Israel. On suede and leather, it is 30 percent, but only if the merchandise is sent to the airport or mailed to your home. However, if you pay by credit card, you lose the 15 percent for dollars.

What's more, you are excused from paying duty on foreign watches, cameras, perfume, alcoholic beverages, tobaccos, and some Israeli products, too, if you buy them at the Eshkar Duty-free Shops at Lod Airport, the King David or other Dan Hotels. Place your order by 10 A.M. the day before you leave, and it will be waiting in the airport exit hall. The most popular items are watches and cameras; you may save 75–100 percent over state-side prices. On perfumes, you save 30 percent.

You can also save money by buying where Israelis buy rather than in tourist stores, but you will not necessarily find the same range of merchandise and services in small neighborhood shops and you will not usually see the reassuring red-spies-bearing-grapes symbol of approval. The symbol does not guarantee the price or quality of specific items, but it does indicate a clean record. Department stores are a good idea. At Shalom in Tel Aviv or at the Hamashbir stores throughout Israel, you will find interesting, off-beat presents, like children's clothes, panty hose, shirts, housewares, records, books.

Since Israel uses the metric system, American sizes are not in common use, although tourist stores understand how our clothing sizes run. A storekeeper can tell you if a dress is close to an American size 10 or 12, but cannot cope with juniors', women's, and other special gradations. If you are shopping for others, bring measurements which can be converted into centimeters, a safer indication than sizes.

For children the best bets are clothes, records, and dolls representing the country's various ethnic strains. There are few Israeli-made toys, except for board games printed in Hebrew. A good gift for all ages are Israel's inexpensive, but ultramod, watches. They start at $10. Perhaps the best presents of all—any age group, any sex—are the Israeli posters that sell for about $2 and cost another $2 if the store air-mails them for you. The all-time classic is the poster called Golda Lisa, showing Prime Minister Meir as the Mona Lisa.

Many women have hopes of buying knits, leather clothes, and furs for themselves, but are disappointed by the stodgy styles and, except for the furs, the high prices. The high styles are created primarily for export, and so are their business-building price tags, although there are a few shops designed for tourists where the styles are comparable to those found back home. Because of the tourist discount, the price will not be higher, but it might not be dramatically lower. The most famous brand of all, Beged Or, does make an effort to provide interesting leather clothes for its visiting customers at the Miss Beged Or shop in Old Jaffa and its showroom at 40 Montefiore Street in Tel Aviv. Don't rush off to the factory in Migdal Ha Emek; the prices are no lower than in Tel Aviv.

For the woman who has everything, bring home some Chutzpah, an Israeli perfume, desirable largely for its name, which is as representative of Israel as it is possible to get. The sales point for the other Israeli perfume, Bat-Sheba, is its lovely bottle.

Keep track of your purchases and hold on to your receipts for Customs when you get back home. "Duty-free" does not mean you are free of the obligation to pay duty or President's surcharges when you return if you have spent more than your duty-free allowance.

For fine *yarmulkes, talayses, mezuzahs,* covers for prayer books, try Mea Shearim first. (The Orthodox section is the first place to look for anything old or traditional, from Yemenite jewelry to Roman glass. The wares are excellent, and the most minimal skill in bargaining will bring you prices 10–50 percent lower than elsewhere).

Menorahs? For fine, old ones, go to Mea Shearim. For modern ones, go anywhere.

East Jerusalem is the place for icons, old crucifixes, old candlesticks. The olive wood carvings and mother-of-pearl inlays that come from Bethlehem are available all over Israel.

Goatskin coats, old Bedouin dresses, new drip-dry Bedouin dresses, copies of Bedouin and Yemenite jewelry classics—these are the specialties of the *souks,* the stalls that line the streets of Old Jerusalem.

Bargaining flourishes in Old Jerusalem, although some Arab dealers say they bargain only because the customers expect it and that, if you knock down the price on one item, they will make it up on the next—or on the large number of Americans who simply refuse to bargain and pay the first price asked. In other parts of Israel, a written price tag appears on everything, but the proprietor might not be immune to a deal. Always try; the seller need only say "no."

To get the hang of bargaining, Mideastern style, practice on an item you definitely do not want. The more obvious your disinterest, the more the price descends. That is the whole secret. Now, move on to something you would like to buy. One hundred pounds? That is ridiculous. Besides it is ordinary. Not well made. Hardly worth ten pounds. You are asking 80? Still outrageous. Good-bye. No, not interested. Sixty? Maybe, for 20 pounds. Thirty? Wrap it up. Do not be afraid to walk out of the shop. In Arab shops the bargaining for an expensive item might start with an invitation for coffee or a soft drink. Courtesy demands that you accept the drink, but does not commit you to a purchase.

*"Did you see 'Never on Sun-
day'?"———"Here it was called
'Only on Weekdays.' "*

—TOURIST AND ISRAELI

10

The Sabbath—Observance and Avoidance

Shabbat—the Sabbath—is one Hebrew word you will master
because it plays a big part in your trip. Each Friday, shops and
offices begin shutting down at noon. By 3 P.M. even the strag-
glers have reached home. By 5:30 the buses have stopped. The
actual stopping time varies with the sunset. To find out, one has
to dial 14 or look at a newspaper. On Saturday, by 5 or so,
the buses have started rolling, the shopkeepers and restaurant
owners are raising their shutters. In between, the residents and
their visitors have kept very busy, not only in prayer.

On the Sabbath very Orthodox Jews do no work of any kind.
They do not handle money, cook, answer telephones, drive cars,
turn on lights. However, most Israelis treat Shabbat like most
Americans treat Sunday, a day for relaxing with family and
friends. For most Israelis it is the only day off, although
Friday has been established as a half-day for government offices,
banks, and public institutions.

Shabbat is the day when beaches, highways and recreational
facilities are totally jammed. Sunday is like an ordinary weekday. All but certain Christian and foreign workers are back at
their jobs. In East Jerusalem, Christian Arab shops close on
Sunday, but Moslem Arab shops close on Friday. It is Friday
that is the Moslem Sabbath, the Arab's day to head for the
beaches and national parks. Mosques are usually closed to outsiders on Friday.

In general Friday is more shut-down than Saturday. Everybody has his own unpredictable quitting time, which might be
several hours before the boss's. Many restaurants stop serving
after lunch. Museums close early. The traffic jam starts at
noon and peaks by 4 P.M. Some movie houses stay open, but
there are no plays or concerts. Night clubs close. Saturday night

70

is the big night for partying, for going out. Tel Aviv's Dizengoff Street is packed with people, and so is its equivalent in every hamlet.

Daytime Saturday is a different story. Especially in Jerusalem, Shabbat is greeted like a Queen, as per tradition, yet on the Sabbath there are more things to do in the Holy City than in Tel Aviv. You can even take a bus within East Jerusalem, although for most tourist destinations you either walk, find an Arab-owned taxi, or hop a hopper. In Tel Aviv you might have to search longer, but you will find taxis and sheruts. In Haifa the regular buses run. In Elat there is also some service. Between cities, there are neither regular buses, planes, nor trains. There are, however, special planes and tour buses. Saturday trips to Elat and Sharm-el-Sheikh are a fine, if expensive, solution to the Saturday problem. Some one-day trips are scheduled only on Shabbat. It is even possible to land or depart from Lod during the Sabbath hours or holidays.

In Jerusalem Friday afternoon is the only time set for the walking tour to the old synagogues and the procession on the Via Dolorosa. On Saturday there are walking tours to the Old City and other sites. As a matter of fact, the Old City is at its liveliest on Shabbat. The Western Wall is thronged with worshipers, many of them proudly clustered around a boy observing his Bar Mitzvah at this holy spot. The Arab shops are bustling. The cafes and restaurants are filled. In the modern city the Israel Museum and Shrine of the Book are open, but you must have bought your tickets in advance. (Sometimes, your hotel will purchase them for you.)

Israelis still use the Jewish calendar for religious holidays and certain national fetes. The Eastern churches have their own religious calendars too, but everybody uses the 12-month Western calendar for all other occasions.

There are no bus tours heading out of Jerusalem on Shabbat, but there are excursions from Haifa and Tel Aviv. Check out multiday trips that keep you busy on the road during the Sabbath.

What is true of Shabbat is true for most of the holidays during the year, except for Yom Kippur. That, the Day of Atonement, is the most sacred day of the Jewish year. Even the national parks close on Yom Kippur, the only time that they do so. On Shabbat one can always find a hotel to provide food and drink. On Yom Kippur not even the hotels serve food, unless prior arrangements have been made.

Of course visitors can always spend the Sabbath and holidays in religious activity. Synagogues welcome visitors. Only during Yom Kippur and Rosh Hashanah, synagogue seats must be reserved and paid for in advance. Be aware that Saturday services start early, usually by 8 A.M., and are over by 10:30 A.M. If you are invited to Saturday morning *Kiddush* in an Orthodox home, the refreshments will be a breakfastlike collation served around 10:30.

There are several new Reform and Conservative congregations scattered around Israel, but expect most synagogues to be Orthodox.

Special Sabbath celebrations are held for tourists, most notably at Hechal Shlomo, the seat of the Chief Rabbinate, 58 King George Street in Jerusalem.

If your hotel is one that has special Shabbat rules for elevators and lights, you will know it. But, except in totally non-Jewish establishments, assume that you are neither to smoke nor write in public, unless everyone else does so.

Few Israelis get truly dressed up on Shabbat, but on Friday night they do don clean clothes and the women wear their prettiest dresses. Beginning on Friday, instead of simply saying *Shalom,* everyone extends the special greeting *Shabbat shalom* for both "hello" and "good-bye."

One more special Saturday activity—throwing stones. Small groups of Orthodox Jews in Jerusalem believe so strongly that it is wrong to perform the work of driving a car on Shabbat that they walk to the Davidka Monument outside Mea Shearim and engage in the work of locating and hurling stones at passing cars. This distresses everybody else in the country, but it still occurs from time to time. If your own beliefs do not preclude driving, let prudence keep you away from the ultra-Orthodox neighborhoods.

"I walked all the way to the top. Then they said it wasn't *Mount Sinai. It was only Mount Zion."*
–Elderly tourist

---

10 BIGGEST MYTHS ABOUT ISRAEL

1. It is a "Jewish" country.
2. It is a little country.
3. It is a very serious place.
4. Israelis have to be nice because you are Jewish and gave money. They have to be nice because you are non-Jewish and are needed as a friend.
5. Teen-agers will be safe from sex and drugs.
6. The food is always Kosher.
7. The people are idealists.
8. The only way to see Israel is on an organized tour.
9. The only place to stay is in a luxury hotel.
10. It is not safe to drive around in a car.

10 MOST FREQUENT COMPLAINTS BY AMERICAN TOURISTS

1. Everybody is rude, noisy, and aggressive.
2. The service is terrible.
3. The food is terrible.
4. The guides have become terrible.
5. You have to get up too early.
6. You have to move around too fast.
7. There is not enough time for shopping. There is too much time for shopping.
8. There is nothing to do at night.

9.   The telephone system does not work.
10. Nobody provides enough information about anything. The street signs are inadequate. Besides, every place has at least two names.

10 MOST UNDERRATED SIGHTS IN ISRAEL

1.   Tel Hai Museum, near Kiryat Shemona.
2.   Museum of Printing, Safad.
3.   Tel Dan archaeological site, springs, and museum, Kibbutz Dan, near Kiryat Shemona.
4.   Jaffa Museum, Jaffa.
5.   Battleground and Memorial, Kibbutz Yad Mordecai, near Ashkelon.
6.   Holocaust Memorial, Mount Zion, Jerusalem.
7.   En Kerem, suburb of Jerusalem.
8.   Ecce Homo, site of the Convent of the Sisters of Zion, Jerusalem.
9.   Corn Museum, Haifa.
10. St. Anne's Church, Jerusalem.

10 BIGGEST BORES IN ISRAEL

For those with special interests, these can be the most fascinating sites in the country. The average tourist can better use his time elsewhere.

1.   Hadassah Hospital, unless you work for Hadassah or adore anything done by Chagall.
2.   Yad Kennedy, unless you plant a tree.
3.   Druse Village, unless you go privately to visit a Druse family.
4.   Safad Artists' Quarter, unless you adore paintings of prancing Hasidim.
5.   Bahai Shrines, unless you are a believer in Bahaism.
6.   Rishon Le Zion Wine Cellars, unless you'll do anything for free wine.
7.   King Solomon's Pillars, unless you are trying to avoid the Red Sea.

8. The Rothschild Mausoleum, unless you adore gardens.
9. The entire town of Tiberias, unless you are a student of Orthodox history.
10. The Beersheba Camel Market, unless you arrive at 6 A.M. and really want to buy a camel.

Part II

BEFORE YOU LEAVE HOME

"Attention, Blue Group—
Call—5:30 A.M.
Breakfast—6:30 A.M.
Departure—6:50 A.M.
Leave bags outside door by mid-
night."

—BULLETIN BOARD,
JERUSALEM HOTEL

12
Pick the Right Trip

WHO MAKES THE RULES?

Israel is a special ball game, with its own benefits and confusions. Not that government restrictions make it difficult; on the contrary, you just stroll in and say, "Shalom." The obstacles are those created by the Pharaohs of international tourism, often working under the impression that they are making it easier or less costly for the prospective visitor. Even if you think you know which arrangement to choose, protect your favorite consumer, yourself, and leap into the sea of travel-ese.

Students and young people have their own set of subsidized blessings, which will be explored later, but for all North American visitors, including the youngsters, the price paid for an airplane ticket is tied to the land arrangements chosen, and vice versa. There are no charter flights between the United States and Israel. The rules of the game are determined by the International Air Transport Association (IATA), to which the world's major carriers belong, and by the carriers' respective governments, plus the hotels, travel agents, and tour operators that are involved in the Israeli tourism industry. The rates and rules apply to all airlines equally, but they are always changing. The basic principles, however, are constant. Airlines try to attract vacationers by promoting off-season, midweek, and volume buying. The best bargains are special fares for groups—either genuine organizations or bands of strangers who agree to the same departure dates—particularly if the group also buys hotel and sightseeing packages.

79

In travel-ese, "tour" and "package" are often used interchangeably to describe a deal that includes air fare plus specific land arrangements. Virtually identical contents are offered to established organizations, departure-date groups, and individuals. "Individual" is used interchangeably with "independent," and can signify a person, couple, family, or quartet of friends, as long as they are traveling independently of a group.

Warning: Package prices, as promoted, may or may not cover lunches, dinners, identical sightseeing. *One constant:* prices are per person, assuming two adults share a room; a single traveler pays at least 10 percent more.

WHICH AIR FARES?

You can buy a First Class ticket, New York to Tel Aviv, round trip for around $1,500. (*Remember, exact fares and accompanying taxes change often.*) An Economy Class ticket costs about $900. For these, there are no whereases about weekend departures or what you do after arrival. Luxury addicts choose First Class because of the big, comfortable seats and elaborate service. Most people are content to fly Economy Class, sitting six across and eating ample, if unspectacular, meals. Among the Economy Class passengers, few actually pay the full flat rate; most pay an amount between $450 and $700. It is completely legal. They get the same plane, seating, food, and service as the full fare payer. The difference is that they accommodate their dreams to fit the requirements of the special fares.

The choice is wide, all the way from totally ad lib travel, going when and where the spirit beckons, to totally preset "land arrangements," that being the industry name for whatever you do after your plane lands. It can cover hotels, meals, rental cars, chauffeured cars, sightseeing buses, even boat rides, or plane flights within Israel. Land arrangements can be custom-made to include whatever you wish, or they can be ordered "Sears–Roebuck style" from a catalogue of packages. Prearrangement limits flexibility, but saves energy, time, and money. An individual has little bargaining power and ends up paying the top rate whether in a youth hostel or a five-star hotel. "Vouchers" are in effect prepaid tickets for tours or hotels.

Your agent gives them to you, and you give them to guides and desk clerks as you proceed.

Individualists can be happy with packaged travel in Israel because the tours are well thought-out and competitively priced. Standards of operation are higher than they are in Europe. Because of the special air fare structure for Israel, there are few "throwaway" packages—that is, bottom-of-the-barrel accommodations that people pay for but never use.

The individual traveler who refuses to preset his itinerary can still save money on his airplane ticket by buying one of the group flight deals described later or by timing his trip to take advantage of Excursion fares. At this writing, there is a 14–21 day Excursion fare that costs about 25 percent less than the ordinary Economy fare and a 22–45 day Excursion that costs about 35 percent less.

Now let's consider the traveler who wants firm reservations and a definite budget, but who still resists donning the tour-member's name badge. By the time you read this, the carriers might have revised their formulas, but chances are they will still offer the Group Inclusive Tour (GIT), familiar to veterans of European and Pacific travel, plus various deals applicable only to Israel and good for as long as one year. These entail rules about how many people constitute a group, when they can fly, and what constitutes high season. Youth fares are also now in effect.

Groups can be composed of members of the same congregation, golf club, or medical society. The individual members can be total strangers who never get to meet each other, even on the plane. Under IATA rules, this is perfectly proper. Long-lived legitimacy of groups is relevant only for certain affinity group fares that have occasionally applied to destinations other than Israel, or for chartering (that is, renting) planes.

So far the Israeli government has forbidden charter flights from the United States and Israel, although not from certain other countries. The absence of charters accounts for Israel's novel group rates.

On a GIT the fare is sometimes as much as 45 percent lower than on a regular Economy ticket. The traveler chooses land arrangements from a list of possible itineraries and departure dates compiled by a travel agent, airline, or organization (American Jewish Congress, Hadassah, and so on). He must fly over, return, make any European stopovers with the same group. Each grouper might have a different itinerary, but it will be one of three: an escorted group tour, an individual tour that he pursues all by himself, or a "no-tour" consisting of at least x-dollars worth of hotels, rental cars, or sightseeing. On individual tours some sightseeing by bus is standard. For an exta payment, a private car with chauffeur-guide or a self-drive car can be substituted.

For most group rates you must fly over, back, and to speci-fied European stopover points whenever the group does, even though between flights you can be on your own. Most depar-tures are from New York, but there are also frequent departures from Boston, Washington, and Baltimore, and at higher fares, from Chicago, Detroit, and Los Angeles.

For certain group setups a travel agent or an organization trip chairman might be able to arrange a return flight with a dif-ferent group.

An air fare that is not tied to a land package is ideal for two traditionally large categories of Israel-goers, people who stay with relatives and repeat-trippers who have already visited the major sights. Another beneficiary is the small but growing number of people who want to travel around on their own, with or without a chauffeur. Of course the fares are one big reason why their ranks are growing. The Youth Fare now covers anyone from 12 through 21 years old, student or not. No land package is required.

FREEDOM VS. SECURITY

Rate deals like the group fares are rare for those affluent travelers who chose what the trade calls Foreign Independent Travel (FIT), which means a custom-made itinerary that has been arranged by a retail travel agent for an individual, family, or quartet of friends. The itinerary is private and personal, but once purchased, as rigid as a group tour. FIT is usually for hang-the-expense devotees of luxury, but not always. FIT clients pay extra for the custom planning but, particularly in Israel, they mix bus tours with their chauffeured forays and they schedule kibbutz guesthouses along with their five-star suites.

"Transfer" means being picked up or delivered to an airport

or other terminal by a representative of a travel agent. People who are traveling by tour bus usually are met by a bus; FIT clients, by a private car. In compact Israel, FITniks are often transferred between cities by car. The cost of each transfer is figured into the total cost for the tour. If you do not mind public transportation, tell your travel agent you do not choose to buy transfers. It will give you a good opportunity to become more familiar with Israelis.

The ultimate in rigidity is the escorted tour package, whether one is traveling with a hometown group or joining fellow tourists who are strangers. You are given several days "at leisure," but on most days, you wake up, eat, admire landmarks, and photograph panoramas in prearranged unison. This can be an advantage, as well as an annoyance.

Throughout the trip, you are under leadership of a guide, who acts as your shepherd, ombudsman, stage manager, social director, and "universal maven." He knows who built the castle, what time you are going to eat, and whether or not you should wear a hat. He sees that your baggage gets carried; you never touch it between hotels. You will also have 40 permanent traveling companions, predominantly female and predominantly over 50. Financial security is part of the bargain, too; so many basic costs are included that you have little to worry about as you go.

Don't be discouraged by the complications. There is an army of pros standing by to help you—the American outposts of the Israel Government Tourist Office, the Vacation Desks and Group Desks of the various airlines, the organizations who keep a steady flow of members bound for Israel, and, of course, the thousands of travel agents around the country. Janet Cushner, of TWA's Vacation Desk in Manhattan, says 70 percent of the people who seek her advice about Israel have already made up their minds to go, but are unsure of what to do next.

The important thing to remember is that, in contemporary travel, more is less. The more people taking the same trip at the same time, the less it costs each one. The more items that are prearranged, the less each item costs. The most expensive trip is a solo jaunt, without plans or reservations.

If you can't turn back the clock and go as a student or as a welcomed relative, then measure the possibilities on the fixed-flexible scale against your tastes, interests, and budget. Kay

Schattman, who handles TWA's Israel desk and who saw the country both as tourist and kibbutz volunteer says that most of the travel agents' bookings she handles are package tours. "The hotel space alone is worth it. There are so many different types of tours that there is something for everyone." To which Janet Cushner adds, "The tours include the high points that everyone wants to see. It would be hard for people to cover that much ground on their own." Hiam Goren, of Tourstars in New York, also stresses the value of confirmed reservations: "The hotel has to find you a place to sleep, no matter what." "You can't expect your relatives to take you around," says Haskell Tydor of General Tours. "They are not on vacation."

HOW PACKAGES WORK

The big question on every traveler's mind is "Who gives the best deals?" The only realistic answer is "It depends." Packages that appear to be the same are often very different. Discrepancies in price are usually due to differences in the number of meals or the amount of sightseeing included or the caliber of rooms within the same large hotel. Then, too, different departure dates (high versus low season) and trips that require fewer fellow passengers will affect price. The travel business is a business. Profit must be built into the package at every step of its preparation. Even charitable groups that sponsor trips often use them not just to cover their operating expenses, but also to create a "profit" that can finance their good works.

Most packages beamed at Americans contain similar ingredients: two-week tours cover 7 or maybe 8 full days of sightseeing; three-week tours cover 10 days, with a two-day jaunt to Elat. Hotels tend to be de luxe (five-star) or first class (four-star). Usually, either no hotels or all hotels are included. Israeli breakfast and dinner are provided on most days. Stopovers in Europe usually feature de luxe or first-class hotels, Continental breakfast, and a sightseeing tour for each city. The individual traveler usually has the option of paying extra to hire a drive-yourself or chauffeured car, instead of sightseeing via bus. Tours sponsored by religious or charitable groups often emphasize visits to the organization's own projects.

Most packages send the traveler to more than one city. The

largest number of days are scheduled for Tel Aviv. Ideally, days at leisure are set for Tel Aviv because people like to shop there. Because of the Sabbath and other practicalities, free days are likely to occur in Jerusalem (wonderful!) or Haifa (what'll we do?).

For individual travelers, packages are often set up on a circle tour basis. Whatever day you arrive, you are fit into the tour operator's weekly agenda of trips. That is what determines whether you go to Haifa before going to Masada.

From the interchangeable building blocks, a vast array of packages is marketed under a variety of names. Whether the tour is in a brochure headed "Airline X's Famous Flight" or "The Heights Temple Annual Trip," it was actually put together by a tour operator or wholesale travel agent (as distinct from the retail travel agent who deals directly with the public). It is the tour operator who lines up the beds, negotiates the deals for guides and buses, arranges the departure date with the airline. The tour operator might maintain its own staff in Israel and the other countries it specializes in, or it might make its Israeli arrangements through a company over there. The retail travel agent's role is to figure out what the tourist wants and to see that he gets it. The actual getting is done by the wholesaler, who circulates a catalogue of his Israel packages, usually in connection with a specific airline. The carrier, in its own promotion and advertising, often calls these wares "our tours."

Any prospective voyager can buy any of these tours at list price from any retail travel agent. A temple's trip committee might choose the same tour or a version aimed at groups, with slightly lower group prices; to the committee, it is "The Temple Tour." A thousand miles away, another trip committee might select the same package to be "our church's." Organization prices are likely to be the same for most organizations.

Who really set up the tour? The only place this appears in print in most brochures is on the last page under "Responsibility" or "Generals Conditions." The company cited there as not being responsible is the company that did the arranging. *This is must reading.* It tells what is and what is not covered. There, too, one will find the several hotel possibilities listed, followed by the really vital words—"or similar."

Brochures are advertisements designed to make one buy an already existing product. They rarely lie, but they often exaggerate and use the English language in very special ways. The words "at leisure" mean that anything you do will cost extra. "You have a chance to" is the same thing as "optional"; that is, you want it, you buy it. "And up" means—well, you know this one; you have been a consumer all your life.

The words that cause the most trouble are "all inclusive." There is no such thing. Travel people use "inclusive" or "all inclusive" to mean a deal that covers land arrangements as well as air fares. Only items specified are included, and even these specifications can be confusing. An included meal is a meal that is preset. Any substitution or addition—including after-dinner tea or coffee—will be paid for by the traveler. Included tips or service refers only to the standard percentage the hotel or restaurant adds to every bills. It does not include the tip expected by the bellman who brings suitcases from the street to the bedroom or the chambermaid who sews up a hem. A package "day" does not include overnight accommodations; a "night" does not necessarily cover meals or daytime activities. If you skip a meal or a sightseeing trip, you cannot be reimbursed.

Single travelers must remember that prices assume double occupancy. Unless you can arrange to share a room with another group member, you will pay a supplement for every night. There is an extra charge for private cars, rented or otherwise.

ORGANIZATIONS

A big attraction of traveling with your organization is that you are likely to be traveling with people you have met before. At least they will be people who share specific interests. The congregation tour is extremely popular with all religious denominations. Most popular of all are tours organized by nationwide charitable organizations. Sometimes you can pay for your tour in Israel Bonds. The trips are supposed to be for organization members and their relatives, but outsiders can often join. The following is a list of where to get tour information from the most active organizations:

American Jewish Congress, 18 East 84 Street, New York, N.Y. 10028 (212) 879–4588

B'nai B'rith, 315 Lexington Avenue, New York, N.Y.
10016 (212) 689–7400

Hadassah, 65 East 52 Street, New York, N.Y. 10021
(212) 355–7900

Union of American Hebrew Congregation Tours, 838
Fifth Avenue, New York, N.Y. 10021 (212) 249–
0100

United Synagogues of America Tour Service, 444 Mad-
ison Avenue, New York, N.Y. 10022 (212) 371–
6170

The United Synagogues Tour Service has prepared an excellent manual on how to organize and conduct a synagogue
tour. Many points will be equally useful to all group planners.
For instance: the booklet states that a tour escort hired in your
hometown can "only see that everything goes well at the airport and on the flight. . . . Upon arrival, a professional tour
guide will take charge. The tour escort then just sits back and
enjoys the trip, and remember, price is important." You can
get a copy of the manual from the United Synagogues address
listed above.

PROTECTING YOUR AIR FARE

To qualify for the various group fares, you must always fly
with the group—over, back, and to stopover destinations. If
you get sick and do not use all your land arrangements, you
should be able to get some or all of the money refunded for
the unused portions, via the travel agent who placed the order.
If you cannot fly with the group, however, you are still responsible for the cost of the flight.

Your only defense is to buy (via your travel agent or insurance broker) what is known as an air fare protector insurance policy, *before you leave home.* This will reimburse you
for the additional flight expense. Some policies also cover a
small amount of hotel expenses.

You are reimbursed if illness or injury strikes you or your
parents, spouse, children, parents-in-law, or siblings under 18
living under the same roof, forcing you to cancel your trip 30
days before departure (assuming you have paid the fare and
cannot get the money back). If anyone in this same cast of

characters is smitten while you are away, you are reimbursed for return Economy fare, one way.

CHARTERS

Yes, there are *no* charter flights to Israel at this writing, but there are charter flights to Europe, from whence you can buy a ticket on a scheduled flight to Israel. If you are a student, you can get a charter flight from Europe to Israel. For non-students there are charters from England, Sweden, Germany, Holland, or France—if you can locate them via foreign newspapers or friends.

SAILING TO ISRAEL

One can still get to Israel by ship, but it takes both time and money. To sail from New York to Haifa on the Greek Line, the last company still serving this run, requires at least 13 days and $400–$500 *one way;* in other words, double the air fare. In the October–March off-season, it is possible to get a 25 percent discount by joining a group of 25 or more persons. Groups are put together by travel agents, as they are for GIT flights.

There are two brighter alternatives—you can sail across the ocean and then fly to Israel from England or France or you can fly across the ocean and then pick up a ship to Israel at Marseilles, Venice, or other Mediterranean port. Transatlantic crossings—if you can book passage on one—cost $250 and up plus 5–7 days each way. The *Queen Elizabeth 2,* it should be noted, has a Kosher kitchen.

Accommodations, prices, and ports of call vary, but the most highly regarded vessels are the Israeli-owned Zim Lines' *Herzl, Dan,* and *Molodet,* Kyriakos Lines' *City of Athens,* and Epirotiki Lines, *Hermes* and *Pegasus.* The Hellenic Mediterranean and Turkish Maritime Lines specialize in more basic accommodations. Zim has definitely abandoned its old New York–Haifa route.

From Marseilles to Haifa, the fare, with all meals, is $90–$175, starting with dorms and going up the scale to two-berth cabins. The lines all give a 10 percent discount for round trips and another 10 percent in off-season, plus assorted discounts for students and families.

HOW TO USE A TRAVEL AGENT

Could a travel agent help you? The answer is definitely yes— *if* you pick the right agent and *if* you watch him like a hawk. The road to Israel is paved with picayune complications. Aunt Millie and Cousin Fred will tell you what you should do (try and stop them), but vacation time is precious. Invest it with a professional. If you are committed to one organization's tour, however, you already have the organization's agent working for you.

Don't be afraid of being sold "a bill of goods." The agent only makes suggestions; decisions are made by you. Even veteran travelers ignore agents because they think they charge high fees, but that is not how the system works. A good agent will probably save you money. A hungry agent will *hahndel.*

On an international plane ticket or packaged itinerary, the retail travel agent charges the traveler nothing at all. The agent is compensated by commissions from the airline and the wholesale tour operator. The airline would sell you the ticket or the tour directly, but not at a price lower than the agent's. The wholesale tour operator won't sell you the package at the wholesale rates. Be aware that many wholesalers have retail divisions that will handle your tour, but at the same retail prices that everyone else charges.

A custom-made FIT itinerary, however, will usually involve fees paid directly by the client. Some retail agents state in advance that they have a flat charge for each reservation made; often, it is $5. Other retailers keep their markup a mystery and become annoyed when the client asks how much their services cost. But it is your money—ask.

Remember that travel agents are agents. The more they sell you before you leave home, the more they earn. Theoretically, their commissions are standardized, so they have nothing to gain from selling you a $1,000 lemon instead of a $1,000 dilly. However, they would have something to lose—your future business.

In actual practice, commissions are not identical. Some tour operators pay an override, which means they give bigger commissions to retailers who push their tours, and wholesale-retail people like to sell their own wares. Theoretically, retail travel agents do not have to be specialists in Israeli travel because they sell arrangements put together by companies that do specialize. Firsthand knowledge of your destination can be helpful, but give a higher priority to a general reputation for good, fair service. Like any growth industry, travel has attracted its share of charlatans and know-nothings.

If you do not have a family travel agent, ask people who share your interests, age bracket, and life style. If need be, contact the American Society of Travel Agents, 360 Lexington Avenue, New York, N.Y. 10017 (212) 661–2424. This is the major professional organization with 3,200 members. They can give you names of members in their area.

Membership in ASTA or in the slightly overlapping Association of Retail Travel Agents (ARTA) is not the same as having a purity certificate or professional license (licensing does not yet exist, although Congress and many state legislatures are considering it). The membership sticker does signify that the principal has been in business at least three years, and has agreed to a code of ethics. ASTA has yet to expel anyone because of consumer grievances, but it does wave its big stick if things go amiss—and this helps.

Talk to several agents before choosing and state openly that you are shopping for a family travel agent and would like to hear his ideas on Israel. Do not compare agents on the basis of price alone. At a preliminary meeting different agents might have completely different approaches to your trip, but when you get down to buying, each can get the same merchandise, from the same factory. Is a large agency better than a small one? Large agencies tend to have more muscle in getting reservations; small agencies often are more personal. If you do go with a large agency, insist on having the same person work with you throughout.

Once you become a client, do your homework. Read. Ask. Check arithmetic. Accept nothing you don't understand. Above all, be honest. Tell the agent the truth about your budget, interests, and dreams. If you would rather swim than see ruins, say so, or else you will spend your vacation looking at ruins. And when you get back home, report on how it worked out.

GROUPERS, BEWARE

So far, most news stories about stranded travelers and absconding trip organizers have involved destinations other than Israel, but still you should find out exactly which group you are going with, what agency is handling the details, and whether or not it is a reputable outfit. Check the airline involved. Be sure you know what kind of deal you are getting, where you will go and under what conditions. Comparison shop. Groups add their own markups to standard tours. "We charge $800," one operator said, "but you'd never know it by the time the churches get through their pricing."

Suppose you want to travel with an organization of which you are not truly a member. Chances are you can get away with pretending you belong, but there is always the possibility that somebody will complain and "bump you" from the flight.

WHEN TO GO

Can I interest you in October through April? Summer is a madhouse. The heat is not much worse than in New York and Chicago—or Rome and the Riviera—but the crowds are. Facilities are swamped, tempers are frayed, decibel levels are painful. The tourist's major activities are waiting and screaming. Passover, Rosh Hashanah, and Christmas are not much better. Then, prices are often higher than in the June to September period.

From the end of autumn's major Jewish holidays (mid-October) until Israeli Independence Day (May), except for Christmas and Passover–Easter, the tourist in Israel pays less and enjoys more. He can still take a dip in the Dead Sea, Red Sea, or Beersheba swimming pools, play golf at Caesarea, water-ski in the Galilee—and ski on Mount Hermon. And he can see or participate in special events—the Mardi Gras-like festivity at Purim or the annual national three-day mass hike to Jerusalem. Spring is the only time when the hills of Israel are green.

Yes, the rainy season goes from October to April and that often means dampish weather, with occasional showers and even more occasional downpours. The truly heavy rains come only in December, January, and early February—the months when it is raining in most other places in the Northern Hemisphere. Even at its chilliest worst, Jerusalem is less uncomforttable than Philadelphia or Toronto. What's more, being so close to the equator, the days in Israel are almost as long in winter as in summer.

Virtually all the sightseeing attractions are available yearround. The concert and theater seasons peak from autumn to spring. Kay Schattman of TWA points out that "fewer tours are offered in winter and fewer different departure dates, but there is a steady stream of opportunities for group flights and a full range of itineraries."

Many church and synagogue groups now choose winter dates on economic grounds. The package tours cost less, fares cost less, hotels cost less. The basic 15-day tour of Israel wholesaled by Sharon Travel costs about $1,000 in the summer, but is closer to $800 in winter. In January you might get a room at the King David for about $10; in July the same room would cost 10–20 percent more—if you could get it.

Nevertheless, most people will continue to go in June, July, and August for the understandable reason that this is when they and their children have vacation. Their consolation prize: more departure dates, more young people on the circuit, incessantly cloudless skies.

TRAVELING ALONE

It beats staying home, even if it is more expensive. If you have doubts about plunging into a demanding itinerary alone, then by all means book yourself into an escorted tour, preferably one that is sponsored by an organization in which you have some interest. Or, enroll in a study-trip or kibbutz worktrip.

Don't expect the members of a tour group to be constant company. Couples tend to stay by themselves or with other couples. You will be thrown up against the other solos in your group, whether you like them or not. Tour operators will try to pair you with a roommate, if you ask.

As a solo traveler, you are more likely to meet new people,

try new things. If you are accustomed to being on your own at home, then you will be equally at ease in Israel. The locals are astonishingly friendly. In Israel, to an even greater extent than in Europe, an unescorted woman can go almost anywhere except an out-and-out night club. To see night clubs, simply join a tour or recruit another adventurous female. Two females will be welcomed without awkwardness.

TRAVELING WITH CHILDREN

Israel is a great place for children, if the parents pick an itinerary with them in mind. Some tours, however, do not accept subteens because most youngsters cannot endure a full day of trekking from monument to monument. Nor do they enjoy trekking from relative to relative. The trip plan, beginning to end, must account for each child's age, taste, personality, and endurance. A fifteen-year-old enjoys most of the things that adults do; a seven-year-old needs a child-sized itinerary. For children six or younger, an extended tour is all wrong; even a one-day trip can be wearing.

A unique solution comes from Archaeological Tours of Israel, an escorted parent-teen-ager 9-night trip, in which the youngsters do some touring apart from their parents and get to meet young Israelis. Parents pay around $700; children are $50 less. The tour operator is at 136 East 57 Street, New York, N.Y. 10022 (212) 421–3320.

Ideally, get your own car, possibly chauffeured, but preferably self-drive, if only for a few days. In any case schedule several days at beaches or country spots. Kibbutz guesthouses are perfect. So are campsites, holiday villages, and offbeat spots like the Vered Hagalil dude ranch.

Look for places that are fun and where other children are likely to turn up. Focus on dramatic, easily comprehended sites; Masada, Megiddo, the Golan battlefields, En Gedi, Caesarea, Acre, Rosh Hanikra. Be sparing about shrines, churches, synagogues, memorials.

One important exception are the various memorials to the six million Jews who were murdered by Hitler. I think every visitor—man, woman, or child—no matter how little or how much he knows of the events should visit at least one of the memorials. Children might be turned off by more than one. Yad Mordecai is the most dramatic of the memorials, and it is coupled with an even more dramatic presentation of the 1948 battle for the kibbutz. Young people cannot be expected to grasp the significance of what to them is distant history, but at Yad Mordecai they can understand what it must feel like to have enemy guns outside your house.

Youngsters will not need real dress-up clothes in Israel, even for religious services, where hats and covered shoulders are sufficient. If you are going to stop in Europe, however, the ties, jackets, and dresses had better come along. Pack sufficient books and toys. It is difficult to find English-language children's things in Israel. Better bring along essential chocolate syrups, vitamins, and so forth. Dry cereal is rarely available, so if necessary, bring that, too. Babysitters can be obtained through hotels or by checking the newspapers.

YOUNG PEOPLE AND STUDENTS

This book is designed for post-college travelers, but as the usher at a Hebrew University lecture told me, "Okay, come in; everyone is a student of something." Many of the "student" trips will interest oldsters.

For different age groups there is a wide spectrum of opportunities—governmental, commercial, and mixed. There are summer camps for those in the 7 to 14 age group; sightseeing tours for those from 10 to 30; summer schools at various universities, some of which are sponsored by American universities and most of which lead to American college credits; study-sightseeing tours; study-work tours and study-archaeological dig tours; kibbutz visits for workers, campers, students, or sightseers; deals involving Bar Mitzvahs.

Start your inquiry by contacting any American outpost of the Israeli Government; the Youth and Student Department, Ministry of Tourism, 24 King George Street, Jerusalem (02) 22 33 61; the Department of Education and Culture, Jewish Agency, 515 Park Avenue, New York, N.Y. 10022 (212) 752–0600; or the Kibbutz Aliyah Desk, 200 Park Avenue South, New York, N.Y. 10003 (212) 477–5653.

Large numbers of those in the 18 to 30 bracket come over

alone and hitchhike around the country, staying at hostels, campsites, and bargain hotels. Those who hope to work on kibbutzim are usually disappointed—unless they arrange a place in advance.

Parents consider Israel a lot safer than Amsterdam or Paris. Yet despite the sternness of the Israeli government, this is the Middle East where the consumption and trade of narcotics are part of an ancient tradition.

At this writing, for those 12 through 21 years old, there is a youth fare applicable between the United States and Israel. Young travelers can also fly across the ocean via charters and then get special student flights for the Europe-Israel leg. Step one is to contact SOFA European Student Travel Center, Ltd., 1560 Broadway, New York, N.Y. 10036 (212) 586–2080 or its Israeli counterpart, Israel Student Tourist Association (ISSTA), 2 Pinsker Street, Tel Aviv (03) 5 96 13. SOFA is an amalgam of various national student organizations, and it operates student charter flights within Europe. A participant between the ages of 16 and 30 can obtain an International Student Identity card by sending a bursar's receipt or a registration form proving that he was a full-time student during the calendar year. For flights between Europe and Israel, students over 30 should apply to ISSTA. Any student should check out ISSTA's trips within the country, as well as the Operation Joshua day trips sponsored by the United Jewish Appeal.

ADDING THE MIDDLE EAST OR EUROPE

Most packages and/or independent itineraries are available two ways, as Israel-only trips or as part of tours that include stopovers in Europe. The various Group and Excursion air fares include these stops at no extra cost, although the airlines could change that at any time. On group flights the regulations specify that everyone make the stopover via exactly the same flight, although as in Israel, they may or may not be expected to stay together on the ground. The European portions are usually made after Israel, although sometimes they are split. Hotels are often in the same category throughout, but the only meal that is included on many packages is breakfast. No matter how many other meals you get, breakfast outside Israel is a Continental breakfast, meaning rolls and coffee, tea, or chocolate. In Holland cheese is sometimes included, and in England eggs might be added. Otherwise, eggs, ham, bacon, toast, or fruit juice cost extra. The sightseeing in Europe usually consists of a half-day at each destination, but might include other local specialties; study the fine print.

At this writing you cannot enter Jordan, Egypt, Lebanon, Syria, or Saudi Arabia directly from Israel, nor can you enter with an Israeli visa in your passport. No problem. You simply go to the Island of Cyprus from Israel, and back to the mainland. Israel dispenses disposable visas, so your visit need not show. There are now packages available that combine Cairo and Beirut with Israeli destinations, just as European itineraries customarily ignore crucial borders. Sunny Land Tours, Inc., 166 Main Street, Hackensack, N.J. 07601 (201) 489–2150, is one tour operator who is making a specialty of Israel–Egypt trips for groups. The tours are either 15 or 22 days and cost $500 to $1,000, with $800 being typical.

*"The only way to do Israel on
$5 a day is the* mishpocheh *sys-
tem—stay with relatives."*

—HAIFA TOUR OPERATOR

13
Make the Right Budget

A QUESTION OF STYLE

The travel industry is like a piano. You can use it to play
"Chopsticks" or Chopin, once you learn how to play. You can
travel to Israel on a 747, spend two weeks sightseeing in Jerusalem, Tel Aviv, Haifa, the Galilee and the Negev, on a basic
budget of $500 or $3,000, covering fare, sightseeing, room, and
meals. The $3,000 takes some striving; one has to fly First
Class, stay in luxury hotels, use private guides. Switch to a
Group Economy Class fare, forego the private guides and some
of the plusher restaurants, and the budget can be between $900
and $1,000, still with five-star hotels. Since Israel's luxury
hotels are not *that* luxurious, it is easy to settle for merely first-
class hotels, dropping basic outlay to $850–$950. Stay in three-
star hotels—there are many comfortable ones, and American-
oriented tour operators have found them—and bring the basics
in for $750–$850. These figures refer to the essential cost per
person, for each of two persons traveling together, whether or
not the items are covered by a package tour.

Because air fare is a large part of the total cost, it is possible
to spend a third week in Israel for only $100–$200 additional.
The third week of a package will contain little or no prepaid
sightseeing, probably just accommodations in Tel Aviv.

For many visitors Israel is the main course and Europe the
dessert. Both two-week and three-week packages are available
in combination with one or more European destinations, the
favorites being Italy, the Greek Islands and/or Athens, and
London. The costs vary enormously, but on one of the many
packages that tack four European nights onto a complete 13
nights (that is, two weeks) in Israel, the extended trip adds

$100–$200 in costs—more sights, more hotels, more meals. On a three-week trip taking the basic 13 nights in Israel and adding on seven days split between two capitals, figure $150–$250 more. A Greek Islands cruise can add $200–$500.

Most of the tours designed for Americans guarantee at least minimal comforts—air-conditioned buses, private showers, clean rooms. For students the $5-a-day philosophy works fine. I say "philosophy" because it is no longer possible to survive in Israel on $5 for a hotel room and three meals. You can get close to $5 only by enrolling in a hostel, camping, school, or work program—or by staying with relatives. For most adults, it is more realistic to think of Israel on $12–$15 per day for room and meals alone. Sightseeing can add $5–$10 each day.

First-timers are often told to choose the kind of accommodations they would back home and to expect to pay the same price. That is bad advice. For one thing, most middle-class Americans are familiar only with resort hotels and roadside motels. They do not know what stateside city hotels charge because they don't stay in them, or if they do, their company pays the bill. Secondly, Israel has cut-rate possibilities that we lack. Thirdly, if money means a go versus no-go decision, it is worth making a few compromises.

THE ECONOMICS OF CHILDREN

There are no universal rules about who is a child and how much he must pay. On regular air fares children under two pay 10 percent of whatever fare an accompanying adult pays, providing they sit on an adult's lap. Children between two and twelve pay half of whatever the adult pays. Unaccompanied children pay full fare but those in the 12 through 21 bracket can get a Youth Fare. There are not now any applicable family fares, like our domestic bring-'em-along rates.

Most Israeli hotels give a room reduction of 30 percent for children up to the age of six and a 50 percent reduction for those between six and twelve, providing the child sleeps in the same room as the parents.

On most package tours, children under two pay nothing for

land arrangements, but they must pay 10 percent of the applicable air fare. Children between two and twelve pay 50 percent of the package total, if they sleep in a room with their parents. If not, they get the discount only on the air fare. At Christmas some packagers charge everybody full price for land arrangements. Other packagers give children over twelve a 50 percent discount if they share a room with their parents.

On package tours involving private cars—self-drive or guide-driven—one has to get the specific charges for his own family. Discounts and required number of passengers are not standard.

20 MONEY-SAVERS

1. Travel off-season.
2. Fly with a group.
3. Tour with a group.
4. Do your homework. Learn about the good deals. Reserve in advance, individually or via a package.
5. Stay in two-star and three-star hotels.
6. Rent an apartment.
7. Stay in the suburbs.
8. Spend time in a kibbutz guesthouse.
9. Go camping.
10. Sleep some nights at hostels.
11. Sightsee by yourself, using regular buses.
12. Purchase an Egged 14-day bus pass.
13. Buy a national parks admission ticket.
14. Have picnics in parks, on beaches, or in your room.
15. Each lunch at felafel stands.
16. Forego special services—do your own laundry, get your own theater tickets.
17. Keep luggage to a minimum to avoid overweight penalties and porter's fees.
18. Rent a small car that is not air-conditioned.
19. Go to a convention or seminar essential to your work. Your boss might pay, or portions might be tax deductible.
20. Stay with relatives or friends (the world's most unbeatable cost-cutter).

A BUDGET-MAKER CHART

Do not take these prices literally. They are based on summer travel, when costs are highest. They do not account for special package and group deals and discounts, for extensive shopping or night life, and for strong personal preferences. Prices are per person, but assume double occupancy by adults, during the period of highest rates. Prices are per day or per occasion.

Air Fares   (Likely Range)
(round trip from East Coast to Israel)

First Class	$1,500
Regular Economy	900
Group fares	450–600

Hotels

*(including Israeli breakfast
15 percent service, local taxes)*

American minimum, no private bath (one- or two-star)	$3–$6
Minimal comfort, some frills, private bath (two- or three-star)	5–12
Reasonable comfort, some frills, private bath (three- or four-star)	6–15
Tops in country, private bath, big public rooms, frills (five-star)	12–23

Restaurants

(first course, main course, dessert, beverage, service, tax)

Simple dinner, evening or midday	$2–$4
Good meal in pleasant, but not luxurious, surroundings	3–7

Best in town,
    notable surroundings   5–15
Light American-style lunch   .50–2

Sightseeing

Half-day bus tour with guide	$4–$8
Full-day bus tour with guide	9–18
Car with English-speaking chauffeur-guide, full day	10–12
Self-drive car, full day	8–25
Museum or archaeological site admission	.75–1.50

Entertainment

(including tips, taxes, and admissions)

Theater, opera, or ballet	$1–$10
Nightclub, two drinks of Scotch and soda	2–10
Folklore evening	2–4

Two Week Package Tour

(13 nights with Israeli breakfasts; sightseeing; basic tips, taxes, and transfers—not including air fare or activities during "at leisure" days)

Top hotels	$300–$550
Very comfortable hotels	250–400
Simple, but comfortable, hotels	185–275

14

Choose the Right Itinerary

STRATEGY

By now, you realize the advantages of a prearranged itinerary. Most package tours follow itineraries that are virtually identical. There are some things that every tourist wants to see, and there are other places which it is profitable for tour operators to take them to. Very often, the two coincide. Kibbutz guesthouses cost less than Tel Aviv hotels, so an operator gets a more alluring price tag by offering a stay in a kibbutz instead of one more night at the Sheraton or Dan. Marvelous. A kibbutz is exactly what the visitors hoped they would see.

Still, you might have your personal list of priorities. You can squeeze in more sights by commuting from one city, than by continually shifting hotels. Tel Aviv or Haifa in themselves are not worth more than one day, but they make good base camps.

As of now, there are no hotels recommended for the general tourist in Bethlehem, Hebron, Nablus, or the Golan Heights, and only limited hotels in Acre, Nazareth, and Caesarea. For the Negev there is nothing between Beersheba and Elat. There is no five-star hotel south of Jerusalem. In the Sinai there are tourist accommodations at several places, but nothing that can be called a hotel.

Lod Airport is 20 minutes from Tel Aviv, but only 60 minutes from Jerusalem, so it is completely feasible to head straight for the main attraction. In checking out package tours, don't be turned off if you can't find Megiddo or whatever else is important to you. That's what days "at leisure" are for—to see your special things. If your list is long or complicated, hire a chauffeured car. The $40 for up to four persons is a small portion of your total cost.

Let's look at the highlights of prefab packages that have been popular in the past. Although one source is given for each tour, each package is available from several. Exact ingredients vary from season to season and even from day to day (the Knesset shut down for repairs, the museum closing early because of a holiday, and so on). Usually, on each leg, you stop to look at more things than are listed here.

The sightseeing routes are fairly standard, whether part of a package or booked on the spot. The Jerusalem New City morning tour traditionally includes Herzl's Tomb, the Military Cemetery, Yad Vashem, Hebrew University, the Knesset. The afternoon New City tour covers King David's Tomb, Dormition Abbey, Room of the Last Supper, Israel Museum, Shrine of the Book. Some packages have only the morning tour and others have both, but the contents do not vary from package to package.

What is listed below as "one night Galilee kibbutz, one night Haifa," is actually what many brochures call "three-day Galilee tour." (Remember, two days equal only one night, three days equal two nights, and so on.)

The first Galilee day covers Nazareth, Capernaum, and Tiberias; the second takes in the Golan Heights, Banias Springs, Safad, and Acre; the third tours Haifa, Caesarea, and the Zichron Yaakov vineyards (with customary side trip to the Rothschilds' tomb at Ramat Hanadiv). The "two-day Galilee" has only one overnight, usually at a kibbutz, and skips Zichron Yaakov and Caesarea. Negev trips can simply go as far as Beersheba, with visits to the Dead Sea, Masada, and Sodom; the night is spent at Beersheba or Arad. Only if Elat is specified does the trip go all the way to the end of the Negev, by plane or motorcoach. If coach, the route probably includes the Ramon Crater, Avdat, Sde Boker, King Solomon's Pillars, and the Timna Mines, plus a trip to the Coral Reefs, Fjord, a swim in the Red Sea, and a ride in a glass-bottomed boat. A trip to "North Sinai" goes no farther than the beach of El Arish, via Gaza and Yad Mordecai. "Sinai" denotes at least a trip to

Sharm-el-Sheikh, and possibly also to Mount Sinai, Santa Caterina, and Abu Rudeis.

A Rehovot excursion is in virtually every tour package. It goes through some of Israel's oldest settlements, but is mostly concerned with a stop at the Rishon Le Zion Wine Cellars and the Weizmann Institute and, sometimes, Kibbutz Giv'at Brenner as well. Jericho trips include the springs of En Fescha, *but not Qumran.* A half-day tour directly to Masada usually includes En Gedi, but when Masada is visited while en route between two cities, neither En Gedi nor Qumran is included. Tel Aviv itself gets only a half-day's circuit, covering a drive past the university and culutral buildings, a visit to the top of the Shalom Tower and the Museum Haaretz (for which the new Tel Aviv Museum might be substituted), and a visit to Jaffa.

Golfers and those who want to attend the Israel Festival concerts in Caesarea's amphitheater can commute from nearby Netanya or from the next closest resort, Herzliya, or even from Tel Aviv or Haifa, each less than an hour away. If you want to skin-dive or try the simpler sport of snorkeling (anyone can do it), schedule time for Elat or Sharm-el-Sheikh. Horseback riding or water-skiing? Try the Sea of Galilee, with accommodations in Tiberias or at a kibbutz. Skiing? From January to late March, stay at Kibbutz Hagoshrim, Kfar Blum, or Giladi to reach the slopes of Mount Hermon. Swimming? You can swim just about anyplace. Inland towns have pools, and Jerusalem is an easy day's trip from the Dead Sea beaches. For thermal baths go to Tiberias or the Dead Sea. The latter is also the place to go for asthma cures.

To compare these itineraries, please remember that (1) the number in front of each city is the number of *overnights,* not the number of days (with one overnight, you can have two full days' visit); (2) the sights listed for the city might be visited en route to the city; (3) even special-interest itineraries include universal elements—art lovers like seeing a kibbutz and action lovers want to visit Jerusalem; (4) these itineraries are feasible whether or not you are going to Europe after Israel; (5) a dagger indicates that you pay extra for the excursion if you buy that itinerary as a specific package.

TYPICAL ITINERARIES

7 days, 6 nights Circular Motorcoach Tour (wholesaled by Caravel)

1   Tel Aviv
                Rehovot
                Weizmann Institute
                Rishon Le Zion Cellars
                Kibbutz Giv'at Brenner
                Ashdod
                Ashkelon

1   Ashkelon (or Tel Aviv)
                Beersheba
                Masada
                Hebron
                Bethlehem

2   Jerusalem
                New City
                Old City
                Jericho

1   Haifa
                City tour
                Banias Springs
                Golan Heights
                Safad

1   Galilee Kibbutz
                Nazareth
                Megiddo

7 days, 6 nights Independent Tour (Author's Choice)

5   Jerusalem
                New City

        Old City
        Bethlehem
        Hebron
        Jericho
        Qumran
        Dead Sea
        Masada
        Tel Aviv (day trip)

1   Galilee Kibbutz
        Haifa
        Megiddo or Hazor
        Safad
        Golan Heights

10 days, 8 nights, United Synagogue Tour Service (wholesaled by Tower Tours)

3   Tel Aviv
        Rehovot
        Weizmann Institute
        Rishon Le Zion Cellars
        City tour

1   Haifa
        City tour
        Caesarea
        Zichron Yaakov

1   Galilee Kibbutz
        Acre
        Safad
        Golan Heights
        Capernaum
        Tiberias
        Nazareth

2   Jerusalem
        Old City
        New City
        Jericho

Hebron
Bethlehem

1   Negev

Arad
Beersheba
Masada

11 days, 9 nights Drive-Yourself-Tour (wholesaled by Master Vacation Associates)

(Traveler can specify how many nights in Jerusalem, Tel Aviv, and Haifa, or all three; author's recommendations given for general-interest traveler.)

5   Jerusalem

Old City
New City
Bethlehem
Hebron
Jericho
Qumran
Dead Sea
Arad
Masada

2   Tel Aviv

City tour
Jaffa
Weizmann Institute
Yad Mordecai

2   Haifa

City tour
Caesarea
Nazareth
Megiddo
Tiberias
Hazor
Kibbutz Ayelet Hashahar
(lunch)

Safad
Golan Heights

15 days, 13 nights (wholesaled by Isram, Ltd., affiliate of Histadrut)

4   Jerusalem
Old City
New City
Bethlehem
Hebron

1   Galilee Kibbutz
Megiddo
Nazareth
Tiberias
Capernaum

1   Haifa
Golan Heights
Safad
Banias Springs
Acre city tour

6   Tel Aviv
Zichron Yaakov
Caesarea
Rehovot
Weizmann Institute
Rishon Le Zion
Kibbutz Giv'at Brenner
Ashdod
Ashkelon
Yad Mordecai

1   Elat
Beersheba
Sodom
Dead Sea
Negev

15 days, 13 nights (wholesaled by Four Star Tours)

6   Tel Aviv
           City tour
           Rehovot
           Rishon Le Zion
           Weizmann Institute
           Yad Mordecai

1   Beersheba
           Market
           Negev
           Masada

4   Jerusalem
           New City
           Old City
           Hebron
           Bethlehem

1   Kibbutz Guesthouse
           Megiddo
           Jericho
           Nazareth
           Nablus
           Tiberias
           Capernaum

1   Haifa
           Caesarea
           City tour
           Golan Heights
           Banias Springs
           Safad
           Acre

22 days, 20 nights American Jewish Congress Tour (prepared by Unitours, Inc.)

5   Tel Aviv (or Herzliya)
           City tour

Modi'im, tree planting
Rehovot
Weizmann Institute
Ashdod
Ashkelon
Yad Mordecai

1   Elat

Negev
Beersheba
Copper mines
Dead Sea

1   Arad

Masada
Hebron

5   Jerusalem

Old City
New City
Bethlehem
† Jericho
† Nablus
† Sebastia
AJC projects

1   Galilee Kibbutz

Megiddo
Nazareth

3   Haifa

Tiberias
Golan Heights
Safad
City tour
Caesarea

4   Herzliya (or Tel Aviv)

At leisure

22 days, 20 nights (wholesaled by Tourstars)

1   Tel Aviv

1   Arad
            Ashdod
            Ashkelon
            Yad Mordecai
            Beersheba
            Masada

3   Jerusalem
            Bethlehem
            Hebron
            Morning, New City
            Jericho
            Dead Sea
            Old City

1   Haifa
            Caesarea
            City tour

1   Galilee Kibbutz
            Acre
            Safad
            Banias Springs
            Golan Heights
            Capernaum
            Tiberias
            Nazareth

13   Tel Aviv
            City tour
            Rehovot
            Rishon Le Zion

MAINLY FOR CATHOLICS

10 days, 8 nights Silver Circle Tour (wholesaled by Caravel Mediterama)

8   Jerusalem
Old City (Mount of Olives, Holy Sepulchre area)
Old City (Temple area)
New City
En Kerem
Bethlehem
Hebron
Masada
Jericho
Galilee
Nazareth

MAINLY FOR PROTESTANTS

10 days, 8 nights Silver Circle Tour (wholesaled by Caravel Mediterama)

6   Jerusalem
Old City (Holy Sepulchre area, Mount of Olives)
Old City (Temple area)
Beersheba
Masada
Bethlehem
Hebron
Jericho
New City
Galilee trip

1   Tiberias or Safad
Nazareth
Kfar Cana
Kibbutzim

                         Tiberias
                         Capernaum
                         Mount of Beatitudes

1   **Kibbutz or Haifa**
                         Banias Springs
                         Golan Heights
                         Safad
                         Acre
                         Haifa city tour
                         Zichron Yaakov
                         Caesarea

DRIVE-YOURSELF TRIPS FOR
PEOPLE WITH SPECIAL INTERESTS

Wings and Wheels Tours (wholesaled by Caravel Mediterama) cover 12 to 22 days, with a confirmed hotel reservation
for only one night in Tel Aviv, plus use of a rental car for the
specified number of days. For subsequent accommodations, you
can take your chances but are advised to arrange reservations.

12 days, 10 nights (for archaeology buffs)

1   **Tel Aviv**
                         Jaffa

1   **Haifa**
                         Megiddo
                         Bet She'arim
                         Bet Alfa
                         Nazareth

2   **Galilee Kibbutz (preferably**
           Ayelet Hashahar)
                         Hazor
                         Tel Dan
                         Banias Springs
                         Golan Heights
                         Capernaum
                         Tabgha

1   Tiberias
> Bet Shean
> Bet Alfa
> Belvoir
> Jericho
> Dead Sea
> Qumran
> En Bokek   or   Arad   or
>   Beersheba
> Masada
> En Gedi

4   Jerusalem
> Bethlehem
> Hebron
> En Kerem
> Old City
> New City

19 days, 17 nights (for archaeology buffs)

2   Tel Aviv
> Jaffa
> Museum Haaretz

8   Jerusalem
> Old City
> New City
> Bethlehem
> Hebron
> En Kerem
> Jericho
> Qumran
> Dead Sea

1   Arad, En Bokek, or Beersheba
> En Gedi
> Masada

1   Elat
> Avdat

King Solomon's Pillars
Coral Reefs
Fjord

1   **Ashkelon**
Ashdod
Yad Mordecai
Weizmann Institute

2   **Galilee Kibbutz (preferably Ayelet Hashahar)**
Capernaum
Tabgha

1   **Haifa**
Caesarea
Megiddo
Bet She'arim
Hazor
Tel Dan
Banias Springs
Golan Heights

1   **Tiberias or Safad**
Bet Shean
Bet Alfa
Belvoir
Meron

12 days, 10 nights (for students of Jewish history, from Bible times to today)

1   **Tel Aviv**
Jaffa
Museum Haaretz
Modi'im

4   **Jerusalem**
Old City
New City

Bethlehem
Hebron
Jericho
Dead Sea
En Gedi
Sodom

1   Arad or Beersheba
Masada

2   Tel Aviv
Cultural institutions
Shalom Tower
Jaffa
Rehovot
Rishon Le Zion
Weizmann Institute
Caesarea

2   Haifa or Galilee Kibbutz
City tour
Megiddo
Bet She'arim
Bet Alfa
Bet Shean
Hazor
Tel Dan
Banias Springs
Golan Heights
Huleh Valley
Capernaum
Tabgha

19 days, 17 nights (for students of Jewish history, from Bible times to today)

1   Tel Aviv
Jaffa
Museum Haaretz
Modi'im
Museum of the Alphabet

9   **Jerusalem**
- Old City
- New City
- Bethlehem
- Hebron
- En Kerem
- Jericho
- Qumran
- Dead Sea
- Sanhedrin Tombs
- Biblical Zoo
- Nablus
- Sebastia

1   **Arad, En Bokek, or Beersheba**
- En Gedi
- Masada

1   **Elat**
- Avdat
- King Solomon's Pillars
- Timna Mines
- Fjord
- Coral Reefs
- Red Canyon

3   **Sinai**
- Sharm-el-Sheikh
- Santa Caterina
- Mount Sinai
- Abu Rudeis
- El Arish

1   **Ashkelon**
- Ashdod
- Yad Mordecai
- Weizmann Institute
- Rishon Le Zion

2   **Haifa or Galilee Kibbutz**
- City tour

Caesarea
Megiddo
Bet She'arim
Bet Alfa
Bet Shean
Hazor
Banias Springs
Golan Heights
Huleh Valley
Tiberias
Capernaum
Tabgha

12 days, 10 nights (for art lovers)

2   Tel Aviv
Jaffa
Museum Haaretz
Tel Aviv Museum
Galleries
City tour

5   Jerusalem
Old City
New City
En Kerem
Bethlehem
Hebron
Jericho
Dead Sea
Qumran
Museums

1   Arad, Beersheba, or En Bokek
Masada

2   Haifa or Galilee Kibbutz
Caesarea
En Hod
City tour

> Megiddo
> Bet She'arim
> Bet Alfa
> Bet Shean
> Hazor
> Golan Heights
> Huleh Valley
> Capernaum
> Tabgha
> Tiberias

12 days, 10 nights (for beach lovers)

4   **Netanya, Nahariya, or Herzliya (instead of Tel Aviv)**
> Jaffa
> Tel Aviv city tour
> Caesarea
> Rosh Hanikra

1   **Galilee Kibbutz or Haifa**
> Harbor city tour
> Golan Heights
> Huleh Valley
> Tiberias
> Capernaum
> Tabgha

3   **Jerusalem**
> Old City
> New City
> Masada
> En Gedi
> En Fescha

2   **Elat**
> Coral Reefs
> Fjord

12 days, 10 nights (for action lovers)

4   Tel Aviv
>   Jaffa
>   Tel Aviv city tour
>   Caesarea

4   Club Méditerranée at Achziv, Netanya or Herzliya
>   Golan Heights
>   Galilee sights
>   Haifa

2   Jerusalem
>   Old City
>   New City

FOR THE AUTOMOBILE-WEARY INDEPENDENT WITH SPECIAL INTEREST

15 days, 13 nights Second-Timers Tour (wholesaled by Tourstars)

This package includes fare plus 7 night of hotels in Jerusalem and 6 nights in Tel Aviv. No sightseeing or car rental is included. The traveler is free to buy a one-day tour, for example, or rent a car for a few days, which is ideal for people who have seen Israel before. More possibilities:

FOR ARCHAEOLOGY BUFFS

7   Jerusalem
>   Old City
>   New City
>   Hebron
>   Bethlehem
>   Jericho
>   Dead Sea
>   Qumran
>   Nablus
>   Sebastia

Masada
Ashkelon

6   Tel Aviv
City tour
Jaffa
Caesarea
Megiddo
Hazor
Galilee kibbutz (lunch)
Haifa
Acre

FOR CHRISTIANS

7   Jerusalem
Old City
New City
Mount of Olives
Bethlehem
Jericho
Dead Sea
Qumran
Nablus
Sebastia
Ramallah
En Kerem
Masada

6   Tel Aviv
City tour
Jaffa
Acre
Nazareth
Mount of Beatitudes
Caesarea
Haifa
Megiddo
Tiberias
Capernaum
Tabgha

15

Getting Organized

PASSPORTS AND VISAS

Allow at least three weeks from the time of application for receipt of the passport. For a first passport you must apply in person to offices of the U.S. Passport Agency of the State Department, certain federal and state courts, or qualified post offices; telephone your postmaster for specifics. Bring proof of birth or citizenship, current identification with description or photo (driver's license is acceptable), two identical 2½-inch square photos showing all adults and children to be covered by the passport, and $12. Actually, separate passports are better for couples.

Already have a passport? Check the dates. Passports are now valid for five years and are not extendable. To get a new one, write to the Passport Office, Washington, D.C. 20524 for an application. Return the form with two regulation photos and $10, or go in person to a Passport Agency. Aliens living in the United States need a sailing permit from Internal Revenue plus possibly a registration card or reentry permit; check Immigration. To enter Israel, no advance visa is needed. You get a free one, a separate card, on landing. Israel is not concerned with whether or not you have visited Arab countries, but Arab countries care if you have been to Israel.

SHOTS AND HEALTH

Shots are no longer required, not even smallpox vaccinations, for Israel, Western Europe, or reentry home. Still, ask your doctor about the advisability of being immunized against smallpox, typhoid, tetanus, polio, malaria, or cholera. Bring your eyeglass prescription and notes on medication and allergies, as well as your hometown doctor's name and your insurance data. Ask the doctor about preventives for travel sickness, "tourist tummy."

TRIP INSURANCE

You might already be covered by an accident policy or home-owner's, tenant's, or personal floater policy. Check particularly for valuables like cameras. Blue Cross is good in Israel, and so are some other health programs. Extra trip insurance for baggage loss and accidents is available from insurance brokers and travel agents. Flight insurance may be purchased for cameras and jewelry. Flying a group rate? Buy a rate-protector, which reimburses you if illness prevents you from flying on the specified dates.

PREPARING YOUR MONEY

Israel is one of the few countries where you do well changing dollars and traveler's checks in hotels, restaurants, or shops; charges are infinitesimal and bank lines are long. Besides, shops can give 15–30 percent discounts on some items only if you pay in traveler's checks or dollars. Nevertheless, take no more than $50–$70 in cash, at least half in singles. The balance should be in traveler's checks or Israel bonds. Hometown personal checks are convenient only (a) by prearranging for them to be cashed (b) by going to the local representative of an international credit card, or (c) by paying extra for an Israeli bank to wire your hometown bank, whether or not they are affiliated.

You will need Israeli currency, and should get a tip-pack or other small amount before leaving home. Familiarize yourself with the coins. The Israeli pound is called *lira* in Hebrew (plural, *lirot*) and at this writing is worth about 25¢, or, for quick figuring, roughly four to the dollar. Each lira contains 100 *agorot*. Consider 5 agorot a penny and 50 agorot, a dime-plus. Caution! When you leave Israel, you cannot change more than about 100 Israeli pounds back into dollars. Another caution! Hometown credit cards might be useless. Only international cards like Air Travel, American Express, BankAmericard, Carte Blanche, and Diners Club are acceptable to charge all or part of the trip or to cash personal checks and buy added traveler's checks. However, using plastic money might cost you the special tourist discount. International car renting companies accept their own or the international cards in lieu of rental deposits. A record of traveler's checks and credit card numbers should accompany you, but do not keep it with your checks or identity papers.

DOUBLE-CHECK YOUR TRAVEL DEAL

Read your agreement with the travel agency or group carefully and ask questions early. Double-check your written itinerary as soon as it arrives. Are scheduling and price as requested? Groupers, do not be upset if tickets and departure times are slow in coming, providing you have checked out the group's reputation.

PLANNING FOR PEOPLE

If you have people to look up, write them before leaving home, explaining your connection to them and your itinerary. To locate persons once in Israel, try the nationwide telephone directory first, then contact Madoor Lechipus Krovimin, a radio program that traces people, by the phoning (02) 22 48 14 in Jerusalem.

Presents? Records, gadgets, clothes, and (discreetly) money are good. No relatives? Arrange to make friends through your professional or fraternal organization (bring business cards, letters of introduction) or, after arrival, contact the local Meet the Israelis operation, which will find you compatible visitees.

LUGGAGE AND PACKING

Do not take more than you yourself can carry: one suitcase, preferably made of fabric with a lightweight frame or, better yet, no frame at all, and also one tote or flight bag (a must for bus-trippers). Big shoppers might also take a folding suitcase. Label each piece inside and out, using the group identification tag if provided. Make your bags easy to spot by putting on a bold design (your initials, perhaps) with colored tape. Because you keep changing hotels, the ideal packing system is to put each dress, suit, or jacket on a slim non-rust hanger and place them inside a plastic garment cover, which can be folded into the suitcase in one swoop.

CLOTHES

The ideal clothing is lightweight, drip-dry, wrinkleproof, and informal. *Indispensable:* two pairs of good walking shoes already broken in, headcovering, bathing suit, and, for women, clothing that covers arms and thighs. *Useless:* neckties, Bermuda shorts, furs. September to June, rain gear is a must. December to March, winter clothes are needed, plus summery clothing for the Dead Sea and Masada. A woman's basic needs for two weeks are: Four daytime outfits (dresses, pants suits, or separates), one slightly dressy outfit, one pair of knockabout slacks or playsuits, swim clothes, two pair of walking shoes, one pair of dress shoes, one pair of sneakers or rubber sandals, one big but light travel pocketbook, one small pocketbook for dress and sports, headcovering, sweater, or stole. A man's basic needs for two weeks are: one sports jacket or blazer, three pairs of slacks, swim clothes, short shorts or jeans, sweater, two pairs of walking shoes, one pair of sandals or sneakers, headcovering. Men, women, or children going to Europe too need another dress-up outfit and, possibly, warmer clothes even in summer. Men and boys will need ties and jackets on the Continent. Two weeks before departure, check out all clothes to see what needs cleaning, mending, or replacement. Do a dress rehearsal on your packing.

OTHER THINGS TO BRING

Definitely bring: washcloth and soap; transformers and plug-adapters for razor and other electrical appliances; laundry soap for drip-dry fabrics, short clothesline or hangers; empty plastic bags for laundry and damp clothes; sticky tape; special shampoos, cosmetics, or medicines, all in plastic containers; spot remover; pants or skirt hanger; pocket packs of paper handkerchiefs; cigarette lighter; transistor radio; shoe polish gear; easy-to-read paperback; small flashlight. Camera buffs, bring plenty of film; it is expensive in Israel.

CUSTOMS CONSIDERATIONS

Considering bringing expensive presents for your relatives? First ask the Israeli Consul about duty. Israel lets each tourist bring in, duty-free, 250 cigarettes or 250 grams of tobacco or cigars, 1.33 pints of whiskey, .44 pint of perfume, cameras for personal use, plus 10 rolls of still and 10 rolls of movie film, 750 yards of recording tape, records, and a record player. To order duty-free tobacco and whiskey to be placed on your plane for your return home, tell your travel agent or go to the airport duty-free shop. Taking cameras or other expensive imports to Israel with you? To be prepared for United States Customs when you come home, register these at the nearest Customs House or at the airport, or bring along a receipt proving prior ownership.

LEAVING YOUR HOUSE

Stop delivery of newspapers, milk, and so forth. Arrange for forwarding or holding of mail; don't let it accumulate where it advertises "empty house." Get plants, pets, and children to their sitters well before your departure. Keep last-minute errands, entertaining, and feasting to a minimum. Keep down the number of people seeing you off; there is much noise, little room, and long waits between the traveler's check-in and the actual departure. Discourage the sending of gifts to the airport, too; flowers, candy, and champagne are nuisances to the laden voyager. Before leaving home, telephone the airport to see if the plane is on schedule. Boarding in New York? Allow 90 minutes to get to the airport from midtown, and be sure you know exactly which terminal to go to. You *can* summon a radio cab in New York, 15 minutes before needed, paying only the metered fare: telephone (212) 786–0707 or (212) 743–8383. For about $20, you can hire a chauffeured limousine.

AT THE AIRPORT

Look for flight number or group insignia. One person checks in for the family, presenting all tickets and passports. The clerk weighs in all baggage, including coats and things you will carry on board. You are allowed 44 pounds of baggage carried free; you must pay extra for each 2.2 pounds at the cashier's window before returning to the check-in clerk to get your boarding passes. Transferring from a domestic flight? Make sure your luggage is put aboard. Either at check-in or at the gate (it varies by airline), you can choose your seat—smoking or no smoking; window, middle, or aisle. (I prefer middle—safe from passing pocketbooks, yet only one body to crawl over to reach the aisle.) Window seat? Not much to see en route. Ordered a Kosher meal? Remind the clerk. After check-in, you can go to the duty-free shop or a currency exchange, but report promptly when your flight is called. You and your hand luggage will probably be searched before boarding. Except for porters, don't tip the airline personnel.

THE FLIGHT ITSELF

You might have to walk or be bused to your aircraft. Movies, if shown, usually come after the first meal; you pay (about $2.50) for the necessary earphones. Except in First Class, you also pay for alcoholic drinks, but soft drinks and coffee are always available free. Check about your Kosher meal as soon as you are seated. Duty-free purchases are brought to you after take off. You can also get tobacco, liquor, and perfume bargains aboard. On overnight flights, brush your teeth, loosen your clothes, and try to sleep. In case of turbulence, keep your seat belt fastened, though loosely. Ask the stewardess for children's toys, writing paper, playing cards, electric shavers.

YOUR ARRIVAL

On landing, follow the signs into the terminal, where you will be steered through Immigration and then, as soon as the baggage is unloaded, through Customs. For most tourists, the answer to "Do you have anything to declare?" is simply "No." Tour escort, travel agent, car renter, or friend—anyone meeting you will wait near the door to the Customs area, sporting a company insignia or singing out your name. Independent travelers can get to Tel Aviv on the special airport bus; buy your ticket (about 50¢) before leaving the terminal. A taxi costs at least $6. To Jerusalem, take a taxi (about $12), a sherut (about $3), or the regular hourly bus (about 75¢).

IF SOMETHING IS AMISS

If weather or equipment problems delay your flight, the airline gives you a free drink, hot meal, or overnight accommodations as needed. If the flight is scrubbed, the carrier will find you an alternative. Even if you check in well in advance, the flight could be overbooked. The carrier then must get you another flight and/or meals and room if needed; he will also wire ahead to people awaiting you. You might also be entitled to compensation of up to $250 for the inconvenience. Check! If your baggage gets lost, tell your airline and your travel agent's representative. The carrier must give you $25–$60 to buy clothes and toilet articles to last until the baggage turns up. If bags are broken, the line must fix them or give you repair money. Completely gone? IATA says they owe you only $330 for 44 pounds of luggage, no matter what the contents.

Part III

ENJOYING ISRAEL

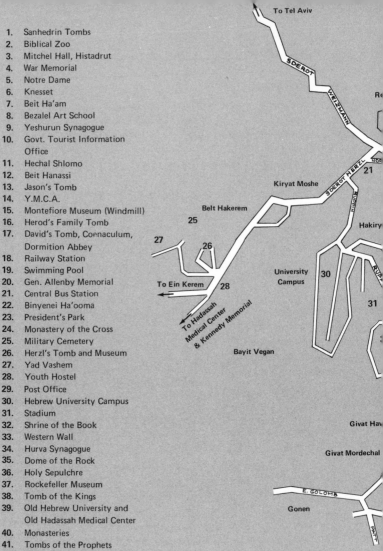

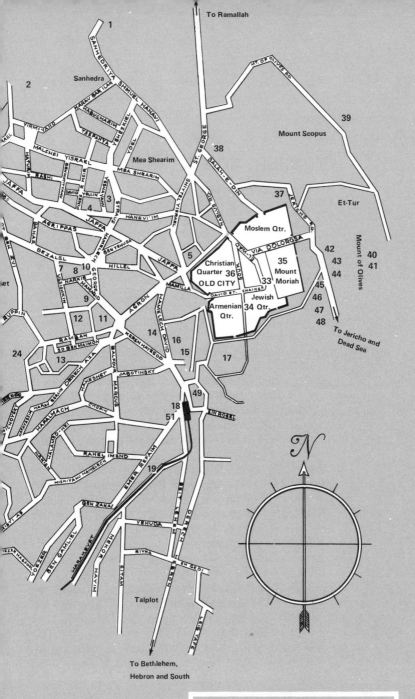

JERUSALEM

16
Jerusalem and Its Neighbors

Hebron, Bethlehem, Jericho, Qumran,
Ramallah–Nablus–Sebastia

The city of David, Jesus, and Mohammed is the most stimulating city on earth. Here one touches the history of man and God, more of it than survives anyplace else. Jerusalem is the capital of a new kind of country, improvised by people from 100 other nations. Temple walls, golden domes, high-rise apartments—a living city of 285,000 that tricks the ordinary visitor into strong emotions and earnest thoughts. No one is certain about the name, but scholars are now sure it does *not* mean "Gate of Peace."

One goes up to Jerusalem, geographically as well as symbolically: the Judean highlands billow up to form a crown, whose points are the rose-brown hills of Jerusalem, 2,700 feet above the sea. This is a city sacred to one billion people. For 19 years it was ripped in two—with the more precious half beyond the borders of Israel. Since 1967 it is one city again, and it is impossible to imagine it otherwise, even when the seam unexpectedly shows. "Is the Diplomat Hotel in Jerusalem or in Israel?" an Arab cabdriver asks, and another asks, "Which Citadel restaurant? The one in No Man's Land?" No Man's Land is now a park and an enclave of craft shops, and there are two Citadel restaurants, two Holyland hotels, two YMCA's, two bus systems, two earthly Jerusalems melded together.

Everything is still organized as West Jerusalem, meaning the New City, the part that has been Israeli since 1948, or as East Jerusalem, which is not quite the same as Old Jerusalem. The Old City usually means the Walled City, the ancient streets inside the walls that Suleiman I built in 1538. East Jerusalem is the Old City, plus Mount Scopus, the Mount of Olives, and a gracious suburb that housed the Jordanian embassies before the Six Day War.

East Jerusalem is definitely Oriental, but even West Jerusalem's garden apartments have an Eastern flavor. Old or new, most buildings are faced in the rosy-beige stone found nearby and are surrounded by greenery.

HOW TO SEE JERUSALEM

Forget what earlier visitors say. Two or three days is no longer adequate to see the city. If necessary, reduce time spent in Tel Aviv to going down by sherut one morning and coming back after dinner. Christians and Jews alike should see both halves of Jerusalem. Wander freely from one to the other. Everybody does. Even bus riders can find routes that go across without having to change buses at the Damascus or Jaffa gates.

For purposes of seeing the most sights, it is practical to start in the eastern portion—the Old City within the walls, the sites just outside the walls, the Mount of Olives, Mount Scopus. Then work west—Mea Shearim, Jaffa Road and the center of the city, the old synagogues and Biblical Zoo, the University–Knesset–museums section, Mount Herzl, En Kerem.

From Jerusalem, Bethlehem and Hebron can easily be seen on the same half-day tour. A trip to Jericho, combined with Qumran and the Dead Sea, requires a half-day. These two are the important out-of-town excursions—providing you visit Masada and the Galilee separately. For lovers of Roman ruins, a Ramallah–Sebastia trip is a pleasant addition.

All these are reached by commercial tours (Sebastia on a full-day trip with Caesarea), as well as by regular buses. Even independent types will do better with guides for the Old City and the synagogues, plus tours to cover widely scattered spots like the Mount Herzl tour or the one combining Mount of Olives, Mount Scopus, and the Second Temple model, even though its dip into the Old City might be repetitious. On the other hand, stalwarts can skip the Mount Zion–Israel Museum tour and see the same places on their own. Free guided tours are offered by Hadassah and its hospital, Hebrew University, the Knesset, WIZO, and Hechal Schlomo.

Sometimes a hot *hemsin* wind blows from the desert; otherwise summer days often require covered shoulders, and the summer evenings definitely do. This works out well because holy places pop up wherever you go, and women must cover thighs, shoulders and, in Jewish or Moslem places, heads. In winter Jerusalem can be very cold and damp, particularly inside shrines. Remember, the Knesset and other government buildings have cafeterias, warm in winter, cool in summer. Fine summer resting places in the Old City are the gardens of St. Anne's, the Temple Mount, the Flagellation or Sisters of Zion. Or, take a long lunch break at the American Colony Hotel. A few sites can be saved for evenings—certain museums, concert halls, the Khan, the Citadel.

On arrival, look at the weekly calendar of special events posted in your hotel, and get a street map, the Jerusalem booklet, and a key to main bus routes. These, and personal direction, are available at the official tourist offices at 24 King George Street and 34 Jaffa Road, inside the Jaffa Gate. The latter is the best place to locate an Arab guide for a very intensive tour of the Old City. Two key attractions compete, the old synagogue tour and the Via Dolorosa procession, both on Friday at 3 P.M. (earlier, during winter). I recommend the synagogue tour to all but those who want to participate in the procession's prayers. It is easier to see and learn about the Via Dolorosa at another time.

In the Old City, particularly, you will be hustled by amateur guides who start in by volunteering directions and often end up by steering you to a relative's shop or even grabbing a purse. They dispense a lot of wrong information, but that could be better than no information at all. If you do accept, agree on a price and guard your wallet.

THE OLD CITY

Anti-guided tour travelers, make an exception this once. Package-buyers, if your itinerary calls for an Old City tour several days after your arrival, don't wait. Get a taxi, a number 18 or 20 bus, or walk—but go right to the Western Wall, the Via Dolorosa, and the Dome of the Rock. The places that everyone yearns to see first are within a half mile of each other in the Walled City, along clearly marked pedestrian-packed streets, some of which also contain *souks*—block after block of stall-like shops. You will return to this section during your free hours, to gawk, shop, and revisit the shrines.

From the New City one approaches the Old City by walking down past the modern shops and office buildings of Jaffa Road or by crossing the valley that used to be No Man's Land, from the direction of the King David Hotel. The city

You can't help seeing sights—like the Old City in the background—on any Jerusalem bus.

Photo by Hans H. Pinn

within the creamy-beige ramparts looks medieval, rather than biblical. Much of it is, having been destroyed and rebuilt haphazardly in layers many times, by many different hands. Some of the buildings are recent—eighteenth and nineteenth centuries. Individually, many are ugly; together, they are superb.

The present walls were built by Suleiman the Magnificent, including stretches from the time of Herod Agrippa and Saladin. The space they encompass is about four-fifths of a mile, east to west, slightly less north to south; it is larger than

Jesus' Jerusalem, about the size of Hadrian's. You can circuit the city atop the ramparts (please do, if only part way) along a two-and-one-half mile orbit.

The walls follow the shape of a diamond, and contain four separate quarters. The Armenian Quarter points south toward Mount Zion and contains David's Citadel; sitting above it is the Christian Quarter of which the Church of the Holy Sepulchre is a part. The upper right-hand section is the Moslem Quarter, site of the Via Dolorosa. The lower right-hand section is the Jewish Quarter, bound by the Wailing Wall. This sacred remnant of the Second Temple also serves as one of the walls of the Old City's fifth portion—the Temple Mount, or Mount Moriah—where the actual temple of the Jews stood until 70 A.D. For centuries it has also been a place holy to Moslems, the site of the Dome of the Rock and El Aqsa Mosque. Christianity is represented here too; the site of the Dome was once a Crusader church. In Jerusalem it is impossible to see the shrines of only one religion at a time.

One enters the Old City by one of seven gates. Once inside, you get to any other spot by going through a maze of narrow, crowded streets. Cars enter through the Jaffa Gate, but they cannot drive far. The Jaffa is the busiest entrance because it is the closest to the New City and the easiest way to reach David's Citadel, the Holy Sepulchre, and many shops. The Zion Gate leads to the Armenian Quarter and the Wailing Wall. The Dung Gate, so-called because it was the gate through which, for centuries, the city's refuse was taken outside the walls, is actually the closest to the Wailing Wall, but it is the farthest from the built-up portions of the city. St. Stephen's Gate, also called the Lion's Gate, is the quickest route going into the Via Dolorosa or, going out, toward Gethsemane. On the long, upper left-hand side of the diamond, leading out to East Jerusalem's traditional "main street," is the Damascus Gate, convenient for locating the main *souks* and the Holy Sepulchre; Herod's Gate (also called Flower Gate) is convenient to the Temple Mount going in and the Rockefeller Museum coming out; (and the New Gate, built in 1889, leads into the Christian Quarter. Outside the walls the chief bus stops are around the Jaffa and Damascus gates. There is no transportation inside the walls.

The Western Wall Now that the sole known remnant of the Temple is back in Jewish hands after 2,000 years, Israelis want it to be called the Western Wall, *Kotel Hama'aravi* in Hebrew. This is not a remnant of the Second Temple itself, but part of a separate outer wall that Herod built to the Temple Court. David first brought the Ark of the Covenant here in 1,000 B.C., when he defeated the Jebusites and captured their city, Jerusalem. Fifty years later, Solomon started to build his temple on Mount

The Western Wall is the scene of dozens of simultaneous prayer services.

Courtesy Israel Government Tourist Office

Moriah, using limestone and cedar. Despite the measurements that appear in the Bible, no one knows what it looked like. (A scholarly guess is visible in the reconstruction of Solomon's city, at the Holyland West Hotel.)

The First Temple was destroyed by the Babylonians in 586 B.C. When Cyrus released the Jews from captivity (those that remained were the ancestors of the modern Iraqi community), they started rebuilding the Temple. It was damaged in subsequent wars (Remember the Chanukah menorah and the story of Judas Maccabeus rekindling the oil?) and extensively repaired by Herod the Great. During the years of Roman rule, the Jews rebelled and Titus destroyed the Second Temple in 70 A.D. (Some of the rebels held out for three more years at Masada, the fortress-palace also built by Herod.) The day on which Titus's troops destroyed the Temple was the same day of the Jewish calendar on which the Babylonians had destroyed it five centuries before—the ninth of Ab, or, in Hebrew, *Tishah b'Av,* which usually falls in August.

Between Tishah b'Av, 70 A.D., and June 7, 1967, the remnants of the Temple stood on non-Jewish soil. During the intervening centuries, Jews came to pray and weep—to wail. On June 7 the Israeli army broke through into the Old City to find hovels and shacks blockading the Wall. These have been removed, creating an oblong sunken plaza, partly fenced off into a large area for prayer. The Wall itself is an unadorned flank of large cream-colored stones.

The area beside the Wall is like a giant outdoor synagogue, with worshipers coming and going day and night, turning toward the Wall to say an individual prayer, to write a "desire" on a slip of paper that is then placed between the stones, to participate with other men in formal services, or to celebrate a Bar Mitzvah. Each man wears a hat and a *tallis,* a prayer shawl. Only the hat is necessary for the visitor, female or male. To the right of the men stands a green plastic screen, separating them from the women. The Bar Mitzah boy's mother must hop up to peer over the screen. The other women, who seem not to have heard about the name change, wail and bob their heads toward the wall, nagging God. Sometimes a *muezzuin* is atop a nearby mosque, calling Moslems to prayer. At other times Black Panthers or dissatisfied immigrants hold protest rallies. On Friday night groups of Hasidim arrive in joyful procession, to dance and sing before the Wall. On Shabbat the soldiers who search all purses and packages barely have time to read their own prayers.

Archaeologists are busy digging under the southern flank, an area closed to the public. The excavations under Wilson's Arch are, however, open to the public, at constantly changing hours, early morning and late evening. There one can see a Crusaders' street, Maccabean walls, and portions of the bridge that connected the Temple with what was known as the Upper City, on Mount Zion. Ask in advance about the hours.

The Temple Mount and Moslem Shrines are reached by a ramp leading from the Wall area up through the Mograbi Gate to the vast garden-plaza that is the chief Moslem site in Israel. A sign erected by the Israeli Ministry of Religious Affairs warns people of the Jewish faith not to set foot on the sacred and beautiful Temple Mount; the sign is not binding, and is usually ignored. Visitors of all faiths explore the Temple Mount because it affords a precious chance to learn about a religion that has become interwoven with everyone else's history.

On a tree-lined esplanade now stand the Dome of the Rock, the El Aqsa Mosque, the Islamic Museum, Moslem prayer niches, remnants of the Byzantine and Crusader eras, and, below the plaza, the ruins of Solomon's stable. This is Mount Moriah, holy soil for 40 centuries. It was here that Abraham prepared to sacrifice his only son to prove his faith, and here that David bought the threshing floor on which to build the Temple. After the Romans destroyed the Jewish Temple, Hadrian built a temple to Jupiter. Later when the area became part of the Byzantine Empire, Justinian erected a church honoring Mary. In 637 A.D. Caliph Omar took Jerusalem from the Byzantines and built a wooden mosque over the rock from which Mohammed is believed to have leapt into heaven, the very rock on which Abraham had been prepared to sacrifice Isaac. The present building is sometimes called the Mosque of Omar, but more often, the Dome of the Rock. Its golden dome dominates the Jerusalem skyline. Inside and outside, the octagonal building is encrusted with marble, tile, stucco, and gold. Inscriptions in graceful Arabic swoop around the walls. The vast interior is aglow from the stained glass windows and brilliant mosaics. Leave your shoes outside and walk in to savor these riches and to see the rock.

Next, visit the El Aqsa Mosque (shoes off, head covered), less opulent, but with a history of catastrophes astounding even in this disaster-prone neighborhood. Since being built in the eighth century, it has been destroyed by successive earthquakes and invasions. King Abdullah of Transjordan was murdered here in 1951; a fire threatened destruction in 1963; and an Aus-

The Dome of the Rock is one of Islam's most sacred and beautiful shrines.

Courtesy Israel Government Tourist Office

tralian blew up part of it in 1969. Its enormous interior seems calm, but somewhat unfinished.

Seek out the staircase, behind a gate, that leads down into the stables, to the pillars where Crusaders, and possibly King Solomon before them, tethered their horses.

From here, you can walk toward the Lion's Gate and the Via Dolorosa or back to the Western Wall and the Jewish Quarter.

The Jewish Quarter should not be confused with Mea Shearim, which is a mere century old. Since the seventh century before Christ, when Jews came to Jerusalem, this is where they came to—the Upper City, once linked directly to the Temple by a bridge. After the Temple was destroyed, none of the conquerors permitted Jews to live close to the Temple grounds, until the Mamelukes in the Middle Ages. Synagogues and *yeshivas* (religious academies) sprang up and flourished in these narrow lanes—until 1948. The Quarter, like all of the Old City, was conquered by Jordan and reduced to rubble. Since 1967 the Israelis have been scurrying to restore the famous synagogues and to put up new institutions and homes. At first they had no plan and little regard for aesthetics, just a compulsion to create a "presence." "Later we can go back and make it look right," was the typically pragmatic explanation. The first results were too ugly even for the pragmatists, so a master design and an architectural control commission now exist.

Stroll through these narrow lanes to look at the old yeshiva buildings and the shelter houses built for nineteenth-century immigrants. Stop in at the Ramban, Yohanan Ben Zakkai, and Hurva synagogues. The Ramban was established by Moses Nahmanides, the Spanish-born philosopher and annotator of the Bible, who came here in 1267. In 1585 it was turned into a mosque. The Sephardic members of the congregation then built the Yohanan Ben Zakkai, which has a cave and "seat" from which some say Elijah will return one day. Both this building and the Ramban have been restored only recently.

Walk in among the ruins of the Hurva Synagogue. The site has been *hurva* (the Hebrew word for "ruin") more often than synagogue. It was built in the eighteenth century atop ruins of a thirteenth-century church, then destroyed, rebuilt in the nineteenth century, and turned to ruins again in 1948, as was the renowned Etz Hayim Talmudic Academy next to it. Both are being rebuilt.

The Citadel and David's Tower are, even for Israel, an exceptionally exciting historical treat. Come by day or at night to see the sound-and-light presentation of *A Stone in the Tower of David*. Dress warmly and check the starting time for the English version. The five towers and most of the present stonework were set on Crusader ruins by Sulaiman in 1540, but tradition says David built the first fortress here and Herod later chose the cite for a magnificent palace. It was he was probably built the tower now known as David's. Climb it for the view. (The minaret is *not* David's Tower.)

Ecce Homo Basilica and Arch can be seen when you retrace the events of Christ's Crucifixion and Resurrection during the Franciscans' Friday procession, or go with a guide. However, a visit inside the Convent of the Sisters of Zion is not included, so allow extra time, preferably before setting off down the Via Dolorosa. The sisters take visitors beneath their nineteenth-century building to see the ruins known as the Lithostrotos, a flagstone street that was inside the Antonia Fortress, where Christ was judged and sentenced. Outside is an arch called the Ecce Homo Arch because medieval visitors thought it the spot where Pontius Pilate said, "Ecce homo," in presenting Jesus to the mob. The arch proved to have been built later and the convent turned out to be the probable site of several of those events surrounding the death of Jesus, which are known collectively as the Passion of Christ.

The sisters lead you down into cavernous rooms that were street-level in ancient times, to see where Roman soldiers crowned Christ with thorns, perhaps in one of the games they drew on the flagstones—the mocking game of Basilicus, or king-for-a-day. The convent museum has fine models of the Antonia and the old city.

The Via Dolorosa (Latin for the "Way of Sadness") is used internationally to denote what in English is the Way of the Cross, the route Christ must have followed on Good Friday, from Pilate's Judgment Hall to Calvary. The actual sites would be layers below the present store-lined streets. They are marked by plaques, chapels, and pillars built mostly in the nineteenth century, which are striking neither for their beauty nor for their portrayal of that era. The route winds through the busy *souk* and ends at the Holy Sepulchre, the giant church built above what was considered to be the actual hilltop of Calvary. (Some think the scene of the Crucifixion might have been outside the present walls. This spot was not always inside.) The Way of the Cross proceeds to 14 stations, or places, where the Gospels or oral tradition say various events occurred. Shortly before 3:00 P.M. on Fridays, one can join the Franciscans' prayer procession at the First Station, or on other days, join Father A. Mertens at the Convent of the Flagellation for a lecture-walk.

The First Station is the Praetorium, or Judgment Hall, a site now occupied by a school. After arriving at the Via Dolorosa through the Lion's Gate, seek out the flight of stairs that leads to the school. Across the street is the Second Station, around the Lithostrotos; this is where Christ received the cross. Go down to the end of this street and turn left to the Third Station, where Christ fell the first time; it is marked by a pillar. The Fourth Station, where Christ spoke with Mary, is outside an Armenian church. Its crypt is worth visiting for its seventh-century mosaic. The Fifth Station, where Simon the Cyrenian took the cross from Jesus, is marked by a Franciscan chapel. At the Sixth, where tradition says Veronica wiped the face of Jesus, whose features were miraculously imprinted on her veil, is a chapel. Go up the stepped street to the Seventh Station, where Jesus fell the second time, through the market and on to the Eighth Station, where a cross stands in the wall of a Greek monastery, at the place where Jesus foretold the destruction of Jerusalem to a group of women. The Ninth Station, marking Jesus' third fall, is reached by backtracking to the market, going up a street the Crusaders named Bad Cookery Street, and climbing a stairway to the door of a Coptic church. Then go down and through the *souk* to the courtyard of the Holy Sepulchre. The next four stations are inside the church on the rock of Calvary or, as it is also called, Golgotha (both words mean "skull," for that is its shape). These are the places where Jesus was stripped of His garments (the Tenth Station), where He was nailed to the cross (the Eleventh), where He died (Twelfth), and where His body was taken down and anointed (Thirteenth). The Fourteenth and final station is the tomb. They are detailed in the description of the Holy Sepulchre.

The Holy Sepulchre is a surprise, a vast tangle of chapels and vaulted aisles, each the domain of a different sect and all awash with people, marching through in processions, religious or curious. To Christians this spot where Christ was crucified, buried, and resurrected is the holiest place on earth. To visualize these events, one must think back through the intricate history that this building anthologizes. Christ's earliest followers knew where the Passion occurred, but when Hadrian turned Jerusalem into his very Roman city of Aelia Capitolina (135 A.D.), he dismissed Christianity as just another Jewish sect and built a temple on this site.

In the Fourth century, when the Roman emperor Constantine embraced Christianity, he and his mother, Helena, came to the Holy Land and searched for the places and objects spoken of in the Gospels. They tore away Hadrian's temple and put a huge church over the site. This, and a subsequent church, were both destroyed. Reconstruction was completed by the Crusaders in 1149. When Saladin defeated them 38 years later, he decreed Christians could once again worship there, provided that Moslems kept the keys (the same family still has the job).

Over the centuries the Moslems gave the Roman Catholics, Copts, Syrians, Armenians, and others the right to maintain and decorate particular corners. During one inter-sect squabble, the Ethiopian monks were chased out of the Sepulchre, so they settled in huts on the roof. They live and pray there still (in ancient Ethiopian). Go up to visit. That accounts for the present jumble and for the scaffolding that has finally been allowed to go up to prevent the whole building from falling down.

Near the entrance, find the stairway that goes to the Franciscan chapel atop Calvary. This, the Eleventh Station, where Jesus was nailed to the cross, is indicated by a Franciscan altar. The Twelfth, where He died on the cross, is part of a Greek chapel, crowded with swaying lamps and gleaming gold icons. The Thirteenth Station is on the main floor below, the tradition-ordained Stone of the Anointing. In the center of the church is the Fourteenth Station, an ornate enclosure indicating the actual tomb. Nothing in the Holy Sepulchre is purely for decoration; each portion memorializes an event or a personage associated with the birth of Christianity. This is dramatically demonstrated every afternoon at 4:00 when the Franciscans conduct a procession (not a tour) through the grounds.

St. Anne's Church is not to be missed, This twelfth-century Crusaders' church is one of the loveliest and oldest in Jerusalem, and its garden is the perfect resting spot amidst the Old City din. Go through the gateway on Burqlaqlaq Street, near the Lion's

Gate. Joachim and Anne, the parents of the Virgin Mary, are thought to have lived here. The White Fathers have uncovered this site and excavated the Pool of Bethesda, a spot near the ancient sheep market, probably where sheep were washed before they were sacrificed in the Temple. At this spot Jesus cured a cripple. You can walk down into the pool. The Fathers' museum is worth seeing too.

Rockefeller Museum shows a disappointingly small fraction of its riches to the public, and these are dully displayed. Still, archaeology or history buffs should go out Herod's Gate and cross Suleiman Street to see the pottery, hand tools, carvings, coins, and best of all, reconstructions of Hisham's Palace. The courtyard is a great place to cool off.

AND, IF THERE IS TIME

Muristan Fountain, a graceful fountain near the Holy Sepulchre, is newly famous because it is the best locale for buying sheepskin coats. *Hezekiah's Pool* is the ancient reservoir off David Street. *St. James Cathedral* and the *Armenian Museum*

In the foreground is Herod's Gate.
Courtesy Israel Government Press Office

are not far from the Jaffa Gate. The chief Armenian place of worship, St. James is decorated with ancient blue tiles, mother-of-pearl, and gold.

MOUNT SCOPUS, MOUNT OF OLIVES, AND GETHSEMANE

These places can be seen in one expedition. A good plan is to take the number 9 bus from the center of Jerusalem straight to Mount Scopus to see the original buildings of Hebrew University and Hadassah Hospital that could not be used from 1948 until 1967. Concentrate on the magnificent views of the Judean hills from the Amphitheater (non-Roman) concert stage. Walk along the saddle of Scopus which connects with the saddle of the Mount of Olives, with its dominant landmark, the Intercontinental Hotel. The impressive building in-between is the Augusta Victoria Hospital (named for Kaiser Wilhelm's wife)—an Arab stronghold in 1967. The most exciting panorama of Jerusalem is the one from in front of the Intercontinental.

Looking down from the cemeteries on the Mount of Olives to the Dome of the Rock and Temple Mount.
Courtesy Israel Government Press Office

The faiths interwine on the slopes of the hill, which is also known as Olivet. Jesus passed this way often, walking to Jerusalem after staying in Bethany. The Palm Sunday procession starts on the far side, at Bethpage. His last evening was spent here and in the Garden of Gethsemane on the lower slopes, and His Ascension to heaven was from a point near the summit. Olivet was already sacred to the Jews, who believed that the souls of the people buried here would be the first to heaven on Judgment Day. That is why for centuries Jews arranged for burial in this spot.

To combine the most interesting shrines and best views, before starting downward, the diligent will visit the Tombs of the Prophets (where tradition says Haggai and Malachi are buried), the Tomb of Hulda the Prophetess, the Dome of Ascension and, with truly ample time, the Pater Noster Church and the Tower of Ascension, as well. Except for the tombs, the structures are considerably younger than the sites. Most visitors will be content to start downward through the olive trees from the Intercontinental to Dominus Flavit ("The Lord Wept"), a graceful chapel memorializing the spot where Jesus wept for Jerusalem. The Byzantines, Crusaders, and modern Franciscans have built near here, as can be seen around the chapel. Go on down to a piece of Old Russia, the onion-domed Mary Magdalene Church built by Czar Alexander III in 1888, and thence to Gethsemane and the Basilica of the Agony, built in 1924 by the architect of the Dominus Flavit. The much-adorned building centers around the Rock of the Agony, where Jesus prayed. Some fine Byzantine (and dismal modern) mosaics can be seen. Outside the basilica is a gemlike flower garden with eight olive trees that are believed to have been in the Garden of Gethsemane when Jesus spent the last night of His life there.

Or, do this tour in reverse, starting at Gethsemane, walking uphill, and ending at the Intercontinental for a panoramic drink at sunset.

AND, IF THERE IS TIME

From the Garden of Gethsemane, return to the Walled City by walking up the Jericho Road, stopping to see the *Tomb of Mary,* from which the mother of Christ ascended to heaven. Going in the other direction, you reach the Kidron Valley's interesting shrines, mostly built during the Christian era to mark the possible tombs of earlier figures. *Absalom's Pillar* was probably built during Second Temple days. The *Grotto of St. James* is actually the Herodian era tomb of a Jewish family. *St. Peter in Gallicantu* is a modern church. Nearby are Byzantine remnants, as well as the path by which Jesus reached Gethsemane.

If you have ample time, visit the *Siloam Pool* by walking down the valley. Time plus nerve? Reach the pool by entering *Hezekiah's Tunnel* at the Gihon Spring. As other rulers did elsewhere and as James Michener described it in *The Source,* King Hezekiah in 700 B.C. safeguarded Jerusalem's water supply by a tunnel from the spring to a reservoir inside the walls.

MOUNT ZION AND YEMIN MOSHE

Mount Zion and Yemin Moshe were from 1948 to 1967 as close as Jews could get to the Old City and the Wall. The summit used to be part of the Old City, but the wall that Suleiman finished in 1546 did not embrace it. So, even though the Arab Legion controlled the Old City during the War of Independence, it was possible for the Israelis to hold the hill, with men and supplies being swung up at night over an iron cable. Today Mount Zion can be reached by walking from the Zion or Jaffa gates or, from the New City, via the "suburb" of Yemin Moshe, a suburb that is now in the center of town. The quarter was built in 1860 to house the first of the immigrants. Still visible are the low arcaded buildings put up by Judah Touro of New Orleans, and the sector's key landmark, a reconstruction of the windmill built by Sir Moses Montefiore who thought a flour mill would give the newcomers a way to earn their living.

A more feasible approach is represented by the Jerusalem House of Quality, a showcase for the city's craftsmen. Here, you can see the silversmiths and weavers at work or rest over a cool snack, or simply shop. Next, you cross a bridge over the Valley of Hinnom, or Gehenna, which became a synonym for hell both because of its heat and its reputation as the place where children were sacrificed to Moloch. From there, you go up to Zion—a phrase that has echoed throughout the ages—to what tradition says is David's Tomb, but which archaeology says are the remnants of a fourteenth-century inn and Crusaders' chambers. Tomb or not, the dim, low room is treated as such; men in prayer shawls moan, weep, and light candles.

Outside, find the staircase leading to the upper chamber, or Cenacle (from the Latin for "eating room"), where Jesus and the Disciples celebrated the Passover feast now known as the Last Supper. Previous shrines have been destroyed. What stands now is a huge pillared room built by the Crusaders. From the minaret atop the roof of this building, the view of the Old City is made even more dramatic by the knowledge that, from 1948 to 1967, this was Israel's frontier.

Again outside, walk to the Dormition Church, built in 1910 on the site of earlier structures commemorating the Virgin Mary's death, or dormition, since she simply went to sleep. (She was then buried in the tomb near Gethsemane before her assumption to heaven.)

Near David's Tomb is the Holocaust Chamber, the most moving of Israel's many memorials to the 6,000,000 Jewish victims of Hitler. Its simple dimly lit displays—a concentration camp uniform, an urn of ashes—have a homemade Ashkenazic quality that seems closer to the victims themselves than the offerings at ultramodern Yad Vashem.

AND, IF THERE IS TIME

Abu Tur: This pre-1967 observation point is now a shop and restaurant catering to bus groups, notable for its long shot of the Old City and for the close-up view of single Arab houses. *The Khan Center:* Mayor Teddy Kolleck thought of turning this old caravansary into an entertainment complex. Colorful and unabashedly commercial, it is an Oriental Lincoln Center housing an arena theater, night club, restaurant, and galleries. *The Source of Folklore, or Artisans Arcade:* Across from the Jaffa Gate in what used to be No Man's Land, this complex of stores, workshops, and The Citadel restaurant is close to other points on a Mount Zion expedition and, psychologically, very New City, having been built since 1967 and featuring avant-garde jewelry, paintings, and clothes. Its Hebrew name is *Khutsot Hayotser,* but saying "Citadel, shops, not David" will get you there.

NEW CITY

"Downtown" is where most visitors spend their time because of the hotels, restaurants, and shops, but it also boasts a few

sights to be seen en route. Independence Park is a quiet, green contrast to the shopping triangle formed by King George and Ben Yehuda streets and Jaffa Road. (Jaffa Road links this section directly with the Old City on one hand and Mea Shearim on the other.) Places worth a visit include the King David Hotel, for tea and a view of the Old City; the YMCA, whose tower provides an even more splendid view; Herod's Family Tomb, Hechal Shlomo, seat of the Rabbinate, with its museum of ceremonial objects and reconstruction of an Italian synagogue interior; the Russian Compound, which still looks very Russian even though many of the buildings are now government bureaus; Artists' House, a national gallery and a restaurant in the lovely old stone house that used to be the Bezalel Museum. Where Ben Yehuda Street meets Jaffa Road is Zion Square, the place to get sheruts or late snacks.

Mea Shearim, the famous ultra-orthodox community, combines together in one outing with the old synagogues, the zoo, and the Sanhedrin Tombs. Mea Shearim looks older than its 100 years, due in part to its stone walls and narrow lanes and in part to the fur hats and earlocks worn by its Hasidic residents, who are perpetually parading to or from the many synagogues and yeshivas, speaking Yiddish, acting and reacting as though they were still in Eastern Europe. Mea Shearim is a Jewish-built ghetto, walled to protect its settlers spiritually as well as physically. The name means "100 gates," but that is a biblical reference unconnected to the fact that the community can only be entered through gateways. The outside streets and surrounding neighborhood are sometimes also called Mea Shearim, but the interior streets are separate and unique. Living among the merely ultra-Orthodox are members of the *Naturai Karta* group who do not recognize the State of Israel because the Messiah did not establish it. Come on Shabbat to view the residents strolling, but also come during the week to see the bustle of the market stalls and to shop for the best and cheapest jewelry and antiquities in Israel. As you enter, signs proclaim "Daughter of Israel, the Torah commands you to dress modestly." They mean it. Avoid slacks as well as shorts and sleeveless dresses. And, do not drive past on Friday night or Saturday!

From Mea Shearim walk out through crowded and colorful streets settled by Jews from Bukhara before the century turned. Bukhara straddled the ancient caravan route from China and its residents were prosperous, two elements that are evidenced in the tapestries and ornate carpeting of the Old Bukharian Synagogue. Worshipers sit on sidewall banquettes, Oriental style. This, and the nearby Persian and Mussaief synagogues are usually on the Friday synagogue tour (as are Cabalistic, Hasidic, and modern congregations). The doors might be locked, so look for the caretaker and then thank him with a small tip.

AND, IF THERE IS TIME

The Biblical Zoo is actually a giant park, complete with boat lake, a half mile from the central bus station and a short ride from Mea Shearim. Here are all the animals, birds, and reptiles mentioned in the Bible, identified not just by name and country of origin, but also by biblical reference. *The Sanhedrin Tombs,* the first-century burial ground of the judges of the Sanhedrin, once Judaism's highest court, are near the zoo. Since 1967, there is too much to see elsewhere, so visitors are few. En route to the Jewish National Fund tree-planting center, this pleasant tree-shaded spot might fit your itinerary better than, say, Yad Kennedy.

Hebrew University, the Knesset, and the museums are another good combination, beyond walking distance from the center, but easily reached by bus or car. They take at least half a day and much interim footwork. Juggle your timetable so that you start uphill at the Knesset and work down while everything is open, or perhaps vice versa. Scheduling is particularly important on Tuesdays when the museum is open from 4–10 P.M. The university's giant Givat Ram campus, which is now much larger than the original Mount Scopus complex, can be strolled through at any time, which is convenient, since the Knesset's visiting hours are as complicated as the museum's.

Among new nations' new parliament buildings, my first prize goes to the elegantly Japanese-ish Knesset, built in 1966 with money willed by James de Rothschild. Other government buildings surround it on a hilltop park known as *Hakirya,* which literally means "the city," but in Israel connotes a government complex. Come to watch the parliamentary sessions or to see the Chagall mosaics and tapestry and the large carved menorah outside. Everyone needs to show a passport, and ladies might have to surrender their pocketbooks (bomb danger). This is surely the world's only parliament with a sign like "The Knesset management is not responsible for money or personal property." Tours are conducted on Sundays and Thursdays, from 8:30 A.M. to 3:00 P.M. Mondays, Tuesdays, and Wednesdays are the days for actual sessions. Check before going.

Unless you have a specific interest or friends to visit, the University is a walk-through tour, to be done with the university guide, weekday mornings at 9 and 11, or by yourself. One big draw: the floating egg-shaped object that turns out to be the world's most avant-garde synagogue, where, nevertheless, lady physics professors and men physics professors sit on separate sides.

The museum complex is worth many hours, preferably divided by a lunch break at the pleasant garden cafeteria. Off by itself is the Shrine of the Book, its white bricks shaped like the lid of the pottery jars containing the Dead Sea Scrolls that had been hidden for 2,000 years. The contents of those precious jars, our most ancient biblical texts, copied out for the library of the Essenes' community at Qumran, are here as well as letters proving the truth of the legend of Bar Kokba's revolt against Rome in A.D. 135. Pottery, tools, and shreds of cloth from those periods are also displayed in cavelike chambers that are entered through a tunnel.

From the shrine walk through the Billy Rose Garden, whose terrace design (by Isamu Noguchi) outshines some of the works. The Bezalel Museum has a minor collection of paintings but fascinating Judaica, a reassembled seventeenth-century Italian synagogue, ancient Torahs, and jewelry. Even more exciting to history lovers is the Bronfman Archaeological and Antiquities Pavilion.

Mount Herzl and the Western Suburbs can occupy earnest Zionists for a whole day, but those less rapt can skip a lot. Realistically a tour bus or car is needed to cover the whole route. Starting uphill from near the Central Bus Station and the Binyanei Ha'ooma Convention Hall, the first attraction is the Military Cemetery, unique for its beauty. Most striking is the underwater monument to those killed at sea. Higher up, walk through the large formal gardens to the austere slab that marks the grave of Theodor Herzl, the Viennese journalist who sparked modern interest in the return to Zion. Noted Zionists—including Zev Jabotinsky—are buried nearby. The small museum contains documents and photographs that will interest even the uninterested. A half mile farther up is Yad Vashem, an austere complex of stark gray containing shrine, museum, archives, and research center memorializing the 6,000,000 dead Jews. In the Hall of Remembrance, an eternal flame set in jagged metal burns in a sunken pit, illuminating the names of the concentration camps. It the Exhibition Hall the story of what happened from 1933 to 1945 is dramatized through photographs and documents. This is the largest such memorial in Israel and the one most visited.

Nearby are two other much-visited sites, the Hadassah Hospital and Yad Kennedy, but the average visitor can skip both. The Hadassah Hospital is a superb medical institution of interest to medical people or the many members of Hadassah whose fund-raising efforts built it. To others, the only attraction is the stained-glass windows done for the synagogue by Israel's nonresident Painter Laureate, Marc Chagall. Yad Kennedy, magnificent when photographed from the air, is a hard-to-reach memorial forest crowned by a concrete and glass building in the shape of a tree stump. This is a good place for panoramic picnicking and for planting trees—the latter to be prearranged through the Jewish National Fund.

Also in the direction of Mount Herzl is the charming suburban village of En Kerem, notable for several churches celebrating its role as the birthplace of St. John the Baptist and also for its lovely terraced fields and stone houses. Time your sightseeing so that you can take lunch at the Goulash Inn, virtually the only restaurant in Israel that is like a European country inn. Particularly for Catholics and lovers of mosaics, important goals are the Church of St. John, built in 1675 above the grotto where he was born, and the Church of the Visitation, on the site of Mary's visit to his parents. The Church of the Visitation, reached by a stone stairway off the road, was built in 1955 but is handsomely traditional. In the lower portion are an ancient well and frescoes. The upper church has both modern mosaics and a section from Crusader times. Nearby is a mosque and a Russian convent, marking the spring for which the village was named, En Kerem, "spring of the vineyard."

There is a fascinating small-scale reproduction of Jerusalem as it was in the days of the Second Temple in a special enclave on the grounds of the Holyland West Hotel. It can be reached quickly from Mount Herzl by car, but you might think it worth a guided half-day tour. The only public transportation from downtown is by Israel Taxi's shuttle service to the hotel. Now that tourists can visit the genuine Old City, the model has lost its must-see status, but I urge those with an historic or a religious bent to make time for it. Ideally, visit the Old City both before

En Kerem, St. John the Baptist's birthplace.
Courtesy Israel Government Tourist Office

and after. The model looks a lot like the existing city, except for the primitive splendor of the Temple, which is startlingly Cecil B. De Mille. Admission is under $1; tickets for Shabbat can be bought midweek at Lean Heerev ticket agency, 8 Rehov Shamai.

THE NEIGHBORING CITIES

Jerusalem is medieval-to-modern. The West Bank is biblical and Arabic. The ancient lands of Judea and Samaria that border the Jordan River below Jerusalem were not Israeli before 1967. Now they are called Administered Territories and the dictates of diplomacy could put them back behind the border, but I think you can count on seeing them as part of an Israel trip. No passes are needed. You can feel safe—before dark and on main roads. Do venture out, if only for a half day, covering Bethlehem–Hebron, Jericho–Qumran–Dead Sea, or Ramallah–Sebastia. The main pull of Bethlehem is Christian-religious, while that of Hebron, is Jewish-Moslem-religious. The lure of the others is historic-archaeological. Scenically, you cannot miss. Climatically, Ramallah alone promises cool breezes, and Qumran in winter is less prone to dampness or cold. If you choose Hebron–Bethlehem, go to Hebron first because it is farther along the same highway that twirls down through terraced fields from Jerusalem. Obstacles along the road are the donkeys overladen with olive wood and Mercedes limousines overladen with men in Arab dress undoubtedly charging off to corner the market in olive wood Madonnas. Women? You will see them, veiled and brightly dressed, toiling in the fields. Up or back, make a corkscrew longcut through history; leave Jerusalem via the Mount of Olives and Abu Dis.

HEBRON

Check your timing. Hebron's main attraction, the Cave of Machpelah which contains the tombs of Abraham, Isaac, Jacob, and their wives, is closed from 11:30 A.M. to 1:30 P.M., except on Fridays and during the entire fast month of Ramadan, when it is closed altogether. No cave, no Hebron, unless you love *souks* and ancient cities per se. Hebron is one of the oldest cities in the world. It has been continually occupied by someone although, since the Arab pogrom of 1929, not by Jews. Only now are young people settling there, despite a hostility that is obvious even to visitors. Hebron still glowers. Until 1967 Jews had been unable for centuries to set foot in the cave.

The 24 miles from Jerusalem take most of an hour. If you look for a cave, you will never find it. The site, also known as the Tomb of the Patriarchs, is surrounded by high walls, like a fortress, which some say were built by Solomon, while others credit Herod. Jews believe that Adam and Eve are buried here, that Abraham bought the cave as a tomb for Sarah and was eventually buried here himself, that Issac and his wife Rebecca were interred here, and so were Isaac's son Jacob with his wife Leah. The burial of the patriarchs also makes the site sacred to Moslems, who have controlled it since Crusader days. One enters via a stairway into the courtyard built over the actual cave, and goes into a mosque that was previously a Byzantine and then a Crusader church. Sightseers maneuver around clumps of Orthodox Jews and veiled Moslem women, deep in prayer near the opening that looks down on the actual cave and at the tombs of Rebecca and Isaac. The interior is very Islamic, decorated with inscriptions from the Koran.

From the large plaza outside the cave, walk to the lively market. Hebron has been famous as a glassmaking center since Bible days, but cheap tourist items are all that is visible now. More intriguing are the unglazed pottery jars and bags made of ropelike fibers. Hungry? Try the Hebron Settlers, a Kosher restaurant opened in 1971 by young Israelis who read their prayerbooks while not fetching the humus. If there is time, also seek out the nearby fountain called the Pool of the Sultan and, farther on, the Oak of Abraham, an ancient tree near which the patriarch might have camped. Ask one of the ubiquitous Israeli soldiers about the prospects for driving through Old Hebron. Near the cave youngsters will tout you on tombs attributed to various biblical personages, but do not bother except from curiosity.

With lots of time, consider going to Bethlehem via the Herodion, to see the fortress built by Herod the Great atop a mountain cone. He is buried there.

BETHLEHEM

On the 16-mile drive back from Hebron, there are points of interest before Bethlehem: the monastery of Hortus Conclusus, the Pools of Solomon (ancient reservoirs attributed to him), and the Etzion Bloc (Jewish settlements that were destroyed in 1948 and where the survivors' children recently settled). Bethlehem, in addition to being the birthplace of Christ, is where Ruth married Boaz and where their descendant, King David, was born. Today it is a city of bustle, catering to tourists with souvenirs of mother-of-pearl and olive wood and enthusiastic guides, professional and semiprofessional. There is not much that is biblical about its modern streets, flanked as they are by churches and convents whose high walls give them a surprisingly militaristic air.

Park your car in Manger Square, where you will also find the official tourist office, market stalls, a shiny shopping center, and a gleaming hamburger joint called the Granada Quick Lunch. At the far end is the main attraction, the Church of the Nativity. Empress Helena, in her fourth-century search for the True Cross and actual scenes of the Gospels, decided this was the spot on which the manger had stood. As usually happened when Helena discovered a major site, her son, Constantine, built a church on it. And, as also became usual, it was destroyed and others came along and built churches on the ruins. The present church was built by the Crusaders and has elements of Constantine's and later Byzantine structures. The result is complex, and warrants expert explanation. You can hire a licensed guide at the entrance. The building itself could not be called beautiful, but it is filled with things of beauty as well as sacred significance.

The Church of the Nativity marks the traditional birthplace of Jesus.
Courtesy Israel Government Tourist Office

One enters through a doorway that is deliberately undersized to deter hostile horsemen. The main hall is divided by four rows of pillars, some of which have paintings of saints. Mosaics are found on the floor and on the pillars. The altar, ornamented with silver and gold, is crowded with icons.

Downstairs, in the Grotto of the Nativity, a silver star indicates the actual spot of birth. ("Catholics, please pray, while I explain to others," says a guide.) The Catholics, Armenians, and Greeks have chapels, convents, and even complete churches inside the walls. Be sure to see the cloister garden and the tomb-like cave where St. Jerome, assisted by St. Paula, translated the Bible into Latin.

From the church, walk on to the Milk Grotto. Down under the chapel is rock that is unusually white, tradition says, because a drop of Mary's milk fell on it. This is particularly a shrine for nursing mothers, who buy cakes made with the ground stone. Keep going, far to the end of the street, for a genuinely exciting view of the Shepherds' Field, where the shepherds lay watching on the first Christmas.

There are several tourist hotels in Bethlehem, but there is little reason to spend the night in what is actually a suburb of Jerusalem. The souvenir shops are interchangeable; price varies with location. Some shops send "guides" out who do a fair job of explaining the churches and then guide you to their bosses.

Back toward the city is Rachel's Tomb, an unimposing limestone building, but sacred to Moslems and Jews. Barren women in particular pray here. They also wind thread around the cenotaph, later rewinding it around their beds.

JERICHO

The lowest city in the world and possibly the oldest, Jericho delivers a gratifying dose of history, complete with Joshua's tumbled walls; beauty, with the ruins of an eighth-century caliph's palace; and exotic scenery, as the road plunges from Jerusalem's 2,740 feet above sea level, winds through 45 minutes of desolate hills, and ends at Jericho, 820 feet below sea level. The road is the best in Israel; before 1967 it was the personal auto racetrack of Jordan's King Hussein. Non-kings better allow 45 minutes, plus time out halfway for a stop at the ancient Khan, or inn, which is where the Good Samaritan of the Gospels brought the man who had fallen among thieves. With ample time Christians might also stop in Bethany to see the House of Mary and Martha and several churches. In winter Jericho's climate is mild and dry, which answers the limp summer visitor's first question, "Why did a rich caliph build a palace here?" This has always been a winter resort. Marc Antony gave it to Cleopatra, but she then sold it to Herod the Great.

The logical starting point is the Old Walls where English archaeologist Dorothy Kenyon unearthed 23 strata going back to 7,000 B.C. A national parks guide is on hand, but despite his best effort, if you don't dig digs, maybe you would rather just cross the street to look at the Spring of Elisha (or, Elijah), where the prophet depolluted a fountain so well that it is still in use. About a mile away is a sixth-century synagogue with a striking mosaic, but I urge you to visit it primarily because it is in a private house. This might be your only chance to enter a comfortable Arab country house and see how arbors, fountains, and descending troughs of water have traditionally been used to create cool gardens.

Drive on to Hisham's Palace (also called Sisham's), which uses the same techniques on an opulent scale. An earthquake destroyed most of it. Mosaics, pillars, a broad esplanade, and remnants of a Turkish bath are all that is left, but it is enough.

At several points you can look up and see the Greek Monastery of the Forty Days, built into the sides of the Mount of Temptation, where Jesus was tempted by the Devil. It is worth a visit, for itself as well as its broad views, but you have to walk partway, so weigh the pleasure against the time. Qumran is more important. The Allenby Bridge and the place by the Jordan where John the Baptist baptized Jesus are both nearby, but the road is usually closed to tourists.

QUMRAN

By driving a few miles out of Jericho (or directly from Jerusalem), you come to the blue waters of the Dead Sea, which is ringed by brown-purple mountains wrapped in mist. The far bank is Jordan. A new road follows the sea and goes on to Elat. The first of the few stopping points along the 210 miles is a national park containing the ruins of an Essene community and some of the caves where they hid their documents. What the world now knows as the Dead Sea Scrolls were found in pottery jars, accidentally, by Bedouin shepherds in 1947. When scholars analyzed the Hebrew script, they knew these were the earliest Bible texts yet discovered, and were also evidence that Essene thought was a forerunner of Christianity. The theological reverberations have not stopped yet. Scholars have taken possession of all the scrolls for study and restoration. You can view several at the Shrine of the Book in Jerusalem.

Here, aided by the park's own guide, you can see how the Essenes lived a communal life, farming, studing, writing their own literature, notably *The War of the Children of Light Against the Children of Darkness.* Their writing room, dining room, and water reservoirs are visible. The sturdy can even climb up and crawl through several caves.

Having come this far, go three miles further to En Fescha Springs where sweet water bubbles out of the barren mountains and provides natural swimming pools on the banks of the Dead Sea. You can swim in either or both. Dressing rooms have been erected on what has become, in effect, Jerusalem Municipal Beach.

RAMALLAH–NABLUS–SEBASTIA

There is no reason to travel the nine miles from Jerusalem to Ramallah, a former Jordanian summer resort, except that it is cool, studded with beautiful villas, and en route to the Roman ruins of Sebastia. Ignore the sign proclaiming the "Ramallah Hilton"; it is a simple hotel that has not yet been stopped from using the name. This hilly region is Samaria, the land of Canaan to which Abraham came. In Hebrew its name is *Shomron.*

Continue past Ramallah to Nablus, which in Hebrew is called *Shechem.* Look over the Hellenic ruins and go on to what is left of biblical Shechem where you can see sites that are supposed to be Jacob's Well and Joseph's Tomb. In modern Nablus live the descendants of the Samaritans, who broke off from the main body of Judaism after the Babylonian captivity. They had been left behind, and the returning Jews felt they had become pagans. To the Samaritans the Bible is the Five Books of Moses; Passover is celebrated by slaughtering a lamb on nearby Mount Gerizim. Their *seder* place and other places of worship can be seen on the mountain, and their synagogue is viewed in the city.

The town of Sebastia was called Samaria or Shomron when it

was the capital of the Kingdom of Israel, nine centuries before Christ. Herod the Great turned it into a grandiose city in the first century, renaming it Sebastia, the Greek version of Emperor Augustus' name. Already unearthed are ruins of a theater, a hippodrome, a street of columns, and a temple. In the village, if there is time, see the Crusader church (there is a mosque inside it) over what could be the Tomb of John the Baptist.

AND, IF THERE IS TIME

There are several additional places in Jerusalem itself that might appeal to you if you have time. North of the walled city in the suburb of Sheikh Jarrah, walk to the *Garden Tomb,* which some Christians consider the true tomb of Christ because it is outside the walls and shaped like a skull (Calvary means "skull"). True or not, it is green and restful. The rooftop of *Notre Dame de France* was a cherished (and chancy) observation point from 1948 to 1967; although in Israel, it is across the street from the Old City. Not needed now, it still offers a striking view. *Mahane Yehuda* is the open-air market off Jaffa Road, particularly busy Wednesdays and Thursdays.

WHERE TO STAY

Important! Please bear in mind that the figures used here are simply indications of what the tourist industry expects price levels to be after 1972. *They are not actual rates.* By the time you go, the rates and facilities of specific hotels might be quite different from what was anticipated at presstime. In this book prices have been put on a comparable basis to help with your planning. (1) Each hotel rate represents the estimated cost per person for two persons sharing a standard double room (*not* suite or "bellevista") with private bath *or shower,* unless bathlessness is specified. (2) Each price includes Israeli breakfast (but no other meals) even though the hotel might charge separately for breakfast or insist you also pay for dinner. (3) A 15 percent service charge will be added to the hotel bill automatically; this charge is not included in the prices given here. (4) The prices are for July and August even if the high season is locally defined as winter. (5) The prices are those available to individuals; group and tour rates are much lower. (6) The prices, facilities, and managements are those expected to prevail in the near future, but they might change at any time. (7) Hotels are listed in each bracket in the order of my preference.

If you are not concerned about Kosher food, consider East Jerusalem—better service, more local color, smaller and quieter tour groups. West Jerusalem's plush hotels are disappointing. The King David is clangingly commercial, and the Diplomat is *Walpurgisnacht* in Miami Beach. (Contrariwise, they have big rooms.) The first-class hotels are better; some are even good. Downtown, modest places are unappetizing; budget watchers, go to the suburbs or the Old City. Under $6 you will not get air conditioning—but fear not, it is needed only 3.4 days and .01 nights each year.

During the summer some lower-priced hotels are preempted by student groups. Families or groups of friends, think about apartments.

The standouts: American Colony, Eden, Jerusalem Tower, YMCA East, YMCA West, Knight's Palace.

$13–$19 (Figure $15–$26 MAP, $19–$28 AP)

The King David is now an appalling hotel, but it pushes itself to the head of the list because in its 40-plus years it has become so famous that it is the only Israeli hotel most people have heard of. Why? An assistant manager said, "Because somebody blew it up once." Yes, the Jewish Underground set off a bomb in 1946, and Paul Newman viewed the Old City from its terrace in *Exodus,* but its popularity zooms because of its hundreds of groups tours, which have also been its downfall. A few rooms are luxurious; the gardens are enormous; the swimming pool, shops, bar, bank, and accessories are dandy; the center-city location is great; but—the food, service, and atmosphere are dismally mechanized. It had 250 rooms, but is almost doubling that. One might find that half board is mandatory.

For those who treasure a swimming pool and garden, but also a gracious touch, consider the St. George, a few blocks from the Damascus Gate. It is a favorite of American Christian pilgrims who are sedate enough to wear ties at night, but not too solemn to enjoy the bar, beauty shop, and decor, which is plushy modern with Oriental flourishes. The 150 bedrooms are good-sized. The dining room is so non-Kosher it serves a non-

Israeli, Continental breakfast. Top rates here and at the Mount Scopus run about 10 percent less than those in West Jerusalem.

The non-Kosher Intercontinental is a chunk of America, which Pan American built atop the Mount of Olives. Its graceful modern arches seem anomalous when you look up, but not when you are looking down. The view is a joy and the 200 bedrooms are topnotch, but that romantic location is also an awesome drawback (infrequent shuttle, costly taxi, or Jordanian bus). No pool yet, but a jewelry, souvenir, and beauty shop; fine newsstand; and a large handsome room that is both cocktail lounge and dancing room.

To provide Israel with needed five-star beds for 1971, the Diplomat opened before it was finished. Cheers? No, it lost one star and found its employees in a war against the Children of Darkness, that is, the clients (we lost). The Diplomat started with 386 rooms and will finish with twice that many, including its basic-to-comfortable annex, the Judea Gardens, but will things get better? They can't get worse. Officially, five-star rank has been restored. The pool is lovely and the bedrooms are large and handsomely decorated with an Israeli flavor (a rarity), but the lobby, elevators, food and service—oh, woe! Add to that an uncorrectable location, a long haul by number 7 bus or taxi into the Judean Hills, and—will there be anyone in the bar and night club but the sorrowing owner!

$9–$13 (Figure $12–$17 MAP, $13–$20 AP)

The American Colony was once the home of a Turkish pasha, and its flower-clotted patio, high domed ceilings, and tacky decor are still pasha-esque enough to make it a favorite with Europeans, journalists, and other good-livers. Service has slipped, but the Continental cuisine holds firm. The location, in a quiet suburb, ten minutes from the Damascus Gate, is workable, thanks to public transportation. Most of the 72 rooms are air-conditioned.

The Jerusalem Tower, with 16 floors, is downtown Jerusalem's shiningest skyscraper and snazziest hotel, which for mysterious reasons merely earned a three-star rating. Nonsense. Its 120 rooms are not huge, but brightly modern, like a fine motel. Public rooms are tiny, but the Kosher food in the self-service restaurant is outstanding. Groups abound, but the standards remain high.

The Hotel Eden is close by, only geographically. Built in 1919, it is virtually Israel's oldest hotel, dowdy, but with genuine class. For Israel, its public rooms are mammoth. Some of the 40 bedrooms are surprisingly chipper. The Kosher food is good enough to keep half the Cabinet as patrons. The topper: no big groups.

The President requires a short stroll into a quiet residential section of West Jerusalem. It is unpretentious, but comfortable. Thanks to its swimming pool and highly regarded Kosher food, its 90 rooms stay filled, largely with American groups.

The Tirat Bat Sheva is the newest and poshest of Israel's ultra-Orthodox hotels. The rooms are small, but bright, almost splashy. The King George Street location is great, but there is no place for evening sitting. On Shabbat, lights and elevators work automatically. (At this point, a reminder: West Jerusalem hotels are Kosher.) Nearby, the Kings is big (150 rooms) and modern, with good-sized lobby and bedrooms. They are needed; it is a favorite with groups. The desk staff is unusually effective; the chef is not.

Back—way back—on Mount Scopus is the five-star hotel of the same name. Beautifully sited and comfortable, yes, but posh and convenient, no. It is about 20 minutes' walk from the Damascus Gate. The 52 modern, balconied studio bedrooms, moderate prices, and calm atmosphere are what attract Protestant groups. Downtown, the Central is an ultra-Orthodox enclave of large, but unlovely rooms. A major plus: soundproof ceilings.

$6–$8 (Figure $9–$13 MAP, $11–$15 AP)

Commendable in this bracket are a quartet of comfortable East Jerusalem hotels that cater to pilgrim groups. In order of their appeal, which happens to be proportional to their proximity to the Damascus Gate: The National Palace has 105 rooms, most of which have balconies and bidets, plus big sitting rooms and both Oriental and Continental dining rooms. The decor at the Ritz is both modern and Arabic, a surprisingly rare combination. Only the dining room is air-conditioned, but everything else about the 104 rooms is shipshape. The Holyland East is not handsome, but serviceable. The Jordan House Hotel is a homey

Arabic villa with only 17 rooms and a delightful garden, but no bar.

Under $6 (Figure $5–$10 MAP, $7–$12 AP)

Tied for first place in this bracket are the YMCA West and YMCA East, which are basically good family hotels, although they are also recreation centers. West has slightly lower prices, 68 rooms (most of which have showers and some of which are singles), tennis courts, a library, an institutional atmosphere, and a tower with splendid views. All this, across the street from the King David Hotel. The East, also known as Aelia Capitolina, has 50 well-kept modern rooms, with tubs, an indoor pool, gym, tennis courts, plush Arabic lobby with classical Muzak, and a top floor dining room with views to match the West's. It is close to where the Mandelbaum Gate once stood. The *yimkas* —Israeli for YMCA—are neither air-conditioned nor Kosher. Yes, the YWCA has rooms, too, 30 of them, all quite modern, but it has no pool, few trimmings, and is way off by itself in East Jerusalem.

The Knights Palace is a lowly one-star hotel, but it is magnificently placed inside the Old City walls. Its rooms are no plainer than most; at least half have showers. It is thronged with young European pilgrims, attracted by the price, $5 or less for bed and Continental breakfast. For minimal-comfort adventures, a find!

Penny pinchers who insist on West Jerusalem, first choice is the Palatin, followed by the Or-Gil, both small, centrally located, and with rates around $5. The Palatin, on a side street above shops, has an ample sitting room. The Vienna nearby has lower prices and very clean, but minimal, bathless rooms.

Good economy entries close to the Damascus Gate: Lawrence, Rivoli, and Metropole, plain but well-run Arabic hotels with $4–$5 price tags. A trio of good, but alas, isolated, hotels are on the road leading up to Mount Scopus. Only the Palace has some (not all) air-conditioned rooms and big modern public rooms. The Palace and Astoria both have balconied rooms and big gardens. The Commodore does not, but compensates with largish, relatively modern bedrooms. Way up top is the smaller, simpler Mount of Olives Hotel, which usually charges around $4.

IN THE SUBURBS

Large, lavish, and resortlike is the Holyland West, which has a huge boat lake as unique as its model of ancient Jerusalem. Some of the 120 rooms scattered around the garden grounds have tiny kitchenettes. The rooms are not plush, but, oh, the accessories—outdoor pool, tennis courts, synagogue, bar, night club. Its prices are in the $6–$11 range. Shoresh is like this, but more modest, as befits a guesthouse that is part of a moshav, cooperative farm. In summer guests must take full board, a good deal but a big drawback, considering that town is a high-traffic ten miles away. Hope that Shoresh will reform because, despite operational kinks, aesthetically it is among the country's best, with great hilltop panoramas, handsome motel-like rooms mixed with less expensive A-frames for families, plus an outdoor pool, tennis courts, and playground.

Nearby are two kibbutz guesthouses that take tourists, although most of their summer clients are Israelis. Both have swimming pools, gigantic grounds, and showers for most rooms. Ma'ale Hahamisha has a rambling outdoor area and 110 rooms that range from plain to downright jazzy. Kiryat Anavim is smaller and simpler, but still resortlike.

The suburb of Bet Hakerem is close to town, a 15-minute bus ride from the center. Here, several pleasant little hotels are scattered among the wooden streets. The Reich is often used by budget-minded tour groups. Like the Margoa and Har Aviv, it has baths or showers for all its rooms. Homey, inexpensive, and quiet.

NEW HOTELS

Progress is slow but maybe by the time you arrive, Hilton and Sheraton might have unfurled their banners in the outskirts of West Jerusalem and the Hyatt House in East Jerusalem. Expect big, modern, air-conditioned Americanism. Definitely to be counted among new entries is the Moriah, near the King David. This used to be a pleasantly modest hotel with a kitchen that local people, if not tourists, rated high. Now its owners, Histadrut, have transformed it into a 100-room extravaganza, aiming for four stars.

WHERE TO EAT

Don't assume that a restaurant is not Kosher because it serves Oriental food. And don't pass up vegetarian restaurants because you are omnivorous. Vegetarian, or dairy, menus feature Israel's triumphs: fish, borsht, blintzes, salads. *Do expect prices, specialties, and standards to change often.*

For fish lovers and Kosher-keepers, Sea Dolphin on Rashid is a lively introduction to East Jerusalem eating. Thronged *and* unair-conditioned, stuffiness is well compensated for by the variety of good $3–$6 fish dinners. Benny's, on Ben Yehuda Street, is a New City spin-off of the Sea Dolphin. For a bang-up feast of Arabic lamb or chicken specialties, the best bet is the Jerusalem Oriental, followed by Hassan Afendi, both on Rashid, and the Golden Chicken of Salah el Din. They have discouraging entrances, but their main dining rooms have festively Oriental carpets, banquettes, tentlike draperies, and low tables. Dinners run around $4. Touristy? Yes, but fun. Bob's, across from the Damascus Gate, is cheaper but similar.

Inside the walls of the Old City, there are many places that would frighten a public health official, but there are also some decent little budget-stretchers. Seek out Uncle Moustache, the student hangout near the Damascus Gate, or the Jerusalem Patisserie, Kosta's, and the Citadel near the Jaffa Gate.

For Kosher Oriental food, walk up Jaffa Road and stop at Marciano, Maadan, or Zabar, or go to nearby Shamai Street, to Palmahi. Each is an informal and lively place where $2–$3 buys a meal. Not Kosher, but close by on Ben Yehuda, is Shemesh, which has a lunch-counter up front and a somewhat fancier and costlier department in the rear.

Homesick? Try the Mandarin on Shelomzion Hamalka, which is crowded, expensive ($5–$10), but presents excellent egg roll, sweet and sour pork, and shrimp, plus some un-American but authentic dishes prepared by two cooks imported from China. Tea costs extra, and orders are not customarily shared.

Fink's is also worth a splurge: it is Israel's miniature Sardi's (on King George Street), serving non-Kosher Central European food. Down the block, the Gondola provides notable Italian fare. In the same $5–$10 bracket are two French-type restaurants, Peer (Kosher) and Chez Simon; they appeal only to those weary of soul food. The Regence Room of the King David is also elegantly and exorbitantly Continental.

A more sensible splurge is an expedition to the garden of the Goulash Inn in En Kerem, where recorded Gypsies serenade you through extraordinary goulash and *palatschinken*. Latins, not Gypsies, are the pacesetters at the Citadel, the one outside the walls. The lowest level serves fine and fancy South American–European food. At midday the Citadel's upstairs dairy cafeteria and outdoor snack bar are devoted to resuscitating sightseers inexpensively. The American Colony does a similar job in its garden and also serves admirable dinners, $4–$6. The Cafe Savion on Ben Maiman is West Jerusalem's answer to garden lunching; stick to its lighter specialties.

Vegetarians have their cool haven at Bavly on Hanavim, off Jaffa. The garden is great, but one can also eat inside, as one can at the Alpin, on King George, where it is well worth waiting for a table. Some dairy enthusiasts like the gigantic Sova, on Histadrut Street. It has self-service and meat restaurants, too.

Nostalgic for an American's idea of Kosher cooking? Report to Feferberg on Jaffa Road, which is un-Israeli enough to serve corned beef sandwiches, but disappointing ones. Stick to the goose, schnitzel, unlaid eggs, or brisket. Bring $2–$3 for a New York-type lunch, $5–$8 for a holiday-type dinner. Hesse's on Ben Shatah is a much more elegant counterpart, and Gerlitz on Malchei Yisrael is a robustly Hasidic version. Leah's on Keren Kayemet is a modest-priced favorite of Old Jerusalem hands.

Two good European-type cafes with commendable pastry are Atara and Alno, both on Ben Yehuda. For ice cream and late snacks, try Alaska on Jaffa Road.

WHAT TO DO AT NIGHT

If you insist on night-clubbing, proceed to the Khan, a handsome cave with dance band and floor show, where admission plus one drink are about $7. (The second drink costs about $1;

that's how things work in Israel, a basically one-drink country.) There is usually dancing every night but Friday at the King David, Diplomat, President, and Holyland West hotels. Discotheques pop up and fade, as they do everywhere, but the favorites have been My Bar, Pop-Op, and Mandy's (founder: Mandy Rice-Davies, whose Tel Aviv establishments are no more).

Outshining night clubs in popularity are the folklore evenings at the Khan, the Shabbat programs at Hechal Shlomo, and the sound-and-light show at the Citadel. Theater exists, but as of now, there are no facilities for English translation. Concerts and dance programs are good and plentiful, a better choice for non-Hebrew speakers.

SHOPPING

Heaven for hagglers! You can chicken out and pay what the price tag says for modern Israeli wares at the shops of Maskit and WIZO on Jaffa Road and the Jerusalem House of Quality. Or shop at the Hamashbir department store, at the Jaffa Gate, or Idit on Ben Yehuda. Jewelry, religious articles, embroidered dresses, glassware, ceramics, carvings—they are in good supply and are done well.

For more adventurous shopping, try the arcade near the Citadel restaurant which houses craftsmen like Jackson, an inventive silversmith, or Jacob Dar, a witty ceramicist.

Old jewelry, Persian miniatures, menorahs, and Roman items are available in many places, but with courage and a little Yiddish, you will get the best prices in Mea Shearim. Try to *hahndel* (Yiddish for "bargain"), even at the souvenir stands here. The shops outside the Mea Shearim wall are ignorable; too touristy.

David Ezra is a widely respected specialist in old brass and copper. If Ezra has left Mea Shearim by the time you arrive, seek him out! Zion Zakai specializes in Persian things, new or old, and Yemenite and Bedouin jewelry. Yemenite jewelry is the specialty at Benayaho, which has a reputation for high prices but wonderful wares, notably the modern pieces made from antique remnants. Ohayon Hayim has exciting modern jewelry. Esfahan has a bit of everything—old silver mirrors, Persian miniatures. Nekker, Israel's famed maker of Tiffanylike glassware, has a factory-showroom close to Mea Shearim at 6 Bet Israel (ask for the Mirer Yeshiva; it is across the street). Here you can watch the factory staff—three men—blow the delicately tinted vases. The wares are sold all over, but are cheaper here.

Bargaining is equally productive in the Old City, and English suffices. To find good Arabic-style dresses, ragged-old or drip-dry-new, head for that part of the *souk* that is near the Holy Sepulchre and Christian Quarter road. Leatherwares headquarters is the Muristan Fountain; for sheepskin coats try Azzam H. Abdeen. For old jewelry you will have to accept the shopkeeper's word, but for ancient pottery and glass you can ask for a certificate of authenticity. Look in at Tabourian Hindlan for carpets or Hadji Babor for assorted antiquities. Around the Holy Sepulchre are shops that have bits of everything—modern jewelry, old jewelry, glass, pottery, carvings, even souvenir key rings and picture post cards. Particularly good assortments are at Salman, Acropolis, Pilgrim's and Old City Bazaar.

Unusual and good: Jerusalem Pottery on the Via Dolorosa makes delightful tiles, doorknobs, and nameplates. If you have two weeks and $5 you can get a name in both Hebrew and English made up as a desktop sign. Among Jerusalem's many fine bookstores, two standouts are Rishon Le Zion Haatikah, close by the Western Wall, and Steimatzky's on Jaffa Road. Embroidered dresses to order can be had from several factory-stores, notably Esther Zeitz on Bezalel Street and Yurmiyahu on Yanai Street, off Jaffa Road. For fine jewelry that is not ethnic, try H. Stern at the Intercontinental or Padini near the Jaffa Gate. Go Israeli with sandals from Nimrod on Ben Yehuda Street. For really fine paintings, not folkloric souvenirs, the place is Rina Gallery, way out on Herzl Boulevard. Phone for an appointment.

KEY ADDRESSES

Sheruts: Get sheruts for Tel Aviv, Haifa, or Beersheba on Lunz Street, off Jaffa Square.

For the airport, the company to contact is Nesher, King George Street.

Information offices: Take your questions to:
Ministry of Tourism, 24 King George
Street (02) 22 72 31
Jaffa Gate (02) 8 22 95
Municipal Tourist Office, 34 Jaffa Road
(02) 22 88 44

Room finding: Promised Land Travel Agency
12 Hillel Street (02) 22 83 11

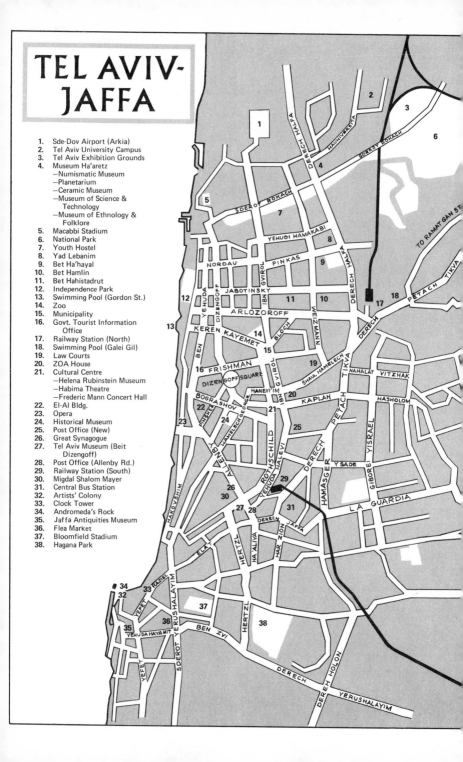

TEL AVIV-JAFFA

1. Sde-Dov Airport (Arkia)
2. Tel Aviv University Campus
3. Tel Aviv Exhibition Grounds
4. Museum Ha'aretz
   - Numismatic Museum
   - Planetarium
   - Ceramic Museum
   - Museum of Science & Technology
   - Museum of Ethnology & Folklore
5. Macabbi Stadium
6. National Park
7. Youth Hostel
8. Yad Lebanim
9. Bet Ha'hayal
10. Bet Hamlin
11. Bet Hahistadrut
12. Independence Park
13. Swimming Pool (Gordon St.)
14. Zoo
15. Municipality
16. Govt. Tourist Information Office
17. Railway Station (North)
18. Swimming Pool (Galei Gil)
19. Law Courts
20. ZOA House
21. Cultural Centre
   - Helena Rubinstein Museum
   - Habima Theatre
   - Frederic Mann Concert Hall
22. El-Al Bldg.
23. Opera
24. Historical Museum
25. Post Office (New)
26. Great Synagogue
27. Tel Aviv Museum (Beit Dizengoff)
28. Post Office (Allenby Rd.)
29. Railway Station (South)
30. Migdal Shalom Mayer
31. Central Bus Station
32. Artists' Colony
33. Clock Tower
34. Andromeda's Rock
35. Jaffa Antiquities Museum
36. Flea Market
37. Bloomfield Stadium
38. Hagana Park

17

Tel Aviv and Its Seacoast

Jaffa, Rehovot, Ashkelon, Herzliya, Bat Yam, Netanya

Tel Aviv is an ugly modern city that lacks even one first-class tourist attraction, yet it is the city every tourist visits and where many spend most of their time. There are reasons. Tel Aviv is Israel's Big Town with the best tourist services in the country— hotels, restaurants, shops—all within day-trip distance of any landmark between Lebanon and the Sinai. Tour groups hover here because the big hotels are here; the big hotels are built because it is where the tourists are.

Jerusalem is the spiritual and political capital; Tel Aviv is in charge of culture, commerce, and sin. Here are the headquarters of publishing, banking, theater, music, painting, fashion, night life. The city rampart is the Mediterranean beach front. On Shabbat it looks as if every one of Tel Aviv's 400,000 citizens is on those beaches. Come sundown, they all adjourn to Dizengoff Street to play the City's favorite outdoor sport—seeing if you can spend more time sipping a fruit juice than the waiter took bringing it to you. In puritanical Israel Tel Aviv is Gomorrah. Actually it is a souped-up subtropical Zurich where everything runs full speed except street cleaning and noise abatement.

The world's first all-Jewish megalopolis is no *Supershtetl*. It is Mediterranean rather than Jewish, perhaps because it is so new. Until 1909, there was no Tel Aviv, just empty sand dunes adjacant to the ancient port of Jaffa. Jewish families left Jaffa's cramped, airless slums and with money from the Jewish National Fund, put up an all-Jewish community of European-style houses. They called the city Tel Aviv (Hill of Spring), which is also the Hebrew title of Theodor Herzl's novel *Altneuland,* in which he imagined the future settlement of Israel. During World War I, the Jews had to leave the city, but when the

British took over in 1917, they returned. Tel Aviv became officially separate from predominantly Arab Jaffa in 1921; now, Jaffa is officially part of Tel Aviv, and the Arab population is small. In the 1929 riots and during the 1948 war, the Jews of both Jaffa and Tel Aviv suffered Arab attacks.

Most of the tourist hotels are strung along the edge of the Mediterranean, on Hayarkon Street. In the rush to build them and the fancy apartment houses, the waterfront was almost forgotten.

The city is ferociously hot and humid in summer, more so than Washington or New York, and chilly-damp in winter. The tourist hotels now have central heating (although some economy entries have room heaters, which aren't the same thing). Many private homes rely on electric room heaters.

Jam-packed hotels, bad climate, noise, dirt—they add up to a suggestion that you think about staying in the chic (for Israel) seaside suburb of Herzliya or its penny pinchers' version, Bat Yam, or Jaffa, rather than Tel Aviv. When they are booked up, consider the Israeli's pet seaside spot farther north, Netanya. The resort of Ashkelon is too far south for convenient commuting to the Galilee and Haifa, but it is acceptable for jaunts to Beersheba, Jerusalem, and Tel Aviv itself. The only tourist facility near Rehovot is the Kibbutz Giv'at Brenner guesthouse. The guesthouse at the Weizmann Institute is for invitees only.

HOW TO SEE TEL AVIV

Several Tel Aviv bus tours are duplicated by tours leaving and returning to Netanya and Ashkelon. Herzliya dwellers can arrange to be picked up and delivered to the Tel Aviv tours. Those staying in Bat Yam and Jaffa must take buses or taxis to reach the starting points for the Tel Aviv tours. From any suburban point, Egged has reasonably frequent regular buses although there might be some changing of buses and some lines stop running early. Handier than the buses, and not much costlier, are the sheruts which go to the Central Bus Station or near Dizengoff Square.

The tourist's Tel Aviv is a strip that starts at the Sheraton and Hilton hotels and runs along the beach front to Allenby Road. The main streets running parallel to the beach are Hayarkon, some of which is right on the sea, Ben Yehuda, and Dizengoff.

The city arcs out around this strip, in all directions, oozing into Jaffa and then Bat Yam on the south, and stretching through the northern suburbs, like Ramat Aviv, up to Herzliya.

If your prepaid arrangements do not include a city tour, foot and bus will get you to the museum, Shalom Tower, University of Jaffa, and so on, in any order you choose. The attractions are not interwoven à la Jerusalem. Save until after dark your expeditions to Jaffa (the fine museum is open Wednesday nights) and to the cultural enclave that includes Mann Auditorium and the Habimah Theatre, which can best be seen by attending a performance.

Looking north from Jaffa to the Shalom Tower.
Courtesy Israel Government Press Office

The Weizmann Institute–Rishon Le Zion–Giv'at Brenner half-day tour is prepaid on most packages. If not, and if you really yearn to see them, buy a bus tour. The places are scattered and rather dull unless you get a good guide who uses the sights in-between as a peg for an exciting explanation of the early settlements and the Rothschild family's role in the creation of Israel. If you are going on a Galilee trip, wait; on that tour you will get a closer look at a kibbutz than the hello-goodbye Giv'at Brenner stop and you will also get another crack at the Rothschild story.

Neither Ashkelon's beach and archaeological riches nor Ashdod's port facilities are really exciting to nonspecialists, but they fit in with a trip to Kibbutz Yad Mordecai, which is universally interesting. A car or tour bus is essential.

If you are not staying at Herzliya or Netanya, there is no reason to go there except to swim, preferably at a friend's hotel.

WHAT TO SEE IN TEL AVIV

Museum Haaretz (Museum of the Land) is a must for museum-haters. No tramping through miles of marble here! At this cluster of museum-lets, strewn across an untamed park in the Ramat Aviv suburb, you walk straight into the exhibition you want. The glass, ceramics, coins, or Jewish history and ethnography pavilions are engrossing even to nonspecialists. The science exhibits are interesting only because they are for local youngsters. A five-museum ticket costs $1. Also on the grounds are a planetarium with irregular hours and the ruins of Tel Qasile. With or without a look at adjacent Tel Aviv University, this is a stimulating half-day excursion. You could add boating on the Yarkon River or a swim in the Mediterranean, both nearby.

Tel Qasile is the excavation of an ancient settlement that goes back at least to the twelfth century. Not as interesting as Israel's other multitiered sites, but the Philistine-through-Roman ruins and adjacent museum are certainly worth seeing when you are in the Museum Haaretz neighborhood.

Shalom Tower is Tel Aviv's first skyscraper, 35 stories high. Considering how little there is in Tel Aviv at ground level, the view from the Observation Tower, 470 feet up, is magnificent. It is open until midnight weekdays; admission is under $1. The Shalom Tower includes a hotel, a highly regarded businessmen's restaurant, offices, and a full-fledged department store, which is an efficient place to shop for gifts.

Tel Aviv Museum opened its Oriental-looking gray concrete halls in 1971 and has yet to acquire much to hang in them, but it is worth seeing for its modern Israeli paintings, its visiting exhibits, and for itself.

Carmel Market is a crowded, colorful, open-air market where unit pricing could not be comprehended. Do stroll down below Allenby Road to see, hear, and—why not?—poke the melons and *hahndel* over brassware.

The beaches start around Allenby Road. They are crowded, dirty, blighted by oil and tar from passing ships, but they are free and lively. Go, even if your bathing suit stays dry. Along Herbert Samuel Esplanade is a nonstop honky-tonk midway and, by gosh, the first all-Jewish red-light district in 2,000 years. If you really want to swim, try the Gordon public pool. Few hotels have private pools, but those that do keep nonguests out.

The serious *art galleries* of Tel Aviv can easily be spotted; they are the ones that are closed on Shabbat. The galleries that specialize in art-as-souvenir of the prancing Hasidim variety are the ones that stay open nights and Saturdays to snare the passing tourist. The following are names and addresses of galleries and specialists that have earned international respect:

> David Bineth, 42 Frug Street (03) 24 85 03; paintings, graphics
>
> Dugit, 43 Frishman (03) 23 75 86; conservative drawings
>
> Gordon #1, 29 Gordon Street (03) 24 74 24; avant-garde, one-man shows
>
> Gordon #2, 4 Natan Hehacham Street (03) 24 03 23; avant-garde
>
> Hadassa K., 33 Frug Street (03) 22 40 22; good conservative
>
> Mabat, 31 Gordon Street (03) 23 68 68; contemporary
>
> Schocken, 59 Hovevei Zion Street (03) 23 70 82; tapestries

Old Tel Aviv is worth strolling through. Easy to find are Herzl Street, near the Shalom Tower, and the Yemenite Section.

AND, IF THERE IS TIME

Tel Aviv's small museums merit attention. Three good ones, all neighbors: *Museum of the History of Tel Aviv* is in the former home of the first mayor, Meir Dizengoff. Its photos and paintings are nostalgic enlightenment. Israel's 1948 Proclamation of Independence was delivered from the balcony. The

178 *The American Traveler's Guide to* **Israel**

Alphabet Museum is of greatest interest to Hebrew speakers, but its clever graphics make the story of written language clearer for all. *Haganah Museum,* in the former home of *Haganah* commander Eliahu Golomb, traces the history of the pre-Independence underground army.

Tel Aviv University in Ramat Aviv has free tours of its campus on weekday mornings. Mondays and Wednesdays, you can arrange to be picked up at your hotel. *Bar-Ilan University,* the stronghold of the Orthodox Zionists, in Ramat Gan, also provides transportation for a tour. *Habimah Theatre* is Israel's national repertory theater. Its curving modern exterior gives no hint that the company was started in Moscow by Stanislavsky, inventor of Method Acting, and moved here in 1928. The once revolutionary group is now very establishment. *Mann Auditorium* is the home of the Israel Philharmonic. Use all the *protectia* you can muster to snare a concert ticket. *Helena Rubinstein Pavilion* was formerly Tel Aviv's major museum of modern art, but now, as an annex of the new one, it presents special interest exhibits.

Tree-planting trips to Modi'im are conducted weekly by the Jewish National Fund. The trip is free; the tree costs about $3.

Free visits—"good deed" tours are offered by several organizations: Hadassah, Mizrachi, WIZO, Pioneer Women.

JAFFA

Jaffa is what Disneyland could be if it had been in the Bible. Tradition says it was founded by Noah's son, Japheth. The cedars of Lebanon for Solomon's Temple were shipped through here. The house of Simon the Tanner, where St. Peter stayed when he made Tabitha rise from the dead, was located here, too. From the 1840's until 1948, it was an Arab town with a few Jews. Now the proportion is reversed. On balmy summer evenings pleasure-bent tourists and Tel Avivniks seem to outnumber the inhabitants. Jaffa is where everyone comes to eat— at side street Arabic steakiyots or at the international restaurants in the fun-and-games redevelopment known as Old Jaffa, or in the Artists' Quarter. There they can also shop, stroll, dance, gaze at panoramas, and contemplate history. History buffs and bargain hunters should come early, for the reasons stated below.

The *Achaeological Museum* houses, in an old Turkish building, the awesome fruits of local excavations going back to Neolithic times.

The *Harbor* requires an imaginative approach to history. One can look out and think of the arriving cedars, pilgrims, and early Zionists. The biggest black rock out there is called Andromeda Rock; supposedly Andromeda was chained to the rock by a dragon until Perseus saved her.

The *Monastery of St. Peter* up on a hill, and the mosque that is near it, en route to the lighthouse, memorialize the site of Simon the Tanner's house and St. Peter's miracle.

The *Clock Tower,* a Turkish building going back to 1810, is the unofficial gateway to Jaffa and a landmark for all visitors.

The *Flea Market* is near the Clock Tower, a melange of tiny shops and stalls where one can haggle for good buys in brass, copper, and Yemenite jewelry.

The *Artists' Quarter* of Old Jaffa has been created by converting old houses in the fortresslike warren atop the port. Between the cafes and crafts shops are some genuine ruins, walls from 1300 B.C. overlooking the harbor. Browsing in the quarter's alley is fun, even if the shopping is spoiled by high prices. The craftwork and manufactured objects achieve high standards, but the paintings are awful. Commercial and obvi-

A Jaffa must—coffee at the Alladin Café overlooking the Mediterranean.
Courtesy Israel Government Press Office

ously phony it all may be, but the stage set looks marvelous in the moonlight and together, the artists and tourists put on one good show. Best place to watch: the terrace of the Aladin or Tarshish.

REHOVOT

The *Weizmann Institute of Science* is a world-renowned center for research in the biological and physical sciences, but all one can see are the outsides of the buildings and a film about what is going on inside them. When the institute opened in 1949, it was named for Chaim Weizmann, first President of Israel and a noted chemist. A small gem of a museum is devoted to Weizmann's life and work, graphically recapping the story of Zionism. Nearby is Weizmann's simple tomb, set in a garden.

Rishon Le Zion Wine Cellars, functioning since 1877, gives free samples, but they will not wow oenophiles. What irritates visitors is the dullness of the winery guides. Rishon Le Zion means "first to Zion"; established by Russian Jews in 1882, the community was not *the* first settlement, but one of them. The Baron Edmond de Rothschild of Paris played a major role in getting the country launched. His first step was to give French vines (and money) to start a wine industry here.

Mikve Israel is the sort of sight you drive right past because what you see are merely farm fields, but this is Israel, and there is nothing "mere" about farms. This is the site of the first agricultural school in the country, started in 1870 by French Jews of the Alliance Israelite (Rothschild? *Oui.*). Fortunately, this makes it hallowed ground, so now it is a permanent green belt containing Tel Aviv's sprawl.

Rehovot itself was a pioneering settlement, and Petah Tikvah came even earlier. One can drive past these Tel Aviv suburbs, but their history is not apparent in the modern streets.

ASHKELON

Ashkelon is two cities now—Migdal, the workaday old settlement, and Ashkelon-by-the-Sea, the new beachside town and resort, a large chunk of which is Afridar Beach, a residential and resort area. This is the tourist's Ashkelon, but at one time it belonged to the original Philistines, those with whom David and Samson contended. Then came Herod, that compulsive builder, followed by those equally compulsive wreckers, the Moslems and Crusaders. The archaeologists have barely started digging; there is a lot of stuff strewn about, most visibly in the National Park.

The *National Park* parallels the sea, providing access to swimming, camping, and ruin-viewing. Clumps of statues, remnants of the old city wall, and a painted cave from Roman times are there.

Yad Mordecai, named for Mordecai Anilevits, a leader of the Warsaw Ghetto Revolt, is a kibbutz about seven miles south of Ashkelon but only two miles north of the troublesome Gaza Strip. The kibbutzniks have preserved the site of their 1948 battle for survival, so that the outsider can grasp how much death and suffering it took to create this pastoral serenity. Stand on the trench-lined hillock and listen to the recorded account of how the Egyptians attacked and surrounded the kibbutz as soon as the war broke out. They held out long enough to prevent an assault on Tel Aviv. The most moving thing about the trenches is that they are so close to the kibbutz houses. Afterward, walk to the stark, angular exhibits dramatizing the fate of Eastern European Jews.

Bet Guvrin and *Lachish* are within 26 miles of Ashkelon, to the east. Both are extremely important excavations, but most of their treasures have been taken to museums, so they are seldom visited. Still, if you are devoted to digs—

Ashdod used to be a Philistine stronghold, but what the tourist sees now is the new harbor, its ships laden with citrus fruit, chemicals, and oil.

WHERE TO STAY IN TEL AVIV

Here one can assume that the hotels, unless specified, are Kosher, although many duck the issue by maintaining only a dairy restaurant. Assume, too, that the large hotels specialize in job lots of American tourists, and have nerve-racking service, noisy corridors, densely populated lobbies, and signs of wear and tear that never disappear. Bedrooms are usually small and plain; the two-star and three-star entries look alike. There are some gems in the $6–$9 range. The primitive little hotels in the

Allenby Road red-light district are only for the gutsiest tourists; they are not included here. Assume rooms have showers or baths, air conditioning, and parking privileges, unless noted. Swimming pools are rare. Don't forget the possibilities for apartments in town or in Herzliya and Netanya. Tel Aviv observes high season during the month of Passover–Easter; low season is from November to March, except for Christmas; and regular season runs from March to October, minus Passover, but plus Christmas.

The standouts: Hilton, Basel, Samuel, Star, Dalia, Shalom, Nes Ziona, the Tadmor in Herzliya.

$13–$19 (Figure $16–$26 MAP, $18–$28 AP)

Tel Aviv's three slick, newish five-star hotels resemble America. The part they resemble most is San Juan—beach, tropical foliage, night club, cost accounting, a kill-the-client approach to service, clients adept at yelling back. The Hilton is no

The apartments may not look large, but they are among Tel Aviv's best.
Courtesy Israel Government Tourist Office

calmer but it is far and away the handsomest hotel in Israel, the biggest—426 rooms to start, plus 190 new ones—and the one that best recovers from wear and tear. Bedrooms and public rooms are outstanding for their sophisticated colors, generous scale, imaginative details, and Israeli art. Each bedroom has a balcony angled for views of the sea.

There is direct access to the beach, but most prefer the pool, which has a restaurant serving virtually the only hot pastrami sandwiches in Israel. For international fare and roast beef, bring $6–$10 to King Solomon's Grill. The hotel boasts a cocktail lounge that is one of the few in Tel Aviv that stays crowded, a night club done up like a Bedouin tent, a dairy restaurant, and a lobby-lounge where even Tel Avivniks come to people-watch over coffee. Shops and services are bountiful—car rental agencies complete with drop-off service, duty-free shop, bookstore, bank, beauty salon, shops for furs, clothes, jewelry.

The Dan cleverly avoids an overwrought lobby by having the yelling space (the desk) separate from the sitting space, where foliage and pools are used to induce calm. There is no outdoor pool for swimming, but one now is in the works. Meanwhile, there is the beach, the shopping arcade, the night club, an attractive little bar, a fancy à la carte grill room ($6–$10), plus the regular dining room and coffee shop. The 400 bedrooms are good-sized and modern.

In the excitement of preparing the Sheraton's 136-room new wing (which was not completed in time for viewing), the 220 "old" rooms (circa 1965) were allowed to get very worn and torn. Let's hope the hotel has licked its housekeeping problems because, from its position at the northern frontier of the seaside hotel strip, it offers many luxuries—a big pool, good shops, à la carte grill, coffee shop, bar, night club, plus a sauna and health club (for which guests pay extra).

The Plaza and Grand Beach have been included as large seaside hotels in this price bracket, but they were not finished in time for the author to see them.

$9–$13 (Figure $12–$17 MAP, $13–$20 AP)

In this bracket night clubs shrink to bars and shopping arcades are glorified newsstands. The Basel must be the best-run hotel in Israel; the staff keeps smiling and so do the guests. Furthermore, it is Swiss-owned. On Hayarkon but blocked from a seaview by the Plaza Hotel, it has 116 small but comfortable rooms, saved from looking too hospital-like by bold splashes of color. There is a small bar next to the lobby and a large downstairs dining room with quite good food.

The Hotel Samuel, on the beach, is a gem of good planning and design. Its 100 colorfully modern rooms have Italian tile baths, shortwave radios, and good paintings. Some are studios.

Highly regarded meals and panoramas can be had if you go to the terrace or the fifth-floor dining room.

Meanwhile, back in Israel, the Park is a big, dull modern hotel close enough to the sea so you can bikini-watch from the dairy restaurant.

The Deborah is an extremely Orthodox hotel with its own synagogue and an elderly clientele, most of whom take all their meals there. The lounge space is very limited. The dairy restaurant is popular with outsiders as well as with house guests.

The Tower Hotel is in the Shalom Tower building, beyond American walking distance of most tourist attractions but in the banking center, which makes it a favorite with businessmen. Its 169 rooms are sprightly; a bar, sauna, and several restaurants are at hand, and, by the time you arrive, perhaps a pool.

The Avia is considered the airport hotel, although it is not *that* close. Guests don't hear the airplanes. Compensating for its inland and suburban location are an enormous pool, extensive grounds, a playground, and a complete pub brought over piece by piece from England. The 110 rooms are popular with air crews and with people with early takeoffs.

The Kessem has many features that are rare in this bracket: beauty shop, stores, a rooftop restaurant 12 stories above noisy Mograbi Square, a few blocks from the sea. It is all shiny new, having opened in 1971.

$6–$9 (Figure $9–$15 MAP, $10–$16 AP)

This bracket has several excellent newish hotels too small to take full-sized groups and reasonably close to the beach. The Shalom and Dalia are both near the Hilton. They have pleasantly modern rooms, little lounges, and terraces. The Shalom's is a sidewalk cafe. The Star, is a bit further along Hayarkon, is equally bright.

Similar in format but not quite so lovable are the Ora, on busy Ben Yehuda Street, and the Adiv on even busier Mendele Street. The Adiv houses a reasonable cafeteria. The Ami not only has a quieter spot but an appealing sidewalk cafe. The Commodore suffers from being right on Dizengoff Square and from having been built 20 years before most of the above, so it tries renovation (the new rooms look great) and charm. Posted at the desk, a nameplate reading, "Greeter on duty."

Similarly, the Yarden on Ben Yehuda Street, which was built in 1934, is bootstrapping itself into three-stardom by redoing rooms, air-conditioning them (but not the halls), and working toward a full set of plumbing. Its downstairs restaurant was highly regarded, but by now it might be in new hands.

The Astor on Hayarkon Street is big and fancy enough to attract large groups. It is not a memorable establishment, but it does have a dining room with a view of the sea and unusually soft beds.

As for the Ramat Aviv Garden Hotel—the name tells the whole story. Near, but not on, the sea, it is a 20-minute ride from Dizengoff, but near the university. The rooms vary in vintage and comfort, but the attractions are the accessories: large grounds, a big pool (with a palm tree in its middle), no traffic noises, beauty shop, weekend discotheque.

Under $6 (Figure $5–$10 MAP, $7–$12 AP)

The Nes Ziona is a bargain hunters' delight—no air conditioning, no breakfast, not always private showers, but clean rooms, good location (off Hayarkon), concerned owner, and tiny lobby with fine Israeli paintings. Near it, the Narciss offers better odds on showers, toilets, and even some air conditioning, plus breakfast and communal TV. The Yarkon is also nearby; it has no frills but acceptable rooms, some without toilet.

HERZLIYA

The town of Herzliya holds no lure for tourists but the nearby community of Herzliya-by-the-Sea does. It is not a town but a scattering of hotels, not all of which are an American's ideal. The big fancy ones are on the beach. From the lesser establishments, a car is needed to reach the good public beaches. Why come here? Because you can't get accommodations in Tel Aviv or because you don't want to sleep in a noisy city or because you have brought the children or yearn for beaches. Except in winter, staying here costs more, not less, than in town. Shuttle service is available from the hotels located here. Modern inland apartments can be prearranged via At Home Abroad, Inc., 136 East 57 Street, New York, N.Y. 10022 (212) 421–9165.

$13–$19 (Figure $11–$26 MAP, $18–$28 AP)

The Accadia is classier, but the Sharon Towers portion of the Israel Land Development Company's Sharon complex is snazzier. The Towers, with its striking balconies, has 132 luxury suits, about one-third of which have kitchenettes. Actually, each has a different owner, condominium-style. The Sharon itself is older and less plush, but is renovated in pleasant, if undistinguished, style and shares facilities with the moderate-priced Eshel Hasharon across the road (see next bracket). These wonders include the beach, outdoor swimming pool, and tennis courts, as well as gleaming white stuccoed lobby, pretty bar, synagogue, hairdresser, and restaurants that serve anything from burgers to banquets. At Accadia the flock of European guests adds to one's illusion of being at an Edwardian spa; the much-renovated hotel has a sprawling leisurely air that, modern trappings aside, makes it seem like it was there long before 1956. It too has extensive grounds, an outdoor pool overlooking the beach, tennis courts, shops, and restaurants. This member of the Dan chain has 195 rooms.

$9–$13 (Figure $12–$17 MAP, $13–$20 AP)

Eshel Hasharon by itself would be a good buy as a motel. As a place to sleep after partaking of the glories of the main tent, it is a wonderful steal.

$6–$9 (Figure $9–$15 MAP, $10–$16 AP)

The Tadmor is a few minutes from the beach and its swimming pool might still be in the planning stage, but this old-fashioned stucco hotel provides miraculous service and astonishing cuisine. It is the official hotel training school of Israel, staffed by the professors and students. Bless them all! Professor Bartender, for example, teaches the 7–1 martini. The 60 rooms have been updated so that they are air-conditioned and very comfortable, if not pretty. They overlook vast gardens. It is quite a deal.

The nearby Validor is a great place for families (of which it gets many), lured by the swimming pool, tennis courts, spacious grounds, and the homey comfort that lets parents stop brooding about their offsprings' behavior. There are special mealtimes for children. Rooms are sparsely but adequately furnished. At night the grownups can escape to the basement tearoom.

JAFFA—BAT YAM

$6–$9 (Figure $9–$15 MAP, $10–$16 AP)

The Scotch House, a former Scottish mission, was built in the Arab style on the beachless Jaffa seafront. Now it is a raffish Tennessee Williams stage set of a hotel suffering from inexperienced management and lack of updating. Still, its patio, high-ceilinged rooms, and exotic location (20 minutes from town) make it a favorite with the different drummer trade. It is not Kosher, not air-conditioned, not centrally heated (but with room heaters), and not even fully "plumbed," but it does have a good French restaurant on the premises.

Compared to the Scotch House, Bat Yam's offerings seem dull. They are, but several small and reasonable hotels have popped up on the street overlooking its beach front about five minutes from Jaffa. (Bus service is frequent, but tours don't pick up here.) The most promising hotel is the Panorama, which has added 22 air-conditioned bedrooms and installed a breezy bar–sitting room–dining room (Kosher). Like the Panorama, the simpler Via Maris and Bat Yam Hotel attract many French guests. The Bat Yam, which is Kosher, has launched a renovation program, but at least half of its 20 rooms have covered balconies. All have air conditioners and colorful modern furniture; some rooms have small bathtubs. The Via Maris is not Kosher nor is it fully air-conditioned, but its seaside rooms can be breezy. It opened in 1969, but it already looks ravaged.

NETANYA

Netanya is the Israeli's own seaside favorite, and with good reasons. The broad public beach is made more inviting by a beautifully maintained public garden that parallels it above a high cliff. On Fridays, the Moslem Sabbath, Netanya's beach is packed with Arab families, an eye-opener for Americans who think there is a total war in progress. Paralleling the park are several streets clotted with small hotels, which tend to be non-Kosher, inexpensive, and packed with Scandinavians, particularly during the winter.

Like Herzliya, Netanya for Americans is a last resort or a place to go because of the children and/or swimming. It is only about 20 miles from Tel Aviv so you can commute to sightsee or, in some cases, start from here.

$13–$19 (Figure $15–$26 MAP, $18–$28 AP)

For luxury-prone Americans, the Canadian-sponsored Four Seasons is *the* hotel in Netanya, but because its 129 kitchenette units are individually owned, condominium-style, it is hard to get in. The owners lock the kitchenettes away. Some of the ample, well-furnished rooms have living rooms and balconies. The picture is filled out by an outdoor pool, beach access, tennis courts, bar, weekly folklore evenings, dining room, and synagogue. This a very Orthodox establishment.

$9–$13 (Figure $12–$17 MAP, $13–$20 AP)

The Orthodox Four Seasons cannot hold a Shabbat candle to the Galei Zans, a resort on the outskirts of Netanya that operates for super-Orthodox and Hasidic Jews. It would be very awkward for anyone else.

The King Solomon, near the Four Seasons, is Kosher too, but what a difference! Brand-new, it is very French, very mod, very nicely planned. Hechal Hamelech David is equally French, but a good bit simpler; still, a good buy.

$6 or under (Figure $5–$10 MAP, $7–$12 AP)

Hakibbutz is a very special treat, a hotel run by the Hashomer Hatzair for their party's kibbutzniks on vacation or attending seminars. *If* you can get in, you will find 108 seaview rooms with showers (some baths); electric room heating, but no air conditioning; nice sitting space, but no room service or bellboys. Hashomer Hatzair is leftwing. Ordinary citizens and foreigners are the clients of the Orli and Palace, each a satisfactory, if uninteresting, spot.

OUTSIDE NETANYA

Shefayim is a kibbutz guesthouse off by itself, about a mile and a half from the beach. It follows the customary plan of motel-like rows around a main house, surrounded by lawns. Shefayim is quiet, favored by older Israelis. No air conditioning, no pool. Expect to pay around $6.

Green Beach is what Israelis call a holiday village, a simple resort. It lures young European couples because it is a low-priced array of beach, pool, tennis courts, riding, playground, and evening activities. The rooms are not fancy, without air conditioning, but bright and well-planned. Half board is mandatory, costing $6–$8 a day.

ASHKELON

The seaside hotels specialize in Israelis, but foreigners will do well in at least three. *Warning:* To do Tel Aviv from here is a deadly commute unless you have your own car. Even then, it is mostly an emergency or budget-spreading alternative.

$9–$13 (Figure $12–$17 MAP, $13–$20 AP)

The three best bets are a few minutes away from the beach. The Dagon is a gardenlike accommodation with bungalows and rows of comfortable rooms. Not all are air-conditioned. It is highly regarded for its dairy buffet and for hospitable touches like an English-language library. It is not Kosher. The King Saul is a shiny-bright establishment with good-sized rooms, a night club that is lively on weekends, a lobby that features a carpeted banquette to sprawl upon, and Kosher food. The Shulamit Gardens is equally Kosher and equally new, with lots of purple and glass in its public rooms. The bedrooms are very comfortable. Note two special features: tennis courts, a sauna.

OUTSIDE TOWN

Club Ashkelon is a holiday village of Catskill-like completeness, run by and for Frenchmen, à la Club Méditerranée. For foreigners, it is a lively buy, *if* they speak French and can forego air conditioning and plush. The seaside grounds are beautifully laid out; gracefully arched houses, each a sleeping unit, are clustered around small patios, beyond earshot of the pool, dining room, and entertainment center. Summers, the deal is full week, full board. For information, you or your travel agent can contact Sirt Tours, 5 Avenue de l'Opera, Paris, France.

WHERE TO EAT IN TEL AVIV AND JAFFA

Beware the cosmopolitan Israeli accustomed to expense account dining! He will urge you to sample restaurants where the European cuisine does not warrant the high price tags. If you are in Israel, be in Israel; eat Arabic and or Eastern European food. For Arabic fare, Jaffa is ideal. Careful! Few downtown or Jaffa restaurants are Kosher.

Assa, on Bograshov Street, is a good place to be introduced to Oriental food, amid air-conditioned comfort, festive decor, fast service, and shashlik or kebab dinners that come in under $6. After this, graduate to the Kosher restaurants in the old Yemenite quarter. The Zion is the best combination of quality and price. Shaul's Inn is very good, but more expensive (as is Mazzawi, the lunch place in the Shalom Tower). Hirbe's on Negara Street and the sidewalk cafe on its corner are ideal budget spreaders. Not Oriental, but highly regarded and Kosher, is Martef Habira, which means "beer cellar" but is a Yiddishe Momma cellar, on Allenby Road.

Central Europe? Opek on Ben Yehuda is Rumanian, has a garden, and will let you out for under $4. Ditto: Mon Jardin, up the street. Cafe Dan, a Ben Yehuda Street sidewalk cafe unrelated to the Dan Hotel, is big for goulash and liver. Keton on Dizengoff has a similar menu and slightly lower prices. Batya, up the street, is reasonable too. Nes Ziona, on the street of that name, is Hungarian, inexpensive, and blessed with a terrace. The Vienna on Ben Yehuda is open only for lunch; if you can consume a main meal then, it is a steal.

Something light? Bon Appetit is for blintzes, fish, or mini-steaks, to be eaten outside or in. Pergola, the cafeteria in the Adiv Hotel, and Bonanza, on Ben Yehuda, are adequate, as is Cafe Frack's dairy cafeteria. Around Dizengoff Square there are many snack bars like Wimpy's, Steak House, and Bar B-Q Chicken House. Most of the sidewalk cafes dispense only desserts and drinks.

Jaffa can be plain or fancy. The plainest of all are the rainbow of interchangeable and inseparable outdoor restaurants off the Clock Tower Square. At any one you walk up to the outdoor kitchen and choose lamb, veal, or liver skewers to be grilled to your order. Skewers and salad cost under $2. Better, more varied, and indoors is Suliman on Yefet Street, a good place to try Arabic-style fish. Yunis, hidden away on a little street called Shisham, is deservedly the most famous of Jaffa's Arabic restaurants. There, dinner might be $3–$5.

The fanciest spot in Jaffa is Chez Roger, a romantically terraced French restaurant in the Scotch House, where a full dinner costs around $10. Some of the flashier restaurants in the Artists' Quarter are more expensive, but ignorable.

If you can only manage one good dinner in Tel Aviv, head for the Artists' Quarter and invest that evening at Tarshish, which not only is the handsomest restaurant in Israel, but also serves outstanding international food, onion soup through moussaka to steak. A big meal will cost $6–$9 and be worth it. Too much? Tarshish also has a large and lovely outdoor terrace for drinks and desserts, but then you must have more drinks or desserts at Aladin, the mosquelike fantasy of a cafe that hovers above the water. The alternatives to Tarshish, in much the same price range, are Taj Mahal, a masterpiece of Indian decor and cooking, or Via Maris, equally handsome but Continental. Down at sea level, Jeanette's is a sound choice for seafood. Make them move a table outdoors for you. Come late if you eat in the Artists' Quarter; it is rarely crowded, but before 9:30 it is empty.

In town, around Ben Yehuda, are a dozen Continental restaurants that achieve acceptable, if not astounding, quality, at $6–$12 per head. The Gondola is the best Italian restaurant in town, and La Barchetta comes close. Casba looks Moroccan, but is French. At Ron, on the seafront, the specialty is shrimp. At Marakesh, the accent is North African. The Dolphin's big lure is its dance band. Shaldag is more Israeli than Continental, specializing in very good fish. The suburban counterparts of these entries are the Casa del Sol and Alhambra, on Jerusalem Boulevard in new Jaffa, which is French.

For Continental food at less stratospheric prices, try La Calvados, which has a terrace looking out on Hayarkon Street.

WHERE TO SHOP

The easy way to round up good modern Israeli jewelry, carvings, embroidery, batiks, and religious articles is to head straight for the giant Maskit cooperative shop on Ben Yehuda. Nearby, the WIZO shop has more sedate offerings from the craftsmen it represents. Exotic crafts and manufactured objects from all over Israel are at Batsheva on Frug Street. Dervish, on Bograshov, specializes in Indian crafts and clothes.

No leather enthusiast can leave the country without inspecting the line whose high styling won international acclaim for Israeli leather—Beged Or, represented here by the flossy new Miss Beged Or in the Jaffa Artists' Quarter and the "plainpiperacks" showroom at 40 Montefiore Street. Other interesting collections of leather for women: the Iwanir chain (conservative), Danaya (slick, young), Tourist Export Center (despite the name, standard prices and wares.)

Furs are a very good buy in Israel because so many skilled workmen have immigrated. The styles are dismal, aimed at a grandmotherly trade, but some of the second-generation's shops can whip up friskier models. Broadtail in the $500–$1,200 range, Persian lamb in the $400–$700 bracket, and mink jackets priced at $500–$1,000 are the favorites. Remember, Americans get a 35 percent reduction here, but pay 12–14 percent duty to Uncle Sam. Inspect Paris–Ur on Mendele, Alaska or Zila on Ben Yehuda. Most of Israel's diamonds are of industrial quality, but diligent shoppers can try the Diamond Exchange in Ramat Gan or jewelers like Tiv, Stein, Padini in the downtown area or Inbar in Netanya.

The lively Artists' Quarter shops have imaginative wares and wild prices. When in Old Jaffa, check out Muza for traditional and modern jewelry, Zion Dahary for Yemenite jewelry and batiks, Au Charme du Passé for antiques, Natiff for splashy modern jewelry, Meisler for carved dolls and humorous statuettes that teen-agers might like, Malka Gabrieli for handwoven fabrics. Two must-see shops: Spilo Jaglom, where the fantasies in gold and precious gems soar to $14,300 for a Tanzanite-and-diamond production, and The Source of Folklore, where the best seller is a photograph of you, snapped in one of the ethnic costumes on hand. Art galleries cluster around Gordon Street. Miscellany: Steimatzky's fine bookstores are all over town. The Shalom department store is ideal for last-minute shoppers. The Jaffa Flea Market might solve your gift problems and so might the Supersol or other supermarket chains which stock Israeli brandy, humus, tahina, and wines. Beauty shops? The hotels are the tourists' best bet, but the David and Lisa chain is a good alternative.

WHAT TO DO AT NIGHT

The best things are free—walking up Dizengoff Street, down Herbert Samuel Esplanade, or through the Artists' Quarter.

Along Dizengoff, the better cafes for people-watching and a pastry are Rowal, the grand old dame; Frack, a newer favorite; Stern, very German; Montana, Savion, and Acapulco, more modern and ice cream-oriented.

For dress-up and dancing, the Hilton, Sheraton, and Dan have night clubs, but the older Israelis go to the Dolphin or out to the Avia. Smart, young Tel Aviv hangs out at The Pub on the waterfront. Go for at least a drink, to grasp the fact that not all sabras are khaki-clad farmers. Discotheques come and go; the famous Mandy's has gone, but you still might arrive in time to try Inbar.

Few tourists get to the Atuna, a rollicking belly-dancing center on the Esplanade. Bar 51 on Hayarkon is a favorite for stripteases, more proof that not all sabras wear khaki.

In Old Jaffa the most popular night club is the Caliph; if you can't get in, try Omar Khayyam or Zorba. Here or in town, most clubs have a cover charge that includes the first drink. Neckties are advisable, but not mandatory.

The big weekly folklore evening for Tel Aviv is held in Herzliya. The tourist office runs buses for the event.

Tickets for concerts and plays are hard to come by. Try your hotel desk first. At Mann Auditorium the Israel Philharmonic or outstanding visiting artists play often, from September on. In summer the schedule is reduced, except during the Israel Festival, when superb concerts are given at Mann, in the easily reached Roman amphitheater at Caesarea, and at other spots around the country.

The Habimah Theatre has earphones for English translation, so you might be able to see them or one of the out-of-town companies that use their hall. Hebrew-speakers have a daily choice of several productions from the Habimah, Ohel, Camerai, or Haifa companies or the privately produced shows, which include Yiddish plays and Hebrew versions of American efforts. Nonspeakers will enjoy the Batsheeva and Bat Dor dance companies and the Israel Opera.

KEY ADDRESSES

Tourist Information: Ministry of Tourism, 7 Mendele Street (03) 22 32 66
Municipal Tourist Office, 42 Frishman Street (03) 22 36 93

Sheruts: For Jerusalem: near the Central Bus Station or Rothschild Boulevard, among other places.
For northern points: Mikve Israel Street.
For southern points: near Yehuda Halevi Street.

18
Haifa and Its Surroundings

En Hod, Caesarea, Acre, Nahariya, Achziv,
Rosh Hanikra

Nobody loves Tel Aviv; *everybody* loves Haifa, which is
equally shy of must attractions. The attraction in Haifa is Haifa
itself, a city rising in three tiers above the Mediterranean, turning Mount Carmel into an amphitheater with the harbor as its
stage. What a show! People say the city is like San Francisco,
but it isn't. Our sophisticated port has many hills, bays, and
bridges. Haifa has one waterfront and one hill, Mount Carmel,
1,800 feet high and broad enough to embrace many suburbs
and villages within its wooded flanks. *Carmel* means "Vineyard
of God" (nobody knows what *Haifa* means). The name suits
the greenery of Carmel, even though the nearest modern vineyards are of Rothschild, about 20 miles away at Zichron Yaakov, at the foot of the Carmel range.

Haifa is Israel with a German accent, bestowed by the
Yeckes, which means "jackets" and refers to the formality-
prone first refugees from Hitler, who arrived just as the new
port facilities set off a boom. The streets are clean, broad, and
bordered by gardens, public and private. Everybody builds to
get a sea view, but nobody is allowed to dominate or mar the
skyline. Haifans are usually good drivers. They have to be, to
get up their hill; there are stop signs at points so steep the cars
seem to be rearing on their hind wheels. The beaches are
crowded on weekends, but relatively clean. The buses run all
day on Shabbat. Simply being Germanic did not create these
blessings; many were the work of the late Aba Khoushy, Haifa's
battling mayor. It is a great place to live. It is not such a bad
place to visit.

Haifa's ground floor is the port area. The second floor is the
business district, called Hadar Hacarmel ("Glory of the Car-

mel"). The topmost layer of streets is called Hod Hacarmel ("Magnificence of the Carmel") or simply Carmel, where most of the hotels, restaurants, good neighborhoods, and panoramas are, clustered around the *mercaz* (center), a shopping street called Hanassi Boulevard. The fastest way up or down is the Carmelit, billed as Israel's only subway, but actually a French-built cable car encased in a diagonal tunnel. It makes several stops between the port and the mercaz; unlike the buses, it does not operate on Shabbat.

Haifa and its port—one of Israel's most magnificent vistas.
Courtesy Israel Government Tourist Office

Conservative Haifa is outgoing to visitors. The Tourist Office has a branch right on the main dock and at the Dan Carmel, plus headquarters in Hadar, at 16 Herzl Street. Alone in Israel, it gives all comers a Guest Card (actually a coupon book) good for free admission to nightly films, fashion shows, local museums, and folklore nights, including a highly recommended Arab Night. Sometimes, too, there are discounts from local restaurants.

After moving on, visitors find themselves continually telling Israelis, "But in Haifa, they—" The response is always "Oh, well, that's Haifa!" *That* is Haifa.

HOW TO SEE HAIFA

Haifa is the gateway to the north and the east. From here one can day-trip along the Mediterranean seacoast to Caesarea, En Hod, Achziv, Nahariya, or Rosh Hanikra, all of which are described in this chapter. Going inland to the Galilee and Golan Heights involves so many possibilities that they are covered in a chapter of their own. Most tours include one half-day and one night in Haifa. The town itself can keep you occupied much longer—swimming, strolling and visiting landmarks that are interesting, if not earthshaking.

You can easily dispense with a guided tour of the city itself but, if you are without a car, a one-day tour is the best way to get north through Acre to Rosh Hanikra. It is also the best way to reach Caesarea *and* the Rothschilds' Tomb *and* a Druse village *and,* if you like, end up in Tel Aviv. However, tomb and village are very dull, as done by the tours, and you can scoot to Caesarea by regular bus or sherut. The Druse village of Daliyat-el-Carmel can be reached by bus, too. Acre is a half-hour by bus; time the trip for lunch or dinner by the sea. By car, a trip to Caesarea can include a meal at the Straton Tower (or adjacent snack bar) and a concert in the amphitheater, with a stop for lunch (or tea) at En Hod. You can drive the long way over Mount Carmel in one direction and see a Druse village and the vineyards en route.

A drive to Rosh Hanikra can allow for a swim there (or at Achziv or Nahariya), a stop at the holocaust museum at Kibbutz Lohamei Hageta'ot, and dinner at Acre.

WHAT TO SEE IN HAIFA

The *Dagon Museum* is an integral part of the port, so first walk into the warehouse area, elbow your way through the throngs of passengers, porters, and black-marketeers, and walk to the dock area through Palmers Gate. As long as you are almost there, you might first stop at the *Maritime Museum* in the Sailors' Home, but it is most important to get to the Dagon, which is open only from 10:30 to 11:00 A.M. Dagon means "corn" and this building, the tallest and best-looking on the waterfront, is actually a grain silo. The free tour of the silo is interesting, but the big surprise is the museum which makes cereal a "hot topic" via Canaanite fertility statuettes, ancient farm tools, and electric models of the silo.

The *Illegal Immigration and Naval Museum* is not on the standard city tour, but to me, it is more meaningful than the *Bahai Temple*. The exhibits recount how many boats tried to break through the British blockade to freedom, but were turned back in the harbor. History moves so fast that it is important to be reminded by seeing photographs and mementos, including an entire ship, the blockade-runner *Af-al-pi*. The museum is often called the *Af-al-pi*.

As Elijah knew, Mount Carmel is riddled with caves.
Courtesy Israel Government Tourist Office

Elijah's Cave is worth a short climb up the Carmel, just outside the *Af-al-pi*. Tradition says it is where Elijah hid when fleeing from Ahab and where the Holy Family stayed after their flight from Egypt. You might find a Moslem group celebrating an impending birth here.

The *Carmelite Monastery,* a favorite place to go for panoramic views, is farther up the hill. One gets here by infrequent city bus or, linking all the sights mentioned so far, by bus and foot.

The *Bahai Shrine* can be reached from the hotels along Panorama Street by walking down through the Allenby Gardens or by bus. Its golden dome forms the city's chief landmark. Bahai is a religion started in nineteenth-century Persia by Baha'u'llah, considered the latest of the prophets sent by God to follow Moses, Christ, Buddha, and Mohammed. The oneness of the human race is its main belief. When persecutions began, the members scattered (there is a major temple outside Chicago), but the leaders chose Acre, and later Haifa, as their headquarters. The shrine is the tomb of Bab, the herald who inspired Baha'u'llah. The building is a graceful combination of East and West set amongst the Persian Gardens, which are rather like an Oriental carpet woven from living plants.

The *Technion* is Israel's MIT, swooping across the top of a Carmel ridge. There is no organized tour, but visitors who stop in the Aeronautical Engineering Building can get explanations of which scientists work there. You aren't permitted inside to watch them, but you can stroll or drive through the campus, as you can at *Haifa University,* way over on another Carmel ridge.

Daliyat-el-Carmel is the village closest to Haifa (15 miles) that is occupied by Druses, the loyal Israelis who are Arabs, but not Moslems. They have a secret religion of their own. The Druses who are not out productively farming their fertile hillsides are busy making baskets, embroidering clothing, and running souvenir shops. The tour groups come mainly to shop for baskets and rugs, which is unedifying even for adept hagglers. However, the trip itself is pleasant, and you will enjoy a real visit with the Druses that might happen at a festivity, by introduction through friends, or by chance conversations at cafes or steakiyot. Another Druse village, Isfiya, is close by.

AND, IF THERE IS TIME

Haifa has a cluster of minor museums, of which the *Museum of Japanese Art,* next-door to the Dan Carmel is the most interesting to tourists. Archaeology fans might also try the

Museum of Ancient and Modern Art, which has some of the treasures dug up at Caesarea.

WHAT TO SEE IN EN HOD

En Hod is an artist's village, sponsored by the government, but run by the artists. It meanders along the Carmel range 14 miles south of Haifa, reachable by interurban bus only in summer. The paintings, sculptures, and crafts sold in the cooperative gallery are only one attraction. Strolling through the tree-lined lanes and spying out the artists' houses hidden in the trees make for a delightful afternoon. Take a refreshment break on the terrace of the only restaurant. Its magnificent view includes the Crusader ruins of Atlit, which are hard to see close up because a naval station is now there. Concerts and dramatic performances are sometimes given in En Hod's small amphitheater.

WHAT TO SEE IN CAESAREA

In the not-too-distant future, Caesarea will be a lively seaside community. The Rothschild interests pushed and pulled at it throughout the 1960's and are still confident it can be done. After all, Herod the Great did it shortly before Christ was born, naming his new city in honor of Augustus Caesar. For five centuries this was the Roman capital of Palestine. Pontius Pilate's headquarters were here. The first Jewish revolt against the Romans broke out here in 66 A.D. and, during the second revolt, Rabbi Akiba was killed here. Talmudic scholars flourished and so did the Byzantines. The Crusaders found the Holy Grail here and took it to Italy. In 1291 the Moslems defeated the Crusaders and destroyed Caesarea.

The Rothschilds decided this sandy soil could grow tourist dollars. Slowly, the ruins became a big national park. A few hotels and a golf club went up. The shoreline became a superb beach. Nothing. Even the most ruin-sated tourist loved the amphitheater and Crusader walls, but hurried back to the bus for the long drive to Tel Aviv. Now the four-lane Tel Aviv–Haifa highway is complete, bringing each city within 40 minutes of Caesarea at the very time when the cities have more tourists than they can house. Now Caesarea Development Company (that is, the Israeli government and the incumbent Edmond de Rothschild—a grandson of the original benefactor) is busy creating vacation home colonies and condominium hotels and a marina and turning the Crusaders' city into an operetta-set village of restaurants and shops, like Old Jaffa or Old Acre.

While touring in Caesarea, it is possible to walk between the various sectors, but a car is preferable.

Caesarea's Crusader City is sort of an archaeological Disneyland.

Photo by the author

The *Crusaders' City* is the name for the new archaeological "playground" whose walls were built in the thirteenth century by St. Louis, who led the Seventh Crusade as King of France. He did not build the minaret or most of the other buildings within the walls; they date from Turkish times. Now they are jewelry and art shops. The stray columns are Roman and so are the arches of the aqueduct that provide shade for swimmers using the golden crescent of beach. The city is particularly beautiful at night, and fun, too. The discotheque and restaurants make it worth a special trip from Haifa. Beyond the walls is the Roman hippodrome, a racetrack big enough for 20,000 spectators. With the Development Company's interest in revivals, maybe night racing will be next.

The *Roman Amphitheater* looks pretty much as it did when it was used for throwing performers to lions rather than to music critics, except that the band shell now makes an ugly, but accoustically useful, fourth wall. During the summer the Israel Philharmonic and visiting musicians perform here under the stars. Day or night, it is a great site. (One of the stones found during the restoration bore the name of Pontius Pilate as governor. It is history's first tangible evidence that such a man existed.)

The *Byzantine Street and Mosaics* are near the amphitheater. The long trough with statues is the excavation of the Caesarea forum as it existed in Byzantine times. The huges statues, now headless, are probably Roman works that the Byzantines plucked from earlier ruins.

The Israel Festival's highlights are concerts in Caesarea's Roman amphitheater.

Photo by the author

The *Caesarea Golf Club* provides a stimulating recess from monuments and miracles. Spend an afternoon on Israel's first and only golf course, a topnotch 18-hole, par 72 course, 6,594 yards long. It is closed Mondays, but open on Saturdays, when it is quite busy. Visitors can play by paying a greens fee of about $10. Clubs, shoes, and golf-bag trolley can be rented for about $6. Don't overlook that trolley; there are no golf cars or caddies. There is a pro shop and a clubhouse with restaurant and bar. The club was launched in 1961 by the English branch of the Rothschild family. Most of the 450 members are Anglo-Saxon Israelis or foreign diplomats and businessmen who pay about $110 in annual dues. The course tends to be flat and sandy, with undulating fairways. The wind cuts across the course from the sea and, according to the members, helps to preserve the challenge for those who play here over and over again. The course is playable all year around; even during the rainy season, the sandy ground never gets waterlogged. Most Israelis consider golf atrociously bourgeois, but are proud to have 100 acres of green grass.

WHAT TO SEE IN ACRE

Acre, or as the Israelis call it, Akko, is a veritable Dagwood sandwich of history. Everybody fought for this port—Joshua, the Phoenicians, the Maccabees, the Crusaders, Saladin, Richard the Lionhearted, Napoleon, and, in 1948, an amphibious Israeli assault force. The city was once a Crusaders' capital, and in the nineteenth century it was the Turkish capital of Palestine.

As you drive the 24 miles from Haifa to Acre through the industrial suburbs that line the curving bay, you glimpse a skyline of minarets and domes. Parts of Acre are new and Israeli, but what lures the tourist is the portion that is old and Arab, with 5,000 Arab residents. There are several landmarks to visit, including Argaman Beach for the compulsive swimmer, but mostly the thing to do is to walk through the *souks* and narrow lanes of the walled city. The Old Acre Development Company, a bureaucratic relative of the Old Jaffa and Caesarea developments, is trying to restore more old buildings and convert the old Khan el-Umdan into a hotel and other spots into restaurants and shops. As of now, there are simple motel-like accommodations in Acre, but it is better to stay in Haifa or further up the coast.

The *Mosque El-Jazzar* is visible as soon as one enters the walled city. It was built atop Crusader ruins in 1781 by the Turkish pasha known as Ahmed el Jazzar, the Butcher, famous for giving his victims hashish before slitting their throats. You can buy a ticket and go in, but the real treats are outside in the courtyards and gardens with sundial, fountain, and colonnades.

The *Knights' Stable* was probably something grander because it now is realized to have been a very large vaulted chamber. It serves as Acre's concert hall. Do go to a performance if you can. It is near the mosque.

The *Municipal Museum* has been converted from Ahmed's magnificent bathhouse to make a uniquely colorful showcase for Islamic art, Persian and local artifacts and, best of all, dramatic scenes "enacted" by statues dressed in costumes of Acre's past. The museum-bath is part of a building complex that portrays overlapping history from Roman times to the present.

The *Crypt of St. John and the Posta* are other parts of the archaeological jigsaw puzzle. A stairway in the museum, or the lane running outside, brings you to an immense Gothic hall with impressively sculptured arches and a vaulted ceiling. This is called the Crypt of St. John, but it is actually the dining hall of the Knights Hospitalers of St. John. Excavations are still going on here. Recently uncovered are a Roman wall and an underground passage that leads to the Knights' hospital, which is known as the Posta because it was a post office in Turkish days. Take a passage and see how the dig has progressed.

The *Citadel and Museum of Courage* are behind the Crypt. The Citadel was Ahmed's fortress, but his successors turned it into a prison for the founder of the Bahai faith, among many others. During the British Mandate, eight Jewish Underground leaders were hanged here and many more served time. In 1947 the Underground conducted a dramatic jailbreak, freeing their key men. Now the Citadel is a mental hospital, but part of it is the Museum of Courage, a touching display of posters and documents about the founding of Israel.

The *souk* is the most interesting route to the fishing port, where modern shops and restaurants have been built into the old stone walls. The *Khan el-Umdan,* a gigantic caravansary that Ahmed built in the eighteenth century, is en route to becoming a modern hotel. Its pillars are made of porphyry and granite, looted from Caesarea. Climb its clock tower for a glorious view. Acre has been a busy port and pilgrim center for centuries, so you will see other khans nearby.

Kibbutz Lohamei Hageta'ot, a few minutes north of Acre, has an excellent museum memorializing not just the Warsaw Ghetto resisters and the Jewish victims of Hitler, but *all* the resisters and victims.

WHAT TO SEE ALONG THE
NORTHERN COAST

Nahariya is a Mediterranean translation of a German seaside resort. Its river runs to the sea, as all rivers do, but this one is neatly wrapped in a stone channel, with pretty little bridges and, at night, colored lights. Horse-drawn carriages ply the streets. The shops, restaurants, and local museum are pleasant, but not worth a stop per se. The attraction is the beach, which is excellent. None of the hotels is on the beach and some are nowhere near it, but it is nevertheless a fine, inexpensive place for families and beach lovers to use as a base for sightseeing forays into the north shore or the Galilee. Most of the guests are Israelis; many are honeymooners.

Achziv is not a town but a beach region, where the Club Méditerranée has its Polynesian-style fun house on a particularly gorgeous stretch of beach and where there is a great camping site. For the average tourist, Achziv has two attractions— the nice public beach and Achzivland, a house and lot that were declared an independent nation by Eli Avivi, an Abbie Hoffman-type whose house is filled with Swedish beauties and objects from the sea. There is a small charge for visiting Achzivland and its national museum.

Rosh Hanikra means "Cape of the Grotto," and that is just what attracts tourists to this northernmost (and possibly nicest) beach in Israel. Driving up to the fenced-off frontier, the road climbs along the tops of seaside cliffs. You take Israel's first cable car, the small bubble type we call "gondolas," and go down to walk inside the dramatic maze of grottoes that have been carved by the sea. It is nature tamed to suit the tourist trade, but still awesome. Up top, there is a restaurant and an observation point.

WHERE TO STAY IN HAIFA

The tourist industry insists that for Americans there are only three hotels in Haifa. The pundits should look again. Haifa has at least eight pleasant little hotels that are attracting many

Yanks. Most are on top of the Carmel. Since not all the luxury lovers in Israel at a given time can fit into the Dan Carmel, the splurgers should consider the alternatives in Caesarea or Nahariya. Beach lovers and families might think about the kibbutz guesthouses and holiday villages along the coast. At the accommodations mentioned, Haifa's high season runs from March to October, plus Christmas. In this section, air conditioning and central heating are prevalent, but not ubiquitous.

The standouts: Dan Carmel, Hod Hacarmel, Wohlman.

$13–$19 (Figure $16–$26 MAP, $18–$28 AP)

Second only to the Bahai Shrine as a landmark on the Haifa skyline, the 222-room Dan Carmel crowns the most built-up part of Hod Hacarmel. Its balcony-pocked modern exterior is undistinguished, but the inside is a surprise—large, well-furnished bedrooms that are genuinely pretty, a football field of a lobby done up in masculine leathers, an outdoor pool area set in an enormous garden, and the Rondo restaurant-night club, which looks like a flying saucer taking off for Haifa harbor. It is a great place for a drink at sunset. The tourist office, airlines, and rental cars have bureaus here, and there are good shops, including a beauty shop. The food is ultra-fancy Kosher. Tour groups abound. Some rates might be below the $13 figure; the same is true for the Shulamit and the Zion.

The Shulamit is much less elaborate, a four-star groupers' favorite, modern, Kosher, air-conditioned, and comfortable, but not special. The newer rooms are bigger and have sitting nooks. It is off on a ridge of the Carmel, beyond strolling distance of anyplace.

The Zion's problem is that it is too close to everything; it is downtown in bustling Hadar Hacarmel. The bedrooms and public rooms are conveniently set up, but the hotel is like a businessman's hotel.

$6–$9 (Figure $9–$15 MAP, $10–$16 AP)

Hod Hacarmel is the name of the neighborhood as well as this wonderfully warm, family-run hotel that has only 23 rooms, a beautiful garden, and a great view. Like each hotel mentioned in this bracket, it has heat, but no air conditioning, and some rooms that cost less than $6. Pension Wohlman is off on a quiet suburban street, but near the *mercaz;* tiny but very pretty, comfortable, and family-run. Pension Korngold is similar, but with a few bathless rooms and a location that is awkward for all but those who will spend time at the Technion. The Dvir does not have the special spark that these do, but the tenants of its 35 rooms have a superb location on Panorama Street, a place other tourists come to see the view. The Lev Hacarmel is good for its price, at the low end of this bracket or below. With 46 rooms, it is big enough to get Economy tour groups. Assets include some air-conditioned single rooms and a lovely garden. On the beach at Acre is a 54-unit air-conditioned motel called the Argamon. It is very basic shelter.

$6 or under (Figure $5–$10 MAP, $7–$12 AP)

The Nesher is a joy, a tiny, well-run hotel above a downtown shop. It has showers and air conditioners for some of its 15 rooms (no private toilets), and a pleasant breakfast room and terrace. Even with air conditioning, you might pay under $5. The Rachel, up on Carmel, is a slightly cheaper version of its neighbor, the Lev Hacarmel. The Rachel is considerably above two-star standards and, if it gets the third star it deserves, its prices will go up.

WHERE TO STAY IN CAESAREA

The Caesarea Hotel is back in the luxury business as a member of the Dan chain after several years as an outpost of the Club Méditerranée. Now you can stay at this handsome Rothschild-built resort hotel for a golf break or whole golf vacation (the course is five minutes away) or for a golfless, see-Israel trip. On the grounds are an outdoor pool, tennis courts, gardens, and the marble-faced, antiquities-stuffed hotel with 110 topnotch air-conditioned rooms. Expect to pay at least $17, with breakfast.

The Semadar started out to be a colony of condominium-style villas clustered around a hotel nucleus, but few of the owners made their units available for rental. So much did they enjoy this magnificent seaside setup—bar, pool, discotheque, Kosher restaurant—that they used the plush apartments themselves. Thus, financial disaster and a flock of solutions. At this writing, it is not known whether it will become more hotel-like or more colony-like. In any case prices *used to be* as high as $30 for a two-bedroom villa.

The alternatives, between here and Haifa, are three seaside vacation villages run by kibbutzim and a kibbutz guesthouse near En Hod. These cater mostly to Israelis, but might suffice for Americans with children or budgets to watch. Kayit Ve'shayit is the only one that is really in Caesarea, on the beach. Guests can try for the 15 rooms with private showers, but the

On the way to Caesarea's beach.
Photo by the author

accommodations are mostly A-frame huts made of pressed wood, just big enough for two cots and a table. Up closer to Haifa, Neve Yam offers better quarters, with better odds on plumbing and even a better beach, plus tennis courts and playground. Hof Dor is close by, on a bay that is beautiful, but shallow. Some of its rooms have private showers, and so do the green cement igloos, which have kitchenettes. Tennis courts are available. Bet Oren, on the slopes of Mount Carmel, has a swimming pool and 81 rooms with private showers. None of the quartet is Kosher or air-conditioned. Expect to be charged full board in summer and to pay $7–$10 AP.

WHERE TO STAY IN NAHARIYA

As I mentioned earlier, Nahariya has no true beach-front hotels. The hotels mentioned here are Kosher. The four-star Carlton is the plushest hotel in Nahariya, which is plush enough for most. It has 75 air-conditioned, amply proportioned rooms, with ampler baths, elaborate European food, an outdoor pool, gardens (terrestrial and roof), and a handsome sitting room away from the desk. In summer expect half board to be required at about $15, but also expect no tour groups. The big flaw: this seaside resort hotel is a long trek from the sea, where one must pay to use changing rooms.

For well under $10, bed and breakfast, the Astar is a well-planned, 26-room, all-new hotel, right next to the Carlton on the river-stripped main street. Air conditioning, a garden, and bright rooms make it the best deal in town.

The Eden Hotel is a simple, old-fashioned place that is popular for tea dancing. It has opened a new air-conditioned wing that is nothing special, but comfortable. The $10 level will apply.

Good economy entries: the Rosenshein, very close to the beach, air-conditioned, fully "plumbed," and with a garden and terrace; bed and breakfast, under $5. The Frank, a block from the beach, is another good bet; plain rooms, but with air conditioning, balconies, and showers.

VACATION VILLAGES AND KIBBUTZIM NORTH OF HAIFA

The Club Méditerranée food is not Kosher, but it is the best in Israel. The club is a French company, backed by Edmond de Rothschild, which operates wildly informal vacation villages around the world. They are like our Catskill resorts in their emphasis on total nonstop activity, but the accommodations are on a simpler scale, particularly those villages, like the one at Achziv, geared to Europeans. There have been affluent Americans who enjoyed it, too. On the Mediterranean shore at Achziv, the club consists of 12 huts that each hold cots for up to 12 people. Showers and sinks are clustered out in the open. No plumbing, but wine with each meal, a night club in the ruins of a stone house, nightly professional entertainment, a boutique owned by a neighboring kibbutz, a beauty shop, skin diving, spearfishing, and boating. For Americans, an all-inclusive, seven-day stay is in the neighborhood of $100 AP. (Or, you can bunk at Achzivland, for a dollar.)

Gesher Haziv is inland, overlooking the Achziv beach. The guesthouse is being upgraded with four-star status for its new carpeted and air-conditioned rooms, and a pool is expected. Perhaps because the kibbutz was founded by Canadians and Americans, it is one of the few places in Israel that serves corn on the cob. The food is Kosher. Expect to pay around $8 for bed and breakfast. Down below Nahariya, Bet Chava is a beautiful, air-conditioned guesthouse that caters to older people. The moshav that owns it discourages children under six years of age. There is no pool, but the beach is nearby. The food is Kosher. Here and at Hanita, full board is usually required; the tab might be $10 or even less.

Way up on the Lebanese border, Kibbutz Hanita opens its guesthouse from April to November. The main building, made of stone, is handsome and so is the mountaintop setting. The sea is about 15 minutes away, but there is a pool. Many tour groups stay here en route to the Golan. A car is almost essential.

WHERE TO EAT IN HAIFA

Add to Haifa's unique virtues the fact that many restaurants serve a fixed-price dinner, as well as the costlier customary à la carte menu. Some of the most pleasant eating in Haifa is done at outdoor cafes up top along the *mercaz* because of the possibilities for light meals, gala pastries, people-watching, and view-gazing. Cafe Carmel is best for people-watching and Swedish plates. Cafe Ron is best for sitting outdoors and gazing at the bay (inside its pseudo-Swiss chalet, one can spend $6–$8 on a full-course dinner).

For a big dine-and-dance occasion, the place is the Rondo of the Dan Carmel, where the tab can easily soar above $10. Another luxury lover's choice is the Bankers Tavern, down in the port. In the suburb of Bat Galim, Haifa's only Chinese restaurant does well enough for $5–$10. Across the street is an indoor-outdoor fish place with similar prices. In this group only the Dan Carmel is Kosher.

The Balfour Cellar in the center of Haifa is one of the most popular Kosher spots in town. It is certainly the most versatile; the table you chose determines whether you will get a snack, a dairy meal, a moderate-priced meat meal, or a fancy dinner. Another Kosher favorite is Korngold, a little bit of Old Second Avenue down near the Haifa docks.

Back up atop Carmel, the Gan Rimon serves big helpings of traditional (but not Kosher) Central European food for as little as $3. You can eat inside or in the lovely little garden. Nearby, a good unpretentious Oriental restaurant is Feenjan, inside the shopping center.

Haifa has many Arabic restaurants, but the most universally favored is Escander on UN Boulevard.

WHERE TO EAT OUTSIDE HAIFA

Acre has several restaurants on the docks of the fishing port where the food does not quite match the scenery, but what could? The fanciest is the Sands, which has an even fancier inside dining room, as well as shops and some of the cleanest rest rooms in the country. Like Tzor, nearby, it serves a standard mix of Oriental and European food. Two neighboring places that are Arabic all the way are the big Abu Christo and the little Ptolemais. Dinner will be $3–$6 here. None of these is Kosher, nor are any mentioned below.

For an elegant version of waterfront dining, drive down to the Straton Tower inside the Crusader's City in Caesarea. Their impressive buffet makes a wonderful lunch. Dinner will cost $5–$10.

The En Hod restaurant looks Arabic, but serves mostly European-Jewish dishes.

In the other direction, just below Nahariya, Fredi's is a lively indoor-outdoor dance spot and restaurant serving fine Central European food. The fixed-price dinners cost at least $5.

WHERE TO SHOP IN HAIFA

There are good shops up near the Dan Carmel and down in Hadar, but nothing super-special. There is a Maskit, WIZO, and Steimatzky. Art? Goldman Gallery is highly regarded and, of course, there is En Hod. Gifts? The Haifa Trade and Exchange center near Palmers Gate, the duty-free shop at the Dan Carmel, or Ludwig Kohen, nearby. Clothes? Browse along Herzl Street. In Acre there is the Sands, the glorified souvenir stand that calls itself "The Emerald Shop," and the Acre Pottery

Center. In Caesarea the Source has a good selection of standard wares. These places are fun to shop, but don't expect bargains.

WHAT TO DO AT NIGHT IN HAIFA

The classic nighttime activity in Haifa is sitting at a sidewalk cafe. Guest Card coupons are usable for free admission to wholesome films and folk dancing. If you can, get to the Oriental folklore evening at the Arab-Jewish Community Center, where young Arabs do a lively job with their traditional songs and dances. For dancing, the Dan Carmel is good. The 120 Club is a discotheque with a nonalcoholic minors' department.

Haifa's Symphony Orchestra is highly regarded; visiting groups, like the Israel Philharmonic, come here too. Haifa's dynamic Municipal Theatre performs around the country, which means other groups often perform here in their place.

KEY ADDRESSES

Tourist Information: 16 Herzl Street, 6 65 21
Port, Shed #12, 6 39 88
Dan Carmel, 8 92 45

Sheruts:

For Tel Aviv and Jerusalem: Baerwald Street and Nordau Street.
For Nahariya: Baerwald Street, Hanevim Street.
For Acre: Hanevim Street.

19

The Galilee

Tiberias, Nazareth, Safad, Golan Heights

The Galilee is the cradle of Christianity, the proving ground of Jewish resettlement, and a battlefield that has been used by everyone from Joshua to Moshe Dayan. The Galilee is more than just the Sea of Galilee's shores. It is a carpet of hilly farmland stretching east from the Mediterranean to the Jordan River and south from the Lebanese border to the Jezreel Valley. The Jordan River is born near its northern tip and plummets down toward near Capernaum, where it disappears under the Sea of Galilee and reemerges on its southern shores. Christians also call it the Sea of Tiberias. In Hebrew the sea is called Lake Kinnert, which means "harp," but no one is sure if this is because it looks like a harp (it does) or sounds like one. This whole area is smaller than the city limits of Los Angeles, but so much history has happened and is happening here that the tourist with only two or three days must work hard.

History is the area's chief crop, but scenic beauty is a close second. Israel's most fertile sector also has its barren hills; some sit like the "before" picture across from the "after" view of green kibbutzim. The malarial swamps have been drained and are invisible now, but there are enough stony hills and Arab villages to help one imagine what it was like for the pioneers who came after World War I to open this area for settlement, simultaneously testing Herzl, Marx, and themselves with the first kibbutzim. Now the kibbutzim look like garden motels. Then they were clusters of tents with towers where sentries watched for Arab attack. The watchtowers have been modernized along with the living quarters; the attacks continued between and during three wars. Standing on the Golan Heights and

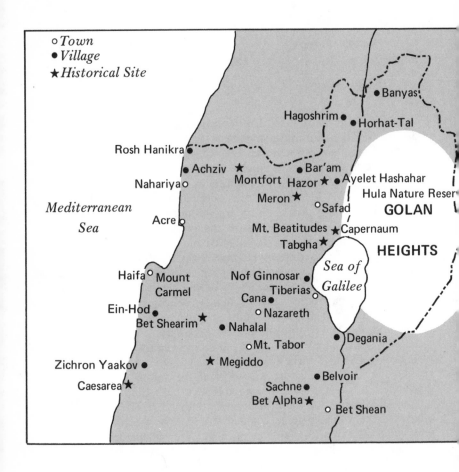

○ *Town*
● *Village*
★ *Historical Site*

● Banyas

Hagoshrim ● ● Horhat-Tal

Rosh Hanikra ●
● Achziv ★
Naharıya ○ Montfort Hazor ★ ● Ayelet Hashahar
Meron ★ Hula Nature Reser
○ Safad **GOLAN**

Mediterranean Sea
Acre ○ Mt. Beatitudes ★ Capernaum
Tabgha ★ **HEIGHTS**

Haifa ○ Mount Carmel
Nof Ginnosar ● *Sea of Galilee*
Cana ● Tiberias ○
Ein-Hod ● ○ Nazareth
Bet Shearim ★
● Nahalal
○ Mt. Tabor ● Degania
Zichron Yaakov ● ★ Megiddo
Caesarea ★ ● Belvoir
Sachne ●
Bet Alpha ★ ○ Bet Shean

Bar'am

looking down into the farmyards below is like standing in a shooting gallery looking at the ducks.

This was fertile land in biblical times; when Jesus Christ lived here, it could support 3,000,000 people. Some of the towns in the Gospels still stand—Cana; the Migdal that was the home of Mary Magdalene; Nazareth, where so many churches and convents and people have huddled that the town has little biblical flavor. That you find in the smaller villages and on the actual shores of the Sea of Galilee.

The Galilee is beginning to lure tourists into staying longer and seeing and doing more than is packaged into a stop-look-reboard sightseeing bus itinerary; one can water-ski on the Sea of Galilee, ski on the slopes of Mount Hermon, hike through the Huleh Nature Reserve or, most popular of all, take a leisurely approach to doing the sights, making base camp in Haifa, Tiberias, Safad, or a kibbutz guesthouse.

Which base camp is for you? The previous chapter explored the alternatives in Haifa and along the Mediterranean Coast, which is also the Galilee. In this chapter we will look at the other possibilities—Tiberias, Safad, and the guesthouses.

HOW TO SEE THE GALILEE

The sights of the Galilee are like the 52 playing cards in a deck. They can be combined in many different ways and still be good. If you are creating your own itinerary, pick one base camp and commute. At the most, pick two. The area is so compact that it can be covered with almost equal ease from Tiberias, Safad, Haifa, or a kibbutz. The Golan Heights, for example, is nearest to Safad, but it is just 70 miles from Haifa and 36 miles from Tiberias.

On guided three-day Galilee tours out of Tel Aviv, one night is spent at a kibbutz guesthouse and one night in Haifa, which is a sound plan, but remember the tours make stops between Tel Aviv and the Galilee itself (they have to feed and water you somewhere). Tiberias is central, but is unbearably hot in summer (although pleasant in winter). Its hotels tend to be unlovable revolving doors for tour buses. It does have some night life. Safad is up at the top of the Galilee and has many advantages—good odds on bearable weather, several nice hotels, a distinctive atmosphere. If swimming is important to you, remember that while Tiberias is on the shores of the Galilee, most hotels are not. Swimming enthusiasts might do better at the kibbutzim (all those mentioned here have pools) or in the Haifa coastal region. Taking the kids? Get thee to a kibbutz. The best guesthouses are found between Tiberias and the Golan, and so are some miscellaneous institutions with similar family appeal.

This chapter divides the Galilee into two sections: the Lower Galilee closest to Tiberias and Haifa, and the Upper Galilee closest to Safad. As you read through, the possible ways of combining them will be more apparent than they are now, but let's sort out the easiest progression. Some possible routings:

From Tiberias

1. Tel Hazor, Tel Hai, Tel Dan, Banias, Golan Heights, Bar'am, Meron, Safad
2. Degania, Bet Shean, Sachne, Bet Alfa, Nazareth, Cana
3. Tabgha, Capernaum, Megiddo, Bet She'arim, Haifa

From Safad

1. Meron, Bar'am, Tel Hai, Tel Dan, Banias, Golan Heights
2. Tel Hazor, Capernaum, Tabgha, Tiberias, Nazareth, Cana
3. Degania, Belvoir, Bet Shean, Sachne, Bet Alfa, Megiddo, Bet She'arim, Haifa

From Haifa

1. Bet She'arim, Megiddo, Nazareth, Cana
2. Bet Alfa, Sachne, Bet Shean, Belvoir, Degania, Tiberias, Tabgha, Capernaum
3. Meron, Safad, Bar'am, Tel Hai, Tel Dan, Banias, Golan Heights, Tel Hazor

WHAT TO SEE IN TIBERIAS AND THE LOWER GALILEE

Tiberias comes across best in long shots. One looks at the blue lake and thinks that these are the very waters around which the events of the Gospels occurred. The fishing boats still bring home carp, mullet, and the fish now known as St. Peter's fish. One sees domes in the foreground and thinks of this as a holy city to the Jews, a center of scholarship from the second century A.D. onward; the Sanhedrin presided and the Mishnah and Talmud were completed here. Close up the inspiration fades. Some domes turn out to be thermal bathhouses. A belt of greenery stretches along the lake on either side of the city, but in town the waterfront is a tiny patch of docks and restaurants. Most hotels are up in Kiryat Shmuel on a hill that is somewhat cooler than the waterfront. Tiberias is 682 feet below sea level, miserable in summer, but from October to May it is just the right temperature to make it the Israelis' favorite winter resort and spa. The Hot Springs, famous since the time of Solomon, are still crowded. Who would stay in Tiberias in July and August? Not even tourists—until recently, when the glut began. The local tourist office is in the middle of town at 8 Nazareth Street.

Considering the city's age, there is not much left to see. Although the Gospels call Kinneret the Sea of Tiberias, the city was built right after the time of Christ by Herod the Great's son, Herod Antipas. From that era, only some wall remnants along the lake shore are still standing. From its golden age of scholarship, all that survives are several marble tombs and some mosaics. Modern Tiberias is up on the hills, but down by the lake there are many houses built of the black basalt quarried nearby. The Sea of Galilee itself is the most important and most gratifying sight in the region. The "harp" is 13 miles long, and Tiberias is located where the harpist's hands would be if she were seated way off in Jordan. The lake is in Israel and has been since 1948, but before 1967, not all of the shore was, and kibbutzniks were frequently attacked in their fields.

Crusader ruins stand along the Tiberias waterfront, and beachside night clubs are on the north edge of town. In the center is a block of wharfside restaurants. Along these shores Christ performed the miracle of loaves and fishes, where He and Peter walked on water and where He preached and healed and spent the last years of His life.

You will get to visit the relevant towns, but to see the Sea of Galilee itself, you should take a boat ride. From the main Tiberias dock there are several daily excursions on the launches of the Kinneret Sailing Co., Ltd., an enterprise run by Kibbutz

En Gev. Its most popular route is the 40-minute ride straight across the seven-mile width of the lake to the kibbutz's rocky beach and dockside restaurant. The round trip is well under $2. At Passover the kibbutz holds a music festival in its concert hall. Speedboats are available at Quiet Beach, for cruising or water-skiing; price is about $2 an hour. Until 1967 the barren brown hills above En Gev were a part of Syria.

Sailing on the Sea of Galilee, toward Tiberias' Turkish ruins.
Courtesy Israel Government Tourist Office

The *Ancient Synagogue of Hammat* is the original settlement close to the Hot Springs and represents the third to eighth centuries A.D. Remnants of the basalt walls are still visible. The fine mosaics, carefully restored, show menorahs and signs of the Zodiac.

The *Tomb of Rabbi Meir Ba'al Haness* is on the hill above the synagogue ruins. Particularly at Shavuot and Lag B'Omer, black-clothed Hasidim come here to the white-domed building to pray at the grave of the second-century miracle worker.

The *Citadel* is where Safad artists go to sell their work in winter. It is an Old Jaffa-type collection of galleries, craft shops, and restaurants built into the old Turkish walls.

The *Hot Springs of Tiberias* might be worth a dip. Many

doctors believe just what the ancients did, that their mineral salts alleviate arthritis, rheumatism, and skin diseases. Less certain: the old belief that a barren woman who sits on the poolside lion will conceive. Men and woman have separate pools, large, small, and mud.

The *Tomb of Maimonides* is not important aesthetically but rather as a place of homage to Rabbi Moses ben Maimon, known in English as Maimonides. He died in Tiberias in 1204. Born in Spain, he spent most of his life in Egypt, part of it as personal physician to Saladin. Working on Jewish theology at the time of the Scholastics, he achieved a synthesis of Aristotle and the Talmud. His importance is measured by the folk saying, "From Moses unto Moses, there was none like unto Moses." The tomb is at the end of Hagalil Street.

The *Tomb of Rabbi Akiba,* of interest because of the man, is on the outskirts of town. Akiba, a scholar who compiled the Mishnah commentaries, participated in the Bar Kokba revolt against Rome. The Romans tortured him to death in Caesarea.

Tabgha, eight lakefront miles north of Tiberias, is the traditional site of the miracle of loaves and fishes. The spot is marked by the *Church of the Multiplication,* built over Byzantine mosaics that depict birds and plants of the Galilee with unusual wit and beauty.

The *Mount of Beatitudes,* two and one-half miles from Tabgha, is the traditional site of the Sermon on the Mount and the choosing of the Twelve Apostles. It is topped by a striking Franciscan church.

Capernaum, two miles from Tabgha, is where Jesus performed many miracles of healing. The Gospels describe how He preached in the synagogue, whose ruins can still be seen. This site is not a national park, but a project of the Franciscans and the Italian government, so one must dress as though for church. The souvenir stand rents skirt-size scarves. At nearby Korazim is another notable synagogue, dating from the third century, on a plateau overlooking the lake. Near here, one can glimpse the pipes and troughs of Israel's national water system.

Vered Hagalil is Israel's seaside dude ranch, launched by a Chicagoan who started to raise roses (the name means "rose of the Galilee"), but ended up with a restaurant specializing in chicken-in-the-basket. One can stay overnight, eat here, or hire a horse and guide (about $3 an hour) for an hour or day trip around the sea or to Arab villages. Both English and Western saddles are available. This Israeli Wild West is 12 miles north of Tiberias.

Karei Deshe is a lovely, grass-bordered beach near Tabgha, open to the public as well as those staying at its hostel (an unusually comfortable one, with community kitchens).

Degania is the first landmark on an itinerary going south from Tiberias. "The mother of kibbutzim", founded in 1911, is now a peaceful garden spot, across the highway from the place where the Jordan comes out of the Sea of Galilee. If you have time, look at the Jordan, then stroll through the kibbutz to Bet Gordon, a science museum memorializing A. D. Gordon, the philosopher who helped launch the kibbutz movement and who lived at Degania, but for complex theoretical reasons refused to join.

Belvoir, about 25 miles from Tiberias, is one of the few Crusader castles that is both well-preserved *and* easy to reach. (Others, like Montfort near Achziv and Nimrod near the Golan Heights are visible, but the average visitor lacks the time to hike there.) To find the road that spirals up to the imposing twelfth-century French fortress, look for road signs saying Kochav Hayarden ("Star of the Jordan"), its Hebrew name. The 360-degree view of the valley is as exciting as the moats and parapets. If you have time between Tiberias and Bet Shean, it is a great stop for children and/or picnics.

Bet Shean, in the Jordan Valley, about 22 miles south of Tiberias, is a development town peopled by recent immigrants, built on top of 18 previous cities (that is the current count) that started 6,000 years ago. The big lure is the splendidly preserved Roman theater on the outskirts of town. Wonderful Canaanite carvings have been excavated from the adjacent Tel, but there is nothing to see on the spot. Some treasures are in the municipal museum downtown, and a striking mosaic from an ancient synagogue is at nearby Tel Etztaba.

Sachne is a marvelous park built around deep natural swimming pools, two miles east of Bet Shean en route to Bet Alfa. The sign to seek is "Gan Hashelosha." Every Friday Sachne is crowded with Arab families.

Bet Alfa, two miles further east, is a miniature national park preserving the glorious mosaic floor of a sixth-century synagogue.

Sachne is a favorite spot for Moslems on Fridays, their Sabbath.
Courtesy Israel Government Press Office

Haifa and its seacoast neighbors—Acre, Achziv, Rosh Hanikra, Nahariya, and Caesarea—are covered in Chapter 18.

The *Jezreel Valley* is called Emek Yizreel in Hebrew, or usually just *Ha'emek,* the valley. This southernmost section of the Galilee, swooping south and east from Haifa, was one of the first places where pioneers settled, drained the swamps, and made the plain as fertile as it had been in biblical times. Coming from Haifa or Tiberias, one passes through here to get to the places mentioned below.

Bet She'arim, 12 miles out of Haifa, is the site of an ancient town where the Sanhedrin (Supreme Court) met in the second century A.D. Now, in a national park set among olive and cypress trees, one can see the synagogue, olive press, and catacombs of that community. As usual, many things are in museums, so the tombs and carved sarcophagi can be viewed in a short time.

Megiddo, about 12 miles south and east of Bet She'arim is, next to Masada, the most interesting archaeological site in Israel. Megiddo is the Armageddon of the Bible and, to a greater extent than any other site, the Tel of Michener's *The Source.* As is known from either book, many battles were fought on this important vantage point above the Via Maris, so Armageddon became a synonym for war. First, go to the small museum to get an idea of what you will see because it takes a lot of imagination to walk through the stones up on the Tel and view them as 20 different eras of settlement, one upon the other, going back 4,000 years. There are remains of Canaanite temples; the walls, gates, and stables of King Solomon's "chariot city"; Israelite granaries; and, the star attraction, the water system. Quite a piece of engineering—for 900 B.C. Climb down the 182 steps and go through the 215-foot long tunnel to the spring that lay outside the town walls. Imagine that you are carrying a large water jar on your shoulder and that, outside the wall, an enemy army is laying siege. Fine, except that you are now outside the wall yourself and must circle the whole Tel to get back in.

NAZARETH

Nazareth, about 25 miles from Haifa, has one of Israel's largest Arab and Christian populations. Half the Arabs are Christians, and these are large numbers of priests and nuns living in the many religious institutions. Allow at least half a day for Nazareth, preferably a full day. The major Christian sites will interest all people, and so will the *souk,* which is particularly colorful here because it swerves uphill to traditional holy sites and is jam-packed on both the Moslem and Jewish sabbaths, since many Arabs work for Jewish companies and have Saturday free for marketing. See the basketballs among the water jugs, the Arab boys riding donkeys and wearing cowboy hats. A happy part of the Nazareth weekend scene is the parade of pickup trucks disgorging nicely dressed Arab families (later one sees the same families enter restaurants carrying plastic shopping bags with new possessions).

Arriving in Nazareth, instinct as well as road signs steer the visitor to Casanova Street, where he will find the tourist office, the entrance to the *souk,* the town's few resturants and shops, and the shrines that are among the most meaningful in the world to Christians—the Basilica of the Annunciation, the Church of St. Joseph, the adjacent museum, the convent of the Sisters of Nazareth and, in a nearby lane, the building known as the Synagogue-Church. Important too are Mary's Well and the Church of Gabriel, a short walk from Casanova Street, and—who would want to miss it—the Frank Sinatra Brotherhood Center, an interfaith recreation building for which the actor helped raise funds. There is a Jewish neighborhood here, too, atop the hill, in Nazrat Ilit. Guides will pounce upon you; look for the brass license button or ask the tourist office to find you one, but beware of the nonprofessionals.

The *Basilica of the Annunciation* celebrates the place where tradition says the Archangel Gabriel appeared to Mary to tell her that Jesus would be born by saying, "Hail Mary, full of grace, the Lord is with thee," the words repeated by Catholics to this day. The church was built by the Franciscans and finished in 1966. Before it, the site was marked by churches built by the Byzantines, the Crusaders, and the Franciscans, who demolished their 1730 church to make way for the present structure. Its lowest level consists of the traditional grotto site of the Annunciation. It can be seen clearly, but none is permitted to enter. Upstairs are modern mosaics from many nations. Poland's representative is particularly pleasing to modern eyes.

The *Church of St. Joseph* is built over the traditional place of Joseph's carpentry shop. Ask and a monk will show you the older church below, with its mosaics, cisterns, and storage places.

Terra Sancta Museum, near St. Joseph's, contains archaeological materials about Nazareth, but it is only open on request. The local guides, however, can get the key.

The Sisters of the *Convent of Nazareth* provide tours to guide visitors through the ruins they discovered when digging a cistern in the draught of 1895. There are Crusader ruins, an old Moslem tomb, a Jewish tomb, and a Byzantine church. An English-speaker might be lacking; your own guide or a knowledge of French will help. The tour is not a three-star must, but the sisters make it wonderfully alive.

The *Synagogue-Church* is in the *souk,* a Greek church built on the site of the synagogue that might have been the one where Jesus and his family worshiped.

Cana, or Kfar Kana, four miles over the mountain from Nazareth, is where Jesus performed His first miracle, turning water to wine at the wedding. There are several churches that could be visited here—the Greek church, which has stone vats that could be related to the miracle, and a Franciscan church with mosaics—but the main attraction is the town itself with typically Arabic stone houses and small lanes set among fertile fields.

WHAT TO SEE IN SAFAD AND THE UPPER GALILEE

Like Jerusalem, Safad (or Safed, Tsefat, or Zefat) is a magnificent stage set of history, where one can walk amidst contemporary bustle to see both present and past. The city curls around a mountaintop, 2,790 feet high, with views (on the few unhazy days) from the Galilee to Lebanon. There is a lot to see, and to learn, about the synagogues, the Roman Crusader Citadel, the Artists' Quarter, and the Printing Museum (a book of Esther, the first book printed in Hebrew, was printed here).

Safad is as holy as Tiberias, but infinitely more beautiful, interesting, and comfortable. It is a favorite summer resort for Israelis, although its midday heat is refreshing only in comparison to Tel Aviv's.

From the thirteenth through the seventeenth centuries, Safad was a capital of Jewish learning, achieving its golden age after the arrival of the Jews who had been expelled from Spain in 1492. This is the birthplace of Cabala, a mystic movement that tried to speed the coming of the Messiah by prayer and magic. Here Rabbi Simon ben Yohai wrote its trailblazing work, the *Zohar.* (His tomb at nearby Meron is worth a visit.) Rabbi Isaac Luria, known as Ari ("the lion"), became the leader of the Cabalists. Today one can see two synagogues, one Sephardic and the other Ashkenazic, named for him, as well as the synagogue of Joseph Caro, who in 1565 wrote the *Shulhan . Aruk,* the definitive codification of Jewish law that is still in use.

These leaders of the Jewish religious renaissance attracted others of religious bent, who have remained the nucleus of Safad's population even though they are now outnumbered by new immigrants and artists. The mild Bohemianism of the artists adds flavor, but Safad is still more Williamsburg than East Village.

On Galilee tours Safad is seen in a few hours. Many people could happily spend a few days here. The local tourist office on Jerusalem Street sponsors modestly priced walking tours, and these are a fine way to see the old synagogues. In September its Arts Month involves film premieres, plays, and special exhibits. The main street is called Jerusalem, and makes a circle around the top of Safad's hill. Up top is the Citadel. Below to one side is the Artists' Quarter and, more or less near it, the old synagogue section.

The *Davidka Monument* on Jerusalem Street is a classically Israeli memorial to a classically Israeli victory. In 1948 the British pulled out, leaving the police station with its supply of guns in the hands of the Arabs. The town had a handful of elderly Jews and 12,000 Arabs, who could command the adjacent valley from their positions. In the middle of the night, 120 men and women *Palmach* commandos entered the city. Using the Davidka, an inefficient mortar that makes much noise, they convinced the Arabs that they were under heavy attack, causing them to flee. Besides, it was raining. This episode is fictionalized by Michener in *The Source,* and is always told to visitors. (In Israeli war stories, luck, not military prowess, wins the day.)

The *synagogues* are scattered amongst a snarl of old lanes running below Jerusalem Street. No matter how old "the synagogue" is, because of earthquake damage, the actual buildings are about 125 years old. The Ari Synagogue of the Ashkenazim was not really the synagogue of Ari, but the place, then outside the walls, where he led his followers to greet the Sabbath. It is at the older, strikingly austere Sephardic synagogue that Ari prayed, studied, and wrote. It is built strong as a fortress, and that is how it was used during 1948. The sixteenth-century Synagogue of Rabbi Joseph Caro is classically Sephardic, with its seats against the walls and colorful decorations. The Bana's Synagogue, named after another famous rabbi, houses an ancient Torah scroll used only in the procession to Meron every year. Regular services for worshipers are held several times a day, when tourists are not welcome. One can visit the tombs of Cabalist scholars and Israeli Underground heroes beyond the synagogue section.

The *Citadel* was built and subsequently destroyed by Romans, Jews, Crusaders, and Mamelukes. Now it is a beautifully cool park. On the walk up, genuine lovers of Israeli art might stop at the Glicenstein Museum, devoted to Jewish art objects and the paintings of the late Professor Glicenstein.

The *Artists' Quarter* can be seen by strolling around and stopping at any shop or studio that is appealing. Serious shoppers should first go to the gallery where all the city's artists display their work, and then look for the studios of their favorites. No need to be shy; Safad's artists are frankly commercial. One man summed up their strategy, "Paint Jewish."

Museum of the Art of Printing, just below Jerusalem Street, will interest booklovers and those concerned with graphics. Organized by the Israeli printers' union in celebration of the fact that Hebrew printing was born in Safad in 1578, it combines exhibits of unusual books, demonstrations of how-to-do-it, and explanations of history.

Meron is a few miles west, at the foot of Mount Meron, 3,926 feet high, and, before the 1967 attachment of Mount Hermon, the highest in Israel. Throughout the year, pilgrims come to camp in and near the tomb of Rabbi Simon ben Yohai, the forerunner of Cabalism, but on the spring holiday of Lag B'Omer, thousands come to light bonfires and dance through the night. Nearby is a large stone gateway from a second-century synagogue.

Bar'am is yet another synagogue. Even if you have had an overdose of second-century synagogues, drive the 14 miles from Safad to see this wonderfully preserved one. The stone building is beautiful, and so is the scenery en route. Whether going on the Golan Heights or not, you can circle back by the road that runs next to the fenced-up Lebanese border, then hits the main road down the Huleh Valley. It is quite safe, but when you come to the "Welcome to Upper Galilee" sign, you will be glad of the reassurance.

The *Huleh Valley* is new. Until the dredging that lasted from 1951 to 1957, it was known as the Huleh Swamp. Members of kibbutzim that ring the area had to contend with malaria and typhoid, but no longer. Good restaurants and lodging are available at Ayelet Hashahar, Kfar Blum, Kibbutz Hagoshrim, and Kfar Giladi. Their fields are as green and lush as an Irish travel poster, spotted with orchards and fish ponds. Try to see the ponds with a kibbutznik; the Israelis are masters of scientific fish-rearing, which is either the result or the cause of the new universal craze for gefilte fish. To preserve some of the animals and plants that flourished in the swamp, about 700 acres have been set aside as the Huleh Nature Reserve, which, if it is open, is a must for bird watchers.

Tel Hazor with its museum, 10 miles north of Safad, is one of Israel's most dramatic excavation sites, 21 layers going down 2,500 years to the Canaanite city, rising to an outpost of King Solomon's. The big excitement is walking down many steps into the cistern. Like the Megiddo cistern, it is the prototype of the cistern in *The Source*. What led to the discovery of Hazor is the fact that the fields outside were abnormally green. There had to be a spring nearby. Tel Hazor is across the road from an even more famous mecca, the guesthouse of Kibbutz Ayelet Hashahar, "blintze lords" of the Galilee. Inside their grounds is the little jewel of a museum that displays the Tel's Canaanite and Israelite knicknacks. See Hazor before mealtime, and phone for reservations.

Tel Hai Museum is the most moving of the monuments to the early settlers. Exhibits showing how eight young kibbutzniks died defending this farmhouse from Arab attack in 1920 are touching. Far more so are displays of their primitive tools and household objects. Facing their daily tasks must have required as much courage as meeting Arab attacks. One of the eight was Joseph Trumpeldor, a pioneer Zionist who lost an arm fighting for Russia before coming to Palestine and leading the Zion Mule Corps that fought with the British in World War I. Near the farmhouse is his grave, marked by the statue of a roaring lion. Tel Hai is about four miles north of the main turnoff from the Huleh Road to the Golan. It is in a town named Kiryat Shemona ("city of the eight"), in honor of the Tel Hai heroes.

Horshat Tal National Park, six miles in from the Huleh crossroads, is an enclave of grass and ancient oaks, with natural pools containing the icy waters of the Dan. It is fine for picnic breaks or swims en route.

Kibbutz Dan and its vicinity have three attractions of interest to the sightseer. In the kibbutz itself is Usishkin House, a museum with an unusually strong emphasis on natural history, showing the plants and animals of the Huleh and Hermon regions. Nearby are the ruins of Tel Dan, where a crosscut through seven levels of settlement gives nonspecialists an idea of how archaeologists work. Seeing the source of the Jordan here is also exciting. Going east from here, one crosses into pre-1967 Syria.

Banias Springs, a few miles past Dan, are a must-see for those going to the Golan because the road passes by. The springs are also a source of the Jordan, with its waterfall and remnants of a Greek temple honoring Pan. In Roman days this was Caesarea Philippi, where Salome danced. The Crusader fortress on the horizon is the hard-to-reach Nimrod's Castle. A few miles on toward the Golan, there is a restaurant (the last one until Kuneitra or Hermon), overlooking a volcanic lake, Birket Ram. Before 1967, Banias was a part of Syria.

Mount Hermon is near the Golan Heights, but it is not a part of them. One reaches Hermon by the new (but twisty) road; it is about 20 miles from the Huleh crossroad through Druse villages to the base station of the ski area. As soon as this became Israeli territory again after 1967, ski enthusiasts began flocking to the 7,000-foot summit that gets Israel's only serious snowfalls from January to March. Another summit is in Lebanon, and one is in Syria. For the first winters security was a major problem, as were the lack of lift facilities and real skiers. (There was a surplus of people sledding on plastic sheets or simply staring at real snow.) Now the 4,000-foot double chair lift with a 1,300-foot vertical drop gives Israelis a fine winter playground, complete with an American-trained ski school, rental equipment, canteen, and ski patrol. Tourists, particularly from April to October, have an exciting time riding that chair lift up and down to see the view that stretches from Beirut to Haifa. Arkia offers day trips from Tel Aviv.

THE GOLAN HEIGHTS

The Golan Heights can be reached via Dan and Banias or by crossing the Jordan on the Bnot Yaakov Bridge, which is the ancient Middle Eastern route to the sea, the Via Maris, or by going up through Kibbutz En Gev. Take different routes each way because they all go past the Syrian trenches to Kuneitra. The Golan is a range of volcanic mountains facing the Galilee hills from the far side of the underground fault known as the Jordan Rift. The highest point is at 3,960 feet. After 1948 the

Syrians fortified the Golan, from which they shelled the kib-butzim below. On the fifth day of the Six Day War, under pressure from the Huleh kibbutzim, Israeli troops were pulled back from the Sinai and sent to attack the Golan Heights. There was only one way to do it—to go straight up on foot, with bulldozers pushing heavy equipment. On the sixth day the Go-lan was taken. By all means come here with a guide, or the battle sites will be meaningless. The guides' versions differ, but they are all good yarns. By now the trenches might be free of mines, but there is nothing wrong with being cautious and strictly obeying all signs.

Kuneitra, the Syrian headquarters town, is deserted except for a nahal settlement called Hagolan, which runs an emergency guesthouse and restaurant. There are now about a dozen com-munal settlements on the heights, and the stony fields are be-ginning to yield crops. Around Kuneitra, one can see Syrian officers' and soldiers' quarters, burned-out tanks, trenches, and now, an Israeli war monument at Mitzpeh Godol, the point a few hundred yards directly above Kibbutz En Gev. From here it is easy to understand Israel's feelings about holding the Golan. The pipeline one passes en route is the T.A.P. pipeline from Iraq to Lebanon that continues to run peacefully through Israel.

WHERE TO STAY IN TIBERIAS AND THE LOWER GALILEE

Hotels in Tiberias (Safad and some kibbutz guesthouses too) usually demand half board. To be comparable with other areas covered in this book, the same price brackets are used, but unless noted, the significant figure is the MAP price, not the bed-and-breakfast cost. Like other prices quoted in the book, they are for summer. For the Tiberias hotels rates are about 20 percent less than what they are in the traditional high season, October to May (for the simpler hotels, December to May). Since the geographical divisions are necessarily arbitrary, be sure to consider the kibbutz guesthouses listed after the hotels, as well as those hotels in the Upper Galilee section. Expect Kosher kitchens and air conditioning unless specified.

The standouts: Galei Kinneret, Kibbutz Nof Ginossar.

$9–$13 (Figure $12–$17 MAP, $13–$20 AP)

The Galei Kinneret is the only true lakefront hotel and the only one with five stars. Sedate, yes, but it has comfort and class—a complete resort hotel mixing rooms that are pleasant with some that are downright fancy, elaborate Kosher Continental cuisine, terraced bar, big lounge, Crusader ruins virtually on the lake step and—if not yet, soon—a swimming pool. Built in 1946 and in 1967, it was acquired by the Israel Land Development Company which seems to have a penchant for undersized luxury hotels like this 66-room house.

$6–$9 (Figure $9–$15 MAP, $10–$16 AP)

From here on in the listing—no swimming pools. The Guberman Grand, Hartman, and Ginton are at the higher end of town, in Kiryat Shmuel, and at the lower end of this price bracket. Summer half board might be closer to $10. Of the trio, the Guberman is far superior to its fellow four-star hotels. The nine-story, Miami-modern tower dominates the skyline. The 72 rooms are plain, but large and attractive. The airy lobby has such a spectacular view of Kinneret that few people go out to the broad terrace. The Ginton and its kichen used to be highly regarded by Israelis, but the establishment has slipped since the tour groups descended. Its public rooms are pleasant, but the 63 bedrooms are Israeli-basic. The Hartman expanded in 1971 to a 70-room house, specializing in Scandinavian pilgrims who stay a full week. Still, you might snare one of the smallish bedrooms and even get a bed-and-breakfast rate.

The Ganei Hamat, on the outskirts past the Hot Springs, has large grounds, with accommodations ranging from "bare bones" shacks to spanking modern rooms that are rated four stars. Five-star rooms are about to be hatched, too. This Israeli favorite is not on the water, but has its private beach across the road. Tennis courts, an amphitheater, cafe, and gardens are close to the living accommodations.

The Astoria gives bed and breakfast, which is its chief selling point beside its view. Its 57 rooms and public rooms have been decorated nicely enough, but the whole has an air of disorganization.

$6 or Under

The Ron is simple, but acceptable; its 30 rooms with showers and air conditioning are not much worse than those in some of the higher-rated hotels hereabout, and its view is much better.

KIBBUTZ GUESTHOUSES AND ETC.

This is socialism? Nof Ginossar is right on the shores of Kinneret, with a private beach as part of the extensive parklike enclave. About two-thirds of the rooms are older and smaller, but all are brightly done up with sheepskin rugs, bamboo blinds,

The guesthouse at Kibbutz Nof Ginnossar, on the Sea of Galilee.
Courtesy Israel Government Press Office

reed furniture, and fresh flowers. Even though three bus groups might descend for lunch at once, the quality of the food is high and the variety is astounding. As in all the kibbutzim, a kibbutznik gives a lecture to groups in the evening and, the group's guide permitting, a walk through the actual kibbutz in the morning. On a bed-and-breakfast basis, expect to pay $7–$9.

Lavi is a kibbutz of a different color. Extremely Orthodox, it caters to long-term visitors by providing simple accommodations, a swimming pool with separate hours for men and women, and frequent religious services. Bed and breakfast, prices should be $6–$7.

The "Etc." is Vered Hagalil, a pure capitalist enterprise mentioned before for its horse tours. There are four rustic stone cabins and some larger "chalets," which are nicely done and have full plumbing. Fine for families, with breakfast, the price works out to $7–$10.

NAZARETH

There are as of now no members of the Israeli Hotel Association here, but there are two modern, non-Kosher, three-star hotels that should be sufficiently comfortable, with air-conditioned rooms and full plumbing. The Grand New is away from traffic noise on a hill. The Nazareth is closer to the center of town, and has a good reputation for food. With bed and breakfast, expect to pay $7–$10.

WHERE TO STAY IN SAFAD AND THE UPPER GALILEE

Safad is also half-board territory, unless otherwise noted. The prices here are for Safad's super-high season, covering mid-July through August, plus the Jewish holidays. Air conditioning is considered unnecessary in Safad, which is continually breezy, at least in theory. Kosher hotel kitchens are the rule. Remember, too, the kibbutz guesthouses listed below.

The standouts: Ayelet Hashahar, Rimon Inn, Motel Canaan, Herzliya.

$9–$13 (Figure $12–$17 MAP, $13–$20 AP)

The Rimon Inn was the old Turkish post office, but in 1968 the Israel Land Development Company converted it into a uniquely beautiful hotel with 36 rooms, like individual stone houses, scattered through a terraced hillside below the Artists' Quarter. The next 58 rooms to be added will be more conventional. Everything done so far has great style, including the panorama from each window and the sophisticated food. The price should stay at the low end of this bracket.

The Herzliya, set back from a garden with ancient olive trees, was the most spectacular one-star hotel in Israel because it kept rates low for its longtime Israeli clients. Now, discreetly adding 50 new rooms with baths to the old stone house, it might have already earned the three or four stars for which it was aiming. I don't know what prices will be, but if the hotel is given four stars, the half-board rate would be in this bracket. With one star, the half-board would be $8–$10. Don't let the absence of stars stop consideration of this delightful spot, famous for its food and warm atmosphere, fostered by the second generation of the family that launched it.

$6–$9 (Figure $9–$15 MAP, $10–$16 AP)

The unique Motel Canaan is way off on a hillside called Canaan B. Its 21 rooms have individual entrances, balconies with stupendous views, kitchenettes, small bathtubs, and clever layouts. Only breakfast is served, but the proprietor can rustle up a Kosher TV Dinner, snack, or drink in the pretty bar-living room. He also hands out picnic ware and shopping bags with towels so his guests won't starve (or steal towels). His son runs a discotheque in the basement. Great for families and nonstop sightseers!

The Tel Aviv, below the main street, has a two-story motel-like wing with 32 rooms, a fine terrace and garden, nice sitting room, and good reputation for food. The Mizpor, built in the 1960's, is on a self-improvement campaign, aiming for four stars and higher prices. At lunchtime it gets tour groups.

Way up on the main peak of Mount Canaan, the Ruckenstein is a comfortable garden hotel favored by older people. Hadassah tours come here for lunch; they're the young folks. The Mines House, also up there, is a comfortable favorite of Israelis. Either of these hotels might provide more quiet than you want.

KIBBUTZ GUESTHOUSES

Ayelet Hashahar is to guesthouses what Rolls–Royce is to cars. In the Huleh Valley, about halfway between the Golan and Tiberias, it gets 600 tour-bus passengers a day for its famous borsht-and-blintzes lunch, then awaits the dinner-and-overnight mob that fills its 104 rooms. Yet, it is not a "factory," but a delightfully warm establishment, an oasis of good design. The swimming pool is next-door in the kibbutz, so one is free to wander over without a guide. The guesthouse complex has an outstanding duty-free shop, art studio, bar and, down the road, the Hazor Museum. Bed and breakfast, expect to pay $7–$10, depending on the room.

Kibbutz En Gev's restaurant is famous for Saint Peter's Fish.
Courtesy Israel Government Press Office

Kfar Blum, farther north, lacks the luster of Ayelet Hashahar, but it has an Olympic-sized outdoor pool where Israeli teams often train, plus extensive grounds and air-conditioned rooms with beds imported from America (many of the kibbutzniks are from the States). New and larger rooms are being added, but the aim is to keep things cozy. The bed-and-breakfast rate is $5–$8.

The Hagoshrim guesthouse is now a ski lodge in winter, since it is the closest accommodation to Mount Hermon, about 20 miles away. Summer tourists like its rustic grounds, complete with loudly babbling brook and natural swimming pool. The bar, dining room, lounge, and crafts shop are in a house built on Roman ruins and Turkish arches. The rooms are small-scale, but air-conditioned and nicely distributed through the trees.

Hagoshrim is also aiming for four stars and more rooms, but with its present three-star status, expect to pay $5–$8 for bed and breakfast.

Nearby Kfar Giladi, after years of catering to Israelis, is now getting into the international tourist business and might affiliate with a hotel chain. Fate and rates unknown, but the setting, at the top of Israel, is great, and so are the pool and outdoor cafe.

Amirim, near Safad, is a special case. A moshav dedicated to organic farming, it invites fellow vegetarians to come live with its families and partake of the Yoga classes and lectures.

WHERE TO EAT IN THE GALILEE

If you never eat another St. Peter's fish, you have to do it in the Galilee. The gala spot in Tiberias is Donna Gracia, amongst the galleries in the Citadel. Its food is European-Israeli, not Spanish. (Donna Gracia was the wife of a Spanish Jew living in Constantinople who talked Suleiman into letting him rebuild Tiberias.) Roses, white tablecloths, candles, the works; and maybe a $5–$10 check. The restaurants on the downtown waterfront have interchangeably decent food, but they are traditionally out of everything on the menu except the biggest, most expensive fish. For honest measure, sail across or drive around to the fish restaurant of Kibbutz En Gev. Try to get to Vered Hagalil, about 20 minutes north of Tiberias, for a fried chicken lunch or, if they will be open that night, for dinner. The apple pie and sundaes could make the homesick weep. Blue Beach and Quiet Beach, on the edge of Tiberias, are lively places to eat St. Peter's fish and then stay on for the folklore show. Budget-stretchers, try Tuv Ta'am for simple inexpensive fare served in Kiryat Shmuel, looking down at the sea from a breezy terrace.

Safad has several plain-faced restaurants along Jerusalem Street where one can be adequately and inexpensively fed, particularly Batia, which is Kosher, and Hamifgash, which is not. The best bets are the restaurants in hotels like the Rimon Inn and Herzliya.

The guesthouses at Ayelet Hashahar, Hagoshrim, Kfar Blum, and Nof Ginossar serve outsiders, and they do it well. Better telephone for reservations.

In Nazareth on Casanova Street, Abu Nasser is a big, dark

restaurant, shop, and guides' hiring hall, where Sidney Green-street eats a $2 shashlik lunch while waiting for Peter Lorre. Next door, at the Israel, one can learn how to say "Eat your humus, Abdul" in Arabic because that is what all the family heads are saying. Tourists and locals mix at both spots, which have interchangeable non-Kosher Oriental food.

WHERE TO SHOP IN THE GALILEE

The pickings are spotty. Tiberias has a burgeoning crop of arts and crafts stores at the Citadel, notably the Yaskil gallery and the Nesher. Safad has a Maskit shop and a flock of galleries and crafts shops, starting on Jerusalem Street and spilling into the Artists' Quarter. The cooperative gallery is a good place to check out prices. Some of the best shopping is at Ayelet Hasha-har's duty-free shop, where the selection for leather clothes rivals those seen in Tel Aviv. Hagoshrim's gift shop has excellent prices for jewelry and knickknacks that come from all over the world, but mostly from east of Suez. In Nazareth the Fran-cisan Fathers sell religious mementos in their museum, and the *souk* sells everything from Roman glassware to Hong Kong toys. When entering the *souk* from Casanova Street, Salim Salem has good brassware and embroidery mixed in with lesser wares.

WHAT TO DO AT NIGHT IN THE GALILEE

In the summertime Tiberias is not the nest of fun-crazed Israelis it is in winter (when all the night clubs are open and swinging fully), but compared to the rest of the nation, it is the Paris of the Galilee. At Blue Beach there are floor shows, some with caller-led folk dancing by the clients, followed by a dis-cotheque session on four nights a week and regular dancing on the others. At Quiet Beach there is folk dancing by professionals and clients and regular dancing, too. Arbel, up in Kiryat Shmuel, has ethnic food, nonethnic dancing.

In Safad the "big deal" is going to the artists' club, the Milo, and having a glass of tea with the painter whose work you have just acquired. In summer there is dancing at the cafe up on the

Citadel. Hashaot Haketanot ("small hours"), down a flight of steps and into the one-time Turkish bath, sometimes features strippers, sometimes jazz.

The guesthouses all have bars and TV rooms, explanatory lectures for groups, films, and sometimes, live local entertainment. However, Pali, the Hagoshrim bartender, says that television has killed the live entertainment business, even up in the Huleh.

KEY ADDRESSES

Tourist Information: Tiberias: 8 Nazareth Street (067) 5 41 44
Safad: Municipality Building, Jerusalem Street (067) 3 06 33
Nazareth: Casanova Street (065) 2 09 92

Sheruts: Tiberias sheruts leave from Kinneret Street.
Safad sheruts leave from near the bus station.
Nazareth sheruts center around the Central Bus Station.

20

The Negev and the Dead Sea

Masada, En Bokek, Arad, Beersheba, Elat

Don't skip the Negev. It is the most exciting part of Israel and has the most spectacular scenery. Everyone goes to Masada, the Dead Sea, and Beersheba, but many scurry back to Tel Aviv without venturing further south. Yes, the Negev is hot and a long ride away, but boring? No. A Bedouin hitches a ride on a tour bus and leans his rifle against your airline tote. A splotch of green turns out to be a kibbutz, near nothing except a hostile border. Another green patch leads to a Nabataean city, whose ancient cisterns taught Israeli scientists about farming the desert. You stop for lunch above a giant crater, unsure whether you are in Israel, Arizona, or on the moon.

The Negev is a miracle that is happening now, before one's eyes. All Israel could be called a miracle, but noble accomplishments are not necessarily good theater. Making the desert bloom is one helluva show, whether seen at the road level or from above. The road bordering the Dead Sea is finished now, and goes straight to Elat and on to the Sinai. Still, fly at least one way, if you can; it intensifies the drama and spares one the minor rigors of the road.

Scholars have not yet decided whether Negev means "dry" or "south," but Israelis use the term for not only the desert, but also for everything between Ashkelon and Elat, including the Dead Sea and the towns of Dimona and Arad. The real desert begins below Beersheba; there are about 4,000 square miles of it, but it is not as empty as it looks. From the main road, one cannot see all the army outposts, pipelines for water and oil, or Bedouin encampments and kibbutzim.

Do not expect the endless sand dunes of the Sahara or the

scrub-covered vastnesses of Utah. This is rock desert, a Technicolor mix of hills, craters, wadis (dry river beds)—some scrub, some sand, all in perpetual variation. There are Bedouin tents, particularly in the upper section, and some points of historic interest, but between Beersheba and Elat, what you see most of is scenery.

Over in the Dead Sea area, history is the main attraction. Qumran and Masada are fascinating and extremely important, and so are Sodom and the Dead Sea itself. Arad and Beersheba are basically bedrooms and staging places. Arad is a beautifully laid-out new development town that provides food and housing for Masada. Beersheba also services the Masada trade and is

Kibbutz in the desert, near the Dead Sea.
Courtesy Israel Government Press Office

the jumping-off point for the Negev. In the 1950's it was a frontier town. Now it is a market and an industrial city thick with high-rise garden apartments.

Elat is different, a military and industrial frontier town that is also a real resort, lacking in finish if not in *chutzpa*. Guess which city is the sister city of this 13,000-person sentry box? Los Angeles. Tour buses often get here before dinner and leave after breakfast. Skin-divers and beach nuts could stay for days or weeks. So can those who would like to explore the desert. Elat, particularly in winter, is Woodstock-by-the-Red-Sea. The Dutch, Scandinavian, and Israeli sun-seekers of all ages start thronging in at Christmastime. Those under 30 camp out on the beach, while their elders check into hotels.

No sand dunes, perhaps, but the other characteristics of a desert are here, including mirages, which are called Fata Morgana(s) and, during the rainstorms that fall every few years, flash floods. The sun and heat are particularly powerful April through October, but can be overwhelming even in winter. If you have never worn a hat or sunglasses in your life, do it now. Drink liquids slowly and frequently. Tour buses carry their own. Private cars should, too; invest in a cooler box, thermos, or canteen. Eat lightly. Dress comfortably. Above all, take it easy, particularly during the heat of the day. In this desert it does not necessarily chill down at night in summer.

This is one part of Israel where distances are no longer miniature. From Tel Aviv to Beersheba is 69 miles. From Beersheba to Elat is another 146 miles. From Elat to Jerusalem is 215 miles, but the kind of 215 miles that takes five hours to negotiate.

The Sinai is covered in a separate chapter because, at this writing, visitors are permitted only as part of tours using bus, plane, or desert command cars. One *can* plan to enter the Sinai from Elat, but it is actually easier to jump off from Tel Aviv.

HOW TO SEE THE NEGEV AND THE DEAD SEA

For the Dead Sea, Masada, and environs of Elat, a car is freedom. The realistic alternatives are tour bus and, for Elat and Masada, a plane-bus tour or a regular flight down to Elat where you can rent a car, hire a local chauffeur-guide, or join a bus tour. Regular Egged buses can get you to Beersheba, Arad, Elat, and even some points on the Dead Sea, but your mobility will be very limited, particularly for Masada. The guided tour possibilities from Beersheba or Arad are very slim—a weekly trip to En Gedi and none to Masada. Licensed guides who live in those towns are rarely available on short notice. Your best hope of recruiting a last-minute guide for Masada—you really need one up there—is to telephone at least 24 hours ahead to the Masada Museum (057) 9 60 16.

If you want a guide for the complete trip, the tour bus is the cheapest deal and the plane-bus the best combination of convenience and coverage. Flying one way via Arkia adds about

$15 to the cost of the two-day Elat junket or three-day Masada–Elat tour. Hurried splurgers can take Arkia to Elat and back again. The round trip cost has been around $40 for a guided one-day tour or $27 just for the flights. Nativ Air, now part of United Israeli, used single- or twin-engine planes for a $75 tour to Elat for a swim and Masada. For a morning at Masada, the tab was about $35. Egged runs day and half-day trips around Elat, but agile adventurers should consider the trips run by an excellent local specialist, Johnny Desert Tours, P.O. Box 261,

En route to Masada by Egged bus.
Photo by Hans H. Pinn

Elat (059) 26 08. Johnny has desert cars—big jeeps—that take small groups into places buses cannot reach, even though buses follow the same general itinerary. Everyone who tried it agrees that the climbing, clambering, and bouncing are a small price to pay for the adventure. The monetary price might be $7–$10.

Johnny's postal box and telephone numbers can also lead one to bigger adventures because the outfit works with Blue Line–Neot Hakikar, an alliance of desert farmers and the Caravan Hotel people, most famous for camping trips into the Sinai. The Blue Line side of the family also runs mini-bus tours. In any case Johnny can custom design excursions throughout the areas. Aqua Sport, P.O. Box 300, Elat (059) 27 88, operates the skin-diving center, charters boats and, by the time you arrive, might already have begun scheduled sailing trips, by night as well as day.

Don't be afraid to drive in the desert. The roads are difficult—narrow, twisted, often clogged with trucks—but they are no more troublesome than most others in Israel. The necessary precautions are simple. They include all those previously mentioned for everyone, plus these: Stock up on fuel and water, for yourself as well as the car; have the car and tires checked out before you enter the area; keep wiping off the sand from the windows and lights; stay only on main roads; when passing one of the few gas stations, fill up; start early, avoiding the midday hours as well as nighttime; if anything goes wrong, stay put. Help *will* come. Some roads are heavily traveled, and all are patrolled. As of now, there is a rental drop-off in Beersheba, but not in Elat, so if you drive all the way down, you have to drive back.

For those driving the entire way, there are two possible routes. Drive down one way, back the other, thereby covering the Dead Sea and Negev in one circuit. From Tel Aviv drive to Beersheba (via Ashdod and Ashkelon, if you want to visit them). Then from Beersheba head over to Dimona if you want to see another development town, or go straight down past Sde Boker, Avdat, Mizpe Ramon, and the craters and on to the Arava Plain. At the Grofit Crossroads join the Dead Sea Highway and proceed past Kibbutz Yotvata to Solomon's Pillars and the Timna Mines, which are just outside Elat. From Elat, side trips can be made to the Fjord, Coral Reefs, and canyons.

The second route, starting from Jerusalem or Tel Aviv, can include stops at Jericho, Qumran, and En Fescha. If these have already been seen from Jerusalem, stay on the road that follows the seashore until you reach En Gedi, then Masada (which is miserably hot after 10:00 A.M., 12 months a year), En Bokek, Arad (Masada can also be reached from the Arad side), Sodom, through the Arava Plain to the Grofit Crossroads, where you join the highway from Beersheba and continue past Yotvata, Solomon's Pillars and Timna to reach Elat.

Two variations: Go Tel Aviv–Beersheba, via Kiryat Gat, and straight to Elat, or over to the southern tip of the Dead Sea. Go Jerusalem–Bethlehem–Hebron–Arad–Dead Sea. Either way, you miss most of the Dead Sea magic, unless you make side trips.

Still another practical system is to make a Masada–Dead Sea circuit, with or without Arad and Beersheba, and return to Tel Aviv or Jerusalem to let a bus or plane transport you through or over the desert to Elat. By the time you get to Israel, it might be possible to continue driving straight to Sharm-el-Sheikh. The road exists, but private cars have not been allowed to wander in and around the waterless Sinai.

WHAT TO SEE IN THE NEGEV AND THE DEAD SEA AREAS

Jericho is usually done as a half-day trip from Jerusalem, so look for the descriptions of Hisham's Palace, the cliffside monastery, ancient walls, and synagogue mosaic in the Jerusalem section. Those coming from Jerusalem can squeeze in an early visit to Jericho, seven miles from the sea, particularly if they plan to stay overnight in Arad or En Bokek.

The *Dead Sea* alone is worth the trip. To reach it from Tel Aviv, you come by way of Jerusalem, dropping 4,000 feet in 25 miles. You can take a more direct, but less dramatic route, driving first to Beersheba, then an hour later reaching the sea's lower end, or via Bethlehem–Hebron–Arad. With either route, you miss the experience of driving along the sea and, unless you backtrack, of seeing Qumran and En Gedi.

The Dead Sea is 1,280 feet below sea level, lower than any other place on earth. The Israeli–Jordanian border runs down its middle. Shaped somewhat like a standing ghost, it is 48 miles long, 11 miles wide, and appropriately framed in barren mountains and shrouded in haze. The Jordan and unseen underwater mountain streams flow into its milky blue waters, and since they are one-third solid, with the aid of science, they evaporate and leave behind their wealth of minerals and table salt. (Its Hebrew name means "Salt Sea.") These are processed at plants clustered at the southern end of the sea. Desalination work is conducted there, too. Rarely is an industrial site spectacular scenery, but this one is also a sculpture park. Stones have been artistically arrayed at several points along the coast. At first one thinks this is Nature's work, but eventually one realizes this is man's doing, which is exactly the effect the sculptor intended. You can swim in the Dead Sea—in fact, you cannot sink—at En Gedi, En Fescha, En Bokek, and Neve Zohar. Not refreshing, but memorable.

Qumran, the national park containing caves where the Dead

Sea Scrolls were found and buildings of the Essene community that inscribed them, is 13 miles from Jericho, virtually on the sea.

En Fescha, less than two miles past Qumran, is interesting because it is the spot where fresh springs pop up and mingle with the Dead Sea waters. Details are in the Jerusalem chapter, but this is a good place to experience the strange sensation of floating in the mineral-laden Dead Sea.

En Gedi has been getting rave reviews ever since Solomon used it as a point of comparison for his beloved in the *Song of Songs.* About 18 miles south of En Fescha and 30 miles north of Sodom, this nature reserve operates like a national park, protecting the wildlife, notably the herds of gazelles, who non-chalantly mingle with the herds of tourists. Before you enter the reserve, you are conscious of the nearby beach, the green fields of Nahal David and other collective settlements, and the greenhouses where members of Kibbutz En Gedi experiment with hydroponic flower growing. The reserve's practically in-visible entrance sign says "To springs." Follow the upward path (the one on the left shows the most) to *David's Spring,* a series of waterfalls carving their way through the gorge to form natural swimming pools and keep the En Gedi oasis green.

Masada is the desolate table-topped peak on which 960 Zealot rebels occupied Herod's palaces and held off 10,000 men of the besieging Roman Tenth Legion from 70 to 73 A.D. Then, rather than be taken as slaves, each man killed his own family and drew lots to choose the ten who would kill the others. Masada is a high point of your trip to Israel. See it properly. Plan your itinerary around it; be sure that you have a guide (brought along or hired via the museum) and that you start up no later than 9:00 A.M. in summer (10:00 A.M., October–March). In summer the wisest climbers start at 3:00 A.M., greet the sunrise amidst the ruins, and are back having breakfast before the first bus passenger faints. Give yourself two hours, preferably three. Tour buses sometimes get here at noon or after lunch, and their passengers suffer.

Masada is hot, and there is no painless way up, not even via the new cable car on the Dead Sea side. It flies you up half a mile in three minutes, but after that you climb 70 steep steps. The alternative from Masada East (the Dead Sea side) is the Snake Path, a safe but spooky 45-minute climb on a narrow zigzag up the precipice. It makes you feel at one with the Zealots or with the members of the Israeli Armored Corps who take their oath of allegiance up top. A hostel and the museum are at Masada East. So, too, on Saturdays and holidays, is a long waiting line for the cable car. The round trip costs about $1.

Probably the easiest approach is via Arad, taking the 13-mile racer-dip road to the side from which the Romans tried to storm the fortress. The walk up takes about ten minutes. But, if you go up Masada West, you must come down the same way, unless you have an obliging driver who, after leaving you at the ramp, then makes the 42-mile circle back to pick you up on the cable car–Snake Path side, which is what some tour bus drivers do. Drinking water and rest rooms are at the top. At the ticket booth you can buy the official booklet and map.

The Masada saga started with Judas Maccabaeus. Then Herod the Great made it into a palace-fort. When the Jews revolted against the Romans in 66 A.D., they occupied Masada. After the Temple was destroyed, they were joined by refugees, including members of the Essene community. They held out until 73. Byzantine monks lived here in the fourth and fifth centuries and built a church. The final epic: for 11 months volunteers from 28 countries did the work of 26 archaeological seasons, excavating all that is now visible.

The finds are marked into three tours, with durations of two, three, and five hours. The highlights: *Western Palace,* with the oldest mosaics in Israel; *Byzantine Church,* with mosaics and decorated plaster; *Synagogue,* the oldest in the world; *Herodian Administration Building and Entrance Gate,* where a pottery "lot" with the name of the Zealot commander, Ben Yair, was found; *Water Gate,* by which water was brought up from the cisterns dug into the precipice below; *Northern Palace,* Herod's spectacular three-level villa built into the cliffside, complete with Roman bath, mosaics, frescoes, terraces; *Herod's swimming pool; enclosed cistern* with stairway, like those at Megiddo or Hazor.

En Bokek is 18 miles below Masada East. By the time you reach here, it is the conventionally modern hotels, bathhouse, and beach that look improbable, not the raw red cliffs fencing in the Dead Sea. Here at nearby Neve Zohar, Israelis come to bathe in the radioactive sulfur springs to ease rheumatism, allergies, and circulatory problems. For tourists, En Bokek is a caravansary for Masada.

Arad offers "nothing to see," but it is an endearing example of what happens when town planning works well. The hotels are away from the city, but stop by the Tourist Office (upstairs from the First Aid Center) to seek someone to walk you around. The drive from the Dead Sea up to Arad is a spectacular 3,000-foot climb. Stop to catch the panoramas. Tel Arad is where a Canaanite temple has been uncovered, but it is difficult to reach and not yet organized for tourists.

Sodom, like Gomorrah, stopped being a town when Mrs. Lot looked backward (she is whichever salt pillar you choose). Now those sinful twin cities are the site of the Dead Sea Potash and Bromine Works. There are some cafes nearby if you want to celebrate your arrival at the lowest point on earth, plus a salt cave that can be visited. Between Sodom and Solomon's Pillars, the terrain is varied, but the desolation is broken only by a scattering of settlements on the Arava.

Dimona is a new industrial town and, if your trip by-passed Arad, you might want to see its neighbor instead. As you drive through the area, you can spot the nuclear reactor at Oron, which guides point out as a military secret being revealed only to you. Skeptics claim that Israel became a nuclear power by instructing its tour guides to point to an empty building.

BEERSHEBA

The city of Beersheba is a staging area for the Dead Sea and Masada, about 45 miles away, as well as for the desert journey to Elat, 139 miles southward. There is very little to see here. The frontier atmosphere of the 1950's has faded into the brisk solidity of the 1970's. The famous Thursday Camel Market still exists, but most of the tourists who strive to get here on Thursdays miss it because the tour groups amble in after 9:00 A.M., and by then the market is over. Get here at 7:00, and you will indeed see a Bedouin spectacular; shop for Bedouin copperware, embroidered bags, woven rugs, and the inevitable souvenirs. The Arid Zone Research Institute and University of the Negev are not open to the public. The Tourist Office is in

Suddenly, in the empty Negev, a group of Bedouins appear.
Photo by Hans H. Pinn

Bet Ha'am on Poalei Binyan Road. For compulsive sightseers, here are some worthy prospects:

Abraham's Well is how Beersheba started. Abraham dug a well, where he made a peace treaty with a chieftain, Abimelech. The well was named the Well of the Pledge, or Beersheba. It has been in use for 4,000 years. You can see it on Hebron Street.

The *Municipal Museum* is in a garden-ringed old mosque. Climb the minaret to get a striking view. Material dug up nearby is organized into a visual summary of what has been happening for the past few millenniums.

Tel Beersheba, recently excavated on the northern outskirts, might have become a national park by your arrival; by then there will be something to see. (At first, the site of an excavation is meaningless to an amateur.) Similarly, the important dig south of Beersheba is not in shape for visitors.

The Palmach War Memorial on a hill north of town is not "another statue," but a cluster of concrete symbols that lets you experience the 1948 battle of the Negev by climbing, stooping, and sidling your way through the flowing structures. Kids love it.

Shivta is 28 miles southeast of town, off the tourist trail, so if you want to see this Pompeiilike array of Byzantine churches and Nabataean houses, do it from Beersheba. Shivta is better preserved than Avdat, but it lacks Avdat's advantage of being on a main road. First be sure the site has been reopened to the public.

Shivta is isolated but worth a side trip for history buffs.
Courtesy Israel Government Tourist Office

TOWARD ELAT

Sde Boker is the kibbutz, 31 miles south of Beersheba, whose early members included Israel's first prime minister, David Ben-Gurion, age 67 when he joined. There are no facilities for visitors, but the adventurous could arrange to hike here from Avdat.

Avdat is a good reason for using this, rather than the faster, Dead Sea route. Above a canyon cut through the Wilderness of Zinn is the hilltop city started around 100 A.D. by the Nabataeans. Their multicity trade route for jewels and gold stretched from Petra, through the desert, to the Mediterranean ports. The Byzantines who came later built the church, fortress, and many of the sights; others were built by the Romans and the Nabataeans themselves. One inscription says that the householder hopes to be remembered. He is, by daily busloads of tourists photographing his doorway. Looking down at the wilderness, one can understand why the Children of Israel gave Moses such a hard time. What a land to be Promised! But—a patch of green catches the eye. It is the experimental station that is duplicating the Nabataean system of storing rainfall.

Mizpe Ramon means "lookout on the Ramon Crater," and that is the reason for stopping at this new settlement—to look down into the crater, a 5-mile by 22-mile stretch of grotesque chasms and lumps, gaudily colored with rich ores. The road goes down into the crater and comes up on the other side.

The *Arava Plain's* crossroads at Grofit is where the Beersheba and Dead Sea routes join. Among the kibbutzim in the Arava is Yotvata, which provides Elat with its drinking water, and whose milk bar dispenses milk shakes to tourists.

Timna, the site of King Solomon's Mines, is now a modern mining installation, with stout Histadrut members replacing slaves.

Solomon's Pillars are at the mines—five huge purple-red pillars that look as if they were disconnected from the Grand Canyon.

Amram's Pillars are a somewhat similar spectacle, an array of redstone pillars and a cave that are closer to Elat, but off the main road.

ELAT

Elat is an outdoor town. The visitor swims, snorkles, skin-dives, and beach-sits. Even the cafes and the few mandatory landmarks are outdoors. Elat is not on the Red Sea, but the Gulf of Aqaba, which swings down along the Sinai Peninsula. The gulf of Suez (and the Canal) comes down the far side of the Sinai. They meet and become the Red Sea. The Elat hotels sit on or above the sapphire horseshoe of a bay, backed by spectacular but strangely soft mountains that seem to be the color and consistency of Wiener schnitzel.

The real Elat is inland, a no-frills mining and shipping center started in a hurry in 1949 to secure an explosive frontier. The distant beachside cluster of Aqaba, Jordan, is where T. E. Lawrence was in such a hurry to get to. Further down the shore is Saudi Arabia. Until 1967 the other side of Elat was Egyptian.

Since its original Jewish settlement 4,000 years back, Elat has often mixed security and pleasure. King Solomon came here to welcome the Queen of Sheba. ("And guys have been making out like crazy ever since," said an American beachnik.) Actually, Sheba came to test the Gulf of Aqaba route from the Red Sea because an Egyptian blockade of Suez had made Solomon a bad business risk. The 1967 war also started with an Egyptian blockade, bottling up the Straits of Tiran, which is where the Gulf of Aqaba breaks into the Red Sea.

The number one tourist hazard in Elat is not the drinking water (it has been improved), not drowning (the sea is remarkably gentle), not sunstroke (even summer tourists learn to stay off the beach from noon to 3, and in winter the temperatures are closer to 60° than to 110°), and not the airplanes which seem to be landing on the beach (the airstrip is only yards behind it). The chief hazard, says the beachfront First Aid man, is broken glass. The beachniks alone cannot be blamed. The best beach belongs to the municipality which, for reasons too complicated for anyone else to grasp, refuses to clean it or let the adjacent hotels clean it. To the necessary sun hat and glasses, add shoes.

Stroll through the town itself to see how its spirited young citizens are getting on. Persistent culture hounds can visit the Philip Murray House, a center named after the late CIO president, and the art museum. The Maritime Museum has a big aquarium, which could interest beach-weary kids. The Tourist Office is in the shopping center known as the New Commercial Building on Tamarim Boulevard (057) 22 89.

Glass-bottomed boats leave from the Coral Reserve (*not* the Coral Island, out in what was formerly Egypt). Regular Egged or tour buses can deliver you for the 50-minute trip over a colorful variety of marine life. (Sailboats and pedal boats can be rented at the main marina back in town.)

Underwater trips for nondivers are conducted by Aqua Sport and Egged. Swimmers can do the underwater tour of the Coral Reserve with snorkel and mask. Nonswimmers can float along on air mattresses. Try it! Underwater is the best part of Elat!

Israel's fjord.

The *Fjord and Coral Island* are eight miles out of town, in what was Egypt until 1967. The fjord is not a Scandinavian-type fjord, but you will not be disappointed by this magnificent circle of beach close to a tiny island containing the ruins of a Crusader fort. One can swim, sail, or scuba to it. The regular buses come here.

The *Canyon of the Inscriptions* is reachable only with a tour. The point of the tour is not just to see the ancient Hebrew and Greek handwriting on the wall, but the trip itself, which includes driving and walking through country even more spectacular than what you have already seen. Many movie companies come here to shoot Westerns. More of the desert can be seen, as mentioned earlier, with Johnny Desert Tours, whose regular trips go to the canyon, the fjord, and beyond.

WHERE TO STAY IN THE NEGEV

Arad and Beersheba observe the customary high and low seasons, with Beersheba adding a super high season for Passover. Elat and En Bokek, however, declare summer to be low season. Every house mentioned is Kosher; they are all air-conditioned. Honeymooners get special rates in Elat. There are no five-star hotels in the Negev, but the Masada in Arad, the Beersheba Desert Inn, and the first four Elat hotels mentioned each have four stars.

EN BOKEK

If you were going to start an oasis in 1971, you would build the En Bokek Hotel, a gleaming white, air-conditioned envelope containing a snazzy bright bar-lounge, synagogue, competent Kosher kitchen, and 96 high-style bedrooms, each with bath and a balcony overlooking the sea. Masada tours come for lunch, and Israelis come to take healing baths in the springs across the road. Maybe not fully broken in, but comfortable. Half board is demanded (there is no place else to go); expect to pay $9–$12. Masada is about 11 miles away.

Down the road is the Galai Zohar, equally new and four-star, equally susceptible to group-lunchers and Israeli cure-takers, but less attractive than its neighbor.

ARAD

In Arad's three tourist hotels, out past the edge of town, two nights is a long stay. Each has a pool, a bar, and a sitting room, with standard-type bedrooms and bed-and-breakfast prices in the $6–$9 range. The Nof Arad has the best reputation and food; the Masada has occasional entertainment, but highly unentertaining cuisine; and the Margoa has particularly pretty grounds.

The alternative to this trio is the Arad in the center of town, a good buy, under $6 for bed and breakfast. Its rooms are minimal, but its public cafe is frequented by people who are not one-nighters.

BEERSHEBA

Arad has stolen Beersheba's claim as the base camp for Masada, so there are no major new entries. The Desert Inn, however, keeps expanding, catering to vacationing Israelis as well as to tour buses. This three-story motel embraces a pool, giant green lawns (in the Negev!), tennis courts, a modern TV lounge-lobby, and a bar done up as the Sheik's Tent, with live music and dancing. The standard rooms are nicely furnished and the de luxe ones are nicer, but still not large. The inn expects to have 175 rooms soon. It is fortunate that its services are so complete; it is way out past town. Bed and breakfast, expect to pay $7–$10.

The other tourist spot is the Zohar, a three-star establishment in a new section of town, where bed-and-breakfast rates are likely to be $5–$7. Some of the 64 rooms are big, but most are small, although comfortable.

The Haneger downtown will appeal to tolerant budget watchers. All of its rooms have showers and are adequate, but the location is noisy.

ELAT

(Tour-resisters, you get a better price on a bus, but if you simply refuse to enlist, did you know you could get good hotel rates via Arkia?) Elat is a resort town, but hotels just don't seem to be its forte. Far and away the best is Red Rock, very mod, very sophisticated, with lots of strong hot colors and matching Israeli-international clientele. On the beach, but with its own pool, Red Rock (the English words are used) has 72 rooms, a nightclub, good-looking lobby, and fresh flowers everywhere. Expect to pay $9–$11 for bed and breakfast for a standard room or about $2 more for a suite, which means standard, plus dressing room and living room.

The Neptune's initial handicaps—a mere 36 rooms and walls programmed for self-destruction—might be corrected now that it is under the banner of Israel Land Development's Sharon Hotels. By now it would have added rooms and a pool and tight reins (its manager is Roger Coster, the second generation of Haiti's legendary Hotel Oloffson). Already on hand are the beachside location and a striking façade, like a tiled egg crate, that gives each balcony a view of the sea.

The Elat Hotel, opened in 1958, is owned by that fine old name in hospitality, the Histadrut, the Israeli labor federation. No tent camp for toilers is this, but a modern beachside enclave, now with 106 rooms, a pool, a bar, and new Scandinavian furniture to welcome wintering Scandinavians, ready for the big tour groups. Expect to pay $11–$13, bed and breakfast in the dressy new rooms. The Solomon, way up on a hill, is also a four-star hotel, but it would take a Solomon to tell why. The rooms in the 1971 wing are indeed large and modern, each with a view of the sea, but balance that against the lack of elevators, pleasant sitting space, or commendable cuisine and the presence of student groups and helter-skelter management. At this writing, a 200-room extravaganza is planned for Coral Beach.

The Queen of Sheba was Elat's first plush hotel. It was stripped of its stars in 1971 and reduced to serving students and other luxury-resisters. The basic plant—pool, 87 rooms, air conditioning, bar—is there and managerial help might already have arrived. Check. The Snapeer, a new entry near the beach, has plain, good-sized rooms, laid out peculiarly with the shower and toilet on a platform next to the window. The Hamifgash Cafeteria next-door is allied for meals; with bed and breakfast, the Snapeer tab will be under $6. The Ophir is a plain-faced little hotel that is often taken over by students, but budget-watchers should be happy here with a bed-and-breakfast rate under $6.

Now for two special cases—the Caravan, which is a motel right across from Coral Beach, and the Sea Star Motel, which is a holiday village way off at the other end of Elat on Lagoon Beach. Both attract student tours. The Caravan is related to the camper-cubicle operation in the Sinai, but this is a motel-like array in concrete, with 60 small but adequate rooms and a main building with veranda, sit-down restaurant, and discotheque; the bed-and-breakfast tab is under $6. Cheaper and simpler is the Sea Star, which has showers and air conditioning for only two-thirds of its 99 rooms, three to a bungalow, but also has plans for improvement. The Sea Star has a private beach, sit-down restaurant, and a pleasant, unbothered atmosphere. A car is a major asset at either place.

Really pinching pennies? Johnny Desert Tours rents out unoccupied flats for around $4. Sometimes a bed is all you get. Check whether or not the apartment is furnished, being sublet to other visitors, with or without utilities.

WHERE TO EAT IN THE NEGEV

Apart from the hotels, Arad and Beersheba each have a few restaurants, and Elat has a comparative galaxy. In Arad the shopping center houses the Cafe, with good European pastry; Yona's, a simple Yemenite restaurant; and the Steakiya, which caused an instant sensation with its European food. In Beersheba the Desert Inn has a surprisingly good kitchen. For the pursuit of elegance, try Patio de Santos, downtown. It has a real patio, real iron grillwork—and stuffed milz, schnitzel, shrimp, and otherwise non-Hispanic fare; $3–$7. Maxim's is big, modern, European, and Kosher, with a fine reputation and a menu requiring $4–$6 for an all-out feast. Morris, off the main drag on Trumpeldor Street, is plain and good. You can put together a meal for $2. The best lunch in the Negev is Morris's fruit and sour cream for about 50¢.

Elat's big deal is the Blue Fish—pianist, maritime decor, fresh roses, candlelight, huge portions, great seafood, and prices that require at least $5 for a full meal. Sauces are extra. This is a good place to try Red Sea shrimp and lobster. Across the road, Yoske's is in back of the kids' outdoor-indoor beer parlor. Its prices and menu resemble those of the Blue Fish, but Yoske's is closed on Shabbat. Among the hotels, the Red Rock has been consistently good; the table d'hôte is about $5. Economy? Try Hamifgash, a lively cafeteria where the daily special is around $2.

WHAT TO DO AT NIGHT IN THE NEGEV

Except for Beersheba and Elat, what you do is count the stars. In Beersheba the main tent is the Sheik's Tent at the Desert Inn or whatever discotheque is in business that week. In Elat the junior celebrants gather at the Red Fish which is the veranda in front of Yoske's, at the big outdoor cafes in the shopping center across the way, at the Half Past Midnight, or at any other discotheque that is functioning. The big night-time splurge is at the Red Rock, which has an Israeli folklore show and conventional dancing. Admission is around $5 and includes the first drink.

WHAT TO BUY IN THE NEGEV

Well, there are post cards. At En Bokek one is limited to souvenirs, but in the towns there are children's wares, household objects, books, and other things Israelis buy for themselves that also make good presents. The bookstore in the Arad shopping center rates five stars, and so do some on Beersheba's main street, where you will also find an outpost of the Hamashbir department stores. If you make it before 9:00 on Thursday, there is the Bedouin market, where you could buy a camel— or a wife. In Elat the big lure is Elat stones. Most guided tours sooner or later end up in a jewelry factory-store where the green-blue stones identified with copper mining are polished and set in bracelets and rings or made into trays and ashtrays. Shops to look for are Azurit, Chen, and Malkit, all near the hotels, or Aladdin, near the Philip Murray Center. Azurit, being the biggest and most convenient, is thought to have the highest prices.

KEY ADDRESSES

Tourist Information: Arad: Magen David Adom Building (057) 9 70 12

Beersheba: Bet Ha'am, Paolei Binyan
Road (057) 22 89
Elat: New Commercial Building (059)
22 68

Sheruts:

In Beersheba: Keren Kayamet Street for
Jerusalem, Tel Aviv, or Elat; Ha'atzmaut
Street for Jerusalem, Tel Aviv.
In Elat: Almogim Street for Beersheba.

21

The Sinai

*Sharm-el-Sheikh, Abu Rudeis,
Santa Caterina*

Date palms and veiled women at the oasis . . . the last of the 734 steps on the climb to where Moses received the Ten Commandments . . . beaches tenanted only by palm trees and Bedouin shepherdesses . . . the icons and skulls shown with equal pride by the last four Greek monks in the desert . . . abandoned tanks and trenches . . . Israeli soldiers drinking orange pop as the offshore dredges on both sides of the Gulf of Suez race for oil.

This is the Sinai. No resorts, no hotels, no boutiques, and perhaps not even much of a future, but nevertheless, the place to see. Until 1967, it was a part of Egypt. Moses and his followers wandered here for 40 years, but you can see it in one to four days. It is easy. Until recently, the alternatives were jeep or bus, but now you can fly in and fly out, getting at least a glimpse of the Sinai in a comfortable 10 hours. You get a sharper understanding by doing it the hard way (which is not *that* hard, as you will see later), but still, a cellophane-wrapped Sinai is better than no Sinai at all.

In this chapter, more so than in the others in this book, please bear in mind that everything described is conditional. Better quarters might have materialized. The Suez Canal might be open to tourists—or boats. Civilian traffic through Gaza and Sinai might have been liberalized—or stopped. This is how things were at the beginning of 1972 and how they are expected to be in the near future.

It has always been difficult to explore this giant desert peninsula thrust between Africa and Asia. It is a big, mean desert, no matter whose flag is flying. Suppose there were no problem of unexploded mines, questionable loyalties, secret installations.

The Sinai is bigger than all of Israel was before 1967—not a good place for Philadelphians or Chicagoans to be rattling around in search of a Howard Johnson, at least not until there is a Howard Johnson.

HOW TO SEE THE SINAI

The only way that Israel will let one into the Sinai is by pre-arrangement—a tour by command car, bus, or plane, or a stay at the holiday village at Sharm-el-Sheikh. To wander alone by private car takes more *protectia* than most tourists—or most

The Straits of Tiran are deserted, except for the tour buses.

Israelis—can muster. The Elat–Sharm-el-Sheikh boat no longer runs. The Elat–Sharm-el-Sheikh road is closed to private cars without special permission. Coming down via the Mediterranean Coast, there is no permanent single barrier. Sometimes the Gaza road is closed, sometimes points farther down. There are very few places to buy gas, food, or lodging within the 10,000 square miles. The rooms that exist are spoken for by Egged–Dan, a two-company coalition that is the only authorized bus tour operator. Two other outfits have organized rugged expeditions, traveling by command car, camping out with sleeping bags. Their main customers are Israelis, so they may or may not be able to provide English-speaking guides or companions. The bigger company is Neot Hakikar–Blue Line, House 320/3, Elat (059) 28 15. Its Tel Aviv representative is Canaan Tours, 113 Ben Yehuda Street (03) 22 91 25. Another outfit is Rekhasim, P.O. Box 3355, Jerusalem (02) 6 86 76.

For most Americans it is the possibility of flying that makes

the Sinai a practical reality. Arkia flies regular flights from Tel
Aviv and Elat to Sharm-el-Sheikh, from Tel Aviv to Santa
Caterina, and from Sharm to Elat. United Israeli charter planes
can take you to these places, too. Theoretically you could buy
a plane ticket without buying a tour, but once you land at Ophir,
the airport for Sharm-el-Sheikh, or at the airstrip ten miles from
Santa Caterina, you cannot get out of the airport without prior
arrangement. There is no taxi, no public bus, no rental car or
camel.

No problem. Through the airlines, tour companies, or travel
agents, you can plan the whole trip at once. Which deal you
choose is a matter of time and money, rather than what you
want to see. There are two main focal points—the swimming
beach and military installation at Sharm and the monastery of
Santa Caterina for the climb up Mount Sinai. Buses, planes,
or command cars go to both. To see the Mitla Pass and the
battlefields of 1967 and 1956, however, one must go by
bus.

The prices range from around $70 for a one-day plane trip
to Sharm-el-Sheikh to $125 for a four-day plane-coach trip.
This is what has been offered in the past:

1 day	Plane:	Tel Aviv—Sharm-el-Sheikh
		Tel Aviv—Santa Caterina and Sharm-el-Sheikh
2 day	Plane:	Tel Aviv—Sharm-el-Sheikh and Elat, overnight; return by bus (or reverse)
2 day	Plane:	Tel Aviv—Sharm-el-Sheikh, flight to Elat for overnight; return by bus (or reverse)
3 day	Bus:	Tel Aviv—Sharm-el-Sheikh, overnight; tour of neighboring points, overnight Abu Rudeis; Mitla and battlefields; return by bus
4 day	Plane:	Tel Aviv—Sharm-el-Sheikh, bus picks up at airport and tours beach, Ras Nasrani, El Tor, overnight Abu Rudeis; bus via Neve Firan, overnight Santa Caterina; climb Mount Sinai, overnight Abu Rudeis; bus to Mitla and battlefield, return to Tel Aviv by bus, or reversed: bus down, flight back
4 day	Bus:	Tel Aviv—Sharm-el-Sheikh, overnight; El Tor, Neve Firan, overnight; Santa Caterina, climb Mount Sinai, overnight Abu Rudeis; bus to Mitla and battlefields, return to Tel Aviv

5 day

Blue Line–Neot Hakikar group of command cars, leaving from Elat, which you reach on your own

Command car Elat to Dahab Oasis, camp overnight; car to Ras Nasrani, Sharm-el-Sheikh, camp overnight Ras Tantur Coral Reef; car to Santa Caterina, camp overnight on plateau; climb Mount Sinai, car to caves, camp overnight En Hudra; car through Wadi Tamile, return to Elat

Arkia also has tours that combine Sharm with Elat and the Dead Sea in various ways.

For the Egged–Dan trips on land, you can take no more than 11 pounds (5 kg) of luggage. You *must* bring a towel, hat, sunglasses, water canteen (for Mount Sinai), and flashlight. You *should* bring bathing suit, camera, binoculars, towelettes, cool and comfortable slacks, one sweater or jacket, sneakers or crepe-soled shoes, and minimal toilet articles. Bring cigarettes. For the command car trips, you will also need a sleeping bag, which can be rented.

Where to stay and eat are prescribed by the conditions. At the bay of Sharm-el-Sheikh, the Caravan Desert Inn has clusters of small, air-conditioned rooms. The Caravan also rents small, stationary trailers. Swimming and skin diving are excellent here; gear can be rented. You can prearrange a protracted stay, at half-board rates in the $12–$14 range. Egged has a colony of yellow air-conditioned fiberglass "igloos" on the other side of the bay. Their object is to provide three-star comfort for tour overnights or longer individual stays.

At Abu Rudeis, Egged maintains several houses in part of the former Italian–Egyptian oil camp. Women sleep, eight to ten to a room, in one house and men, similarly distributed, sleep in another. The rooms are air-conditioned, neatly painted, and clean. Showers are in a third building, and toilets in a fourth. There is a large terraced bar-restaurant used by soldiers and oil workers, as well as by tourists. Considering that supplies must be brought in across the desert, the food is good.

At the monastery of Santa Caterina, they try to discourage tourism by keeping their accommodations simple. (Maybe that is why they also keep them dirty.) Egged has been trying to broaden their viewpoint, but no luck so far. There are no showers or hot water. The toilets and sinks are in one coeducational room and do not work very well. You sleep four to eight to a room, under dirty quilts. Still, it is not every night that you brush your teeth between a bus driver and a monk, and by the time you reach the comparatively Hiltonian Abu Rudeis, the discomfort is forgotten. The thrill of Mount Sinai is not.

The Straits of Tiran, whose blockade started the Six Day War.

During the day, lunch is often a picnic brought along on the bus. Cold water and cold soda are continually available and you are urged to keep imbibing to avoid desiccation. There are beach stops on most days, and pauses at oases. There are only two or three rest rooms encountered while in transit during the four days, and these are rather primitive.

The bus may not be air-conditioned; in the breezy Sinai, that is not fatal. When you see the roads, you will understand why there are problems keeping equipment on hand. For Santa Caterina, the bus leaves the paved highway and takes off over sand tracks.

Because of the relative roughness, the groups attract an interesting mixture of tourists from many countries, including Israel.

WHAT TO SEE IN THE SINAI

Having established that there is little choice, let us look at the most important possibilities.

Elat to Sharm-el-Sheikh is 149 miles, four to six hours by bus, allowing for stops at oases like Nuweiba and Dahab (fine swimming and snorkeling) and Nabek (mangroves growing out of the sea, the farthest north this has ever been found). The bus proceeds alongside the straits of Tiran to the point known as Ras Nasrani, facing the island of Tiran off the shore. (Here one leans against rusting Egyptian guns, suitably impressed by the mine warnings.) That tiny bit of open water is the Straits of Tiran—Israel's route to Asia and Africa and the trigger that started the Six Day War. Like many historic sites, its smallness is its most dramatic feature. Its scenery is also impressive. For several hours one has been looking at the forbidding walls of mountains, rising beyond the sea, but the surprise never fades. Sharm-el-Sheikh's superb beach and nearby coral reef look so appropriate for a vacation setting that you forget you are on a strategic military outpost on the edge of an empty desert. If you fly to Ophir, you pick up the route at Ras Nasrani.

El Tor is deserted now, but once it was the quarantine station for Moslem pilgrims returning to Africa. Its size gives an idea of how many people passed this route by foot and camel.

Abu Rudeis is the center of the Sinai oil industry. Rounding the southern tip of the peninsula, after El Tor, one sees oil wells, offshore rigs, and oil tanks. The oil camp for the pre-1967 Italian technicians has great strategic importance now, and is ringed with barbed wire. Yet, this is where Israelis were accused of holding orgies. *That's* improvisation! *Abu Zeneima,* about seven miles away, has an excellent beach, the perfect place to recover from the rigors of Santa Caterina.

The *Road to Santa Caterina* is a journey into a sixth-grade geography book, across a desert track, through a gorge, up past Wadi Firan to where you picnic near the mud-walled houses and orchards of the oasis known as Neve Firan. The Bedouin women shyly turn away, but their children clamber over the tourists, asking for coins, food and, most persistently, the nylon shopping bags that hold the lunches. In the Sinai it might not rain for years, but the ground stores the water and, brackish though it often is, it makes life possible. Going into the interior, one passes Bedouin holy places and the rock where, the Bible says, Moses directed the war against Amalek. Climbing up through the mountains, the road suddenly turns into a narrow valley, and there is the monastery, like a fortress with nothing to command.

Santa Caterina is a Greek Orthodox monastery that has been functioning since the sixth century. The Byzantine emperor, Justinian, built it to honor St. Catherine, a martyr whose bones were believed to have been transported here by angels. The monastery is at the base of the 7,362-foot high peak known as Jabal Musa, Mount of Moses. Many believe this is the Mount Sinai of the Bible; it is one of 13 possible ones. The biblical account of the Exodus could make this the place where the Golden Calf was worshiped while Moses received the Ten Commandments.

En route to Mount Sinai, the Firan oasis

Despite the simple quarters of the monks (some have wives and families), the monastery has great wealth. It owns much land, including that at Neve Firan. The Bedouins who live near here are believed to be descendants of the European troops hired to protect the monks several centuries ago. Until recently, the gate of the monastery was open only during visits of the Archbishop. In between, visitors entered by being hoisted up in a basket.

The riches of the monastery are most apparent in the Library, a storehouse of rare and beautiful manuscripts and hundreds of superb icons. Within the walls are an eleventh-century mosque, used by neighboring Bedouins, a bell tower, and a cathedral marking the site where Moses saw the Burning Bush. Brilliant icons and mosaics decorate the church. The monks also display their collection of skeletons. Their predecessors, after a brief underground burial, are dug up and stored in bins in the Room of Skulls. The Library and the sleeping quarters are set along the galleried upper stories of the main building. Everything else is in the courtyard. The lights go off at 9:00 P.M.

Mount Sinai might not be *the* actual Mount Sinai, but it will do. Your ascent starts with a 3:00 A.M. wake-up call, 3:15 coffee, and 3:30 rendezvous outside the walls. The walk takes two hours, mostly on a well-graded path, easily followed by flashlight. You can choose to ride halfway up by camel. It only costs a few dollars, but at the end of the bumpy ride (some people get seasick), you still must walk up 734 steps, carved into the rock, to reach the summit. By then it is daylight. Resting by the little stone Chapel of the Holy Peak, you think about Moses and marvel at the purple-brown mountains around you. On some, there are chapels and crosses, but no inhabitants now. Coming down, you take a different route, following a canyon in which the monks have cut steps and entrance arches. Now, you are served the Israeli breakfast for which Egged–Dan has supplied the food.

Mitla Pass winds across the central Sinai, chosen by the Egyptians as their unassailable attack route. In 1956 Israeli paratroopers landed behind Egyptian lines and, after heavy fighting, cleared the way for the thrust toward the Canal. In 1967 Israeli planes and tanks again surprised the Egyptians, turning their fine Russian-made tanks into fiery traps. Most of the burned-out tanks have been removed (to be used by the Israelis), but one can see many signs of the fighting, including memorials to individuals and units.

El Arish is an oasis-town on the Mediterranean that is sometimes visited by tour buses on their way out of the Sinai. The beach is a five-mile palm-dotted expanse, completely unspoiled —yet. The town is very Arabic.

Gaza is also on one northern route out of the Sinai, but tours usually avoid it, not just because of possible danger—it *has* quieted down—but because there are few interesting landmarks and the area is very poor and depressing, virtually the only place within Israel's borders that is.

The *Suez Canal* and the towns along its banks are not now open to tourists.

*"I do not speak well English.
Please try instead French, Ger-
man, Yiddish, or Rumanian."*
—SIGN IN HAIFA HOTEL

Appendix A
Speaking Israeli

HOW TO SPEAK ISRAELI

If you can't already speak Hebrew, don't bother trying to learn.
Of course, you should learn to read the alphabet so that you can
sound out the street signs, and memorize the customary tourist
words: greetings, directions, numbers, and so forth. Get a Dover
or Berlitz phrase book and keep it with you. Then, in emergencies,
open it and point. That takes care of the Hebrew. What you
should concentrate on learning is Israeli, the Hebrew geographic
and historic terms and daily expressions that the country's most
fluent English-speakers cannot live without. Herewith, Basic Israeli:

ESSENTIAL HEBREW TERMS

Rega	Literally, "a minute;" actually, "Come on," "Stop shoving," or "Make room for me"
Beseder	"All right," as in "All right, already"
Nachon	"All right," in the sense of "Okay"
Achod, shtayim	Literally, "one-two"; actually, "Make it snappy"
Shabbat	Eleven A.M. Friday to 4:30 P.M. Saturday
Hag	Holiday, starting like Shabbat on the preceding afternoon
Sabra	Native Israeli, named for the cactus fruit, which is tough on the outside, sweet inside

267

Olim	Immigrants; the singular is *olah* or *oleh*
Olim Hadoshim	New immigrants
Kosher	Food prepared according to biblical dietary laws; a place or person that follows the laws is said "to be" or "keep Kosher"

POSSIBLY, ENGLISH

A short walk	Twenty minutes uphill
So?	May I help you?
Administered Territories	Places that came within Israel's borders in 1967, but are not officially integrated—Sinai, West Bank, Golan Heights
B.C.E.	B.C. (letters stand for Before Common Era)
C.E.	A.D.
Dairy	A meal that can include fish, but no meat
Tender	Pickup truck
Anglo-Saxon Jews	Jews from English-speaking countries

GEOGRAPHY

The Negev	The desert, including the Dead Sea, from Beersheba to Elat; sometimes, the nondesert Ashkelon–Beersheba is included
The Sinai	The peninsula, starting at the pre-1967 Israel–Egypt border, which is a straight line across the open desert
The Galilee	Not just around the Sea of Galilee; anything north and east of Haifa, except the Golan Heights
Lake Kinneret	Sea of Galilee

The Golan	The low mountains running above the eastern side of the Sea of Galilee
Sharon	The costal plain north of Tel Aviv
The Emek	The Valley of Jezreel, in the Lower Galilee

INSTITUTIONS

Knesset	Israel's one-house parliament
Bet Knesset	A synagogue
Suchnoot	The Jewish Agency: before Independence, Israel's shadow government, but now the link between the State and non-Israeli Jews; concerned with immigration, settlement, and economic development
Keren Hayesod	The fund-raising umbrella for the Jewish Agency, whose American arm is the United Jewish Appeal
Keren Kayemet	The Jewish National Fund: the nation's chief landlord, owning nine-tenths of the actual land, which it assigns via 49-year-leases to everyone else; responsible for land development and reclamation, which includes planting of trees
Histadrut	Israel's Labor Federation
Zahal	Israeli Army
Naturai Karta	The extreme Orthodox group which does not recognize the State of Israel (because the Messiah was supposed to come first) and whose members do not speak sacred Hebrew for daily matters; their passion for Sabbath observance has led them to stone nonobservers
Kibbutz	Collective farm, probably also involved in industry, where work and

property are collectively organized, members eat in communal
dining room, and children live in
communal nurseries

Moshav Shitufi   Collective farm, with or without
industry, where each family has its
own house and kitchen for children as well as parents, but where
work and pay are collectively organized

Moshav Ovdim   An agricultural village where every
family has its own house and leased
land, but buying and selling are
done cooperatively

Kupat Holim   The national Health Fund, deliberately pronounced as Kaput Olim,
or "broken immigrant"

Ulpan   Intensive Hebrew-language course
for immigrants

Appendix B
Landmarks of 4,000 Years

Adapted from "Facts About Israel" prepared by Israeli Ministry of Foreign Affairs

I.   **The Biblical Period—B.C.**

first half of second millennium
   Patriarchs: Abraham, Isaac, and Jacob
thirteenth century
   Exodus from Egypt
twelfth to eleventh centuries
   Israelites return to the Promised Land; Judges: Deborah, Gideon, Samson, and so on; King Saul

ca. 1000	David makes Jerusalem the capital
ca. 960	Solomon builds the Temple in Jerusalem
ca. 930	Kingdom divided into Judah and Israel
721	Conquest of Israel by Assyrians
586	Conquest of Judah by Babylonians; sacking of Jerusalem and destruction of First Temple
538–515	First return from Babylon; rebuilding of Temple

271

II.   The Second Temple Period

457–424	Second return to Zion; Ezra and Nehemiah
333	Conquest by Alexander the Great
323–168	Hellenistic rule
168	Revolt of the Maccabees (Hasmonaeans)
63	Beginning of Roman rule
37	End of Hasmonaean dynasty
37–4 B.C.	King Herod

A.D.

66	Jewish revolt against Rome
70	Destruction of Second Temple
73	Last stand of rebels at Masada

III.   Alien Rule

132–135	Bar Kokba's rising against Rome
ca. 200	Completion of Mishnah (codification of Jewish Law)
352	Jewish rising against Rome in Galilee
395–638	Rule by the Byzantines, the Emperors of the eastern half of the Roman Empire
ca. 400	Completion of Jerusalem Talmud
ca. 500	Completion of Babylonian Talmud

614	Persian invasion, supported by Jewish army
636	Beginning of Arabic rule
1072	Seljuk conquest
1099	Crusaders take Jerusalem and massacre its Jews
1267	Nahmanides revives Jewish community of Jerusalem
1291	End of Crusader rule; Mameluke conquest
1517	Ottoman conquest
1565	Publication of Rabbi Joseph Caro's *Shulhan Aruck,* written in Safad
1799	Napoleonic expedition

IV.   The Return

1870	Agricultural school founded in Mikve Israel
1878	Petach Tikva, first pioneering village, founded
1882	Pinsker's "Autoemancipation"; First Aliyah begins; Rishon Le Zion, Nes Ziona, Zichron Yaakov, and Rosh Pina founded
1895	Theodor Herzl's *Der Judenstaat* published
1897	First Zionist Congress in Basel —World Zionist Organization founded
1904–14	Second Aliyah—start of labor movement
1909	Tel Aviv, first all-Jewish city,

founded and Degania, first collective village founded

1917   Balfour Declaration; cornerstone of Hebrew University laid in Jerusalem

1917–18   British Army, with Jewish contingents, liberates the Holy Land from the Turks

1920   Third Aliyah begins; Histadrut (General Federation of Jewish Labor) founded

1921   Nahalal, first moshav (cooperative smallholder's village), founded

V.   The Mandatory Period

1922   British Mandate over Palestine and Transjordan confirmed by League of Nations; Britain excludes Transjordan from area of Jewish National Home

1925   Hebrew University opens on Scopus

1937   Peel Commission proposes partition, one part to be Jewish State

1939   British White Paper limits Jewish immigration and land purchase

1947

Nov. 29   United Nations General Assembly adopts Partition Plan, pro-

viding for establishment of Jewish State

VI.   Independent Israel Reborn

1948

May 14	Proclamation of State
May 15	British withdraw; invasion of Is-rael by Arab armies; large-scale immigration begins

1949

Feb. 16	Dr. Chaim Weizmann elected President
Feb. 24	Armistice Agreement with Egypt (first to be signed)
March 10	First regular government, under David Ben-Gurion
May 11	Israel admitted to United Na-tions
July 20	Armistice Agreement with Syria (last to be signed)
Nov. 20	Jewish population reaches first million

1950

July 5	Law of Return passed, confirm-ing right of every Jew to dwell in Israel
Sept.	Airlift of 45,000 Jews from Ye-men ends
Nov. 29	500,000th immigrant since 1948

1951
July
Airlift of 110,000 Jews from Iraq

1952
Dec. 8
Itzhak Ben-Zvi elected President

1954
Jan. 26
Moshe Sharatt becomes Premier

1955
Feb. 21
Ben-Gurion rejoins Cabinet as Minister of Defense
Sept. 22
Oil struck at Leletz, in Negev
Sept. 27
Egyptian-Czech arms deal announced
Nov. 3
Ben-Gurion again becomes Premier

1956
Oct. 29
Israel, in self-protection, clears Egyptian guerrilla bases and regular troop concentrations in Sinai

1957
March 8
Israel completes evacuation of Sinai and Gaza Strip on receiving assurances of free passage in Tiran Straits; U.N. Emergency force stationed in Gaza and Sinai

May 23	Arrest of Adolph Eichmann announced
July 4	Atomic reactor, for research and medical use, activated

1964

Jan. 5	Pope Paul VI on pilgrimage to holy sites in Israel
May 12	Israel and West Germany agree to establish diplomatic relations
Dec. 10	Shmuel Yosef Agnon receives Nobel Prize for Literature

1967

May 19	U Thant rebuts allegations of Israeli troop concentrations near Syrian frontier; U.N. Emergency Force in Sinai and Gaza Strip withdraws at Nasser's demand
May 23	Nasser declares Tiran Straits closed to Israeli shipping and cargoes; announces readiness for "all-out war"
May 30	Hussein of Jordan signs anti-Israel pact with Egypt, placing his forces under Egyptian command
June 2	Iraqi and Saudi-Arabian troops enter Jordan
June 4	Iraq signs anti-Israel pact with Egypt
June 5	Egypt moves Sinai armor toward Israel and shells border villages; Israel counterattacks, smashing enemy air power; Jordan and

	Syria join in assault on Israel; Israel forms National Unity Government
June 6	Israeli forces advance into Sinai, occupy Gaza Strip
June 7	Israel clears Jordanian offensive out of Jerusalem and areas west of Jordan River
June 8	Israeli forces reach Suez Canal
June 10	Israel storms Syrian fortifications on Golan Heights
June 29	Jerusalem, Israel's capital, reunited

1969

Feb. 26	Death of Prime Minister Levi Eshkol
March 17	Golda Meir installed as Israel's fourth Premier

Index